Books are to be returned on or before
the last date below.

**Stars and Masculinities
in Spanish Cinema**

OXFORD STUDIES IN MODERN EUROPEAN CULTURE

GENERAL EDITORS

Elizabeth Fallaize, Robin Fiddian, and Katrin Kohl

Oxford Studies in Modern European Culture is a new series conceived as a response to the changing modes of study of European literature and culture in many universities. Designed to combine focus with breadth, each title in the series will present a range of texts or films in dialogue with their historical and cultural contexts—not simply as a reflection of history but engaged in a mediation with history, conceived in broad terms as cultural, social, and political history. Flexible, interdisciplinary approaches are encouraged together with the use of texts outside the traditional canon alongside more familiar works. In order to make the volumes accessible not only to students of modern languages but also to those studying the history or politics of modern Europe, all quotations are offered in both the original language and in English.

STARS AND MASCULINITIES IN SPANISH CINEMA

From Banderas to Bardem

Chris Perriam

OXFORD
UNIVERSITY PRESS

OXFORD

UNIVERSITY PRESS

Great Clarendon Street, Oxford OX2 6DP

Oxford University Press is a department of the University of Oxford.
It furthers the University's objective of excellence in research, scholarship,
and education by publishing worldwide in

Oxford New York

Auckland Bangkok Buenos Aires Cape Town Chennai
Dar es Salaam Delhi Hong Kong Istanbul Karachi Kolkata
Kuala Lumpur Madrid Melbourne Mexico City Mumbai Nairobi
São Paulo Shanghai Taipei Tokyo Toronto

Oxford is a registered trade mark of Oxford University Press
in the UK and in certain other countries

Published in the United States
by Oxford University Press Inc., New York

British Library Cataloguing in Publication Data
Data available

Library of Congress Cataloging in Publication Data
Data available
ISBN 0-19-815996-X

1 3 5 7 9 10 8 6 4 2

Typeset by Graphicraft Limited, Hong Kong
Printed in Great Britain on acid-free paper by
T.J. International Ltd, Padstow, Cornwall

Preface

In this book I study the careers of Spanish film actors Imanol Arias, Antonio Banderas, Javier Bardem, Carmelo Gómez, Jordi Mollà, and Jorge Sanz who all had their first big successes in major films of the post-Franco period. A further four younger actors, Eduardo Noriega, Fele Martínez, Liberto Rabal, and Juan Diego Botto are also covered, but less extensively. In all cases I look at details of performance in specific scenes, and study the formation of star personae and star qualities in these men, particularly in relation to certain constructions of masculinity in film and print media. Fairly extensive use of popular and intellectual press coverage of these actors grounds what I have to say in some Spanish specificities and helps take into account the tastes, aspirations, and fantasies of Spanish audiences across the period chosen—more or less from Almodóvar's *Labyrinth of Passion* to the latest premières of 2001. What I intend is a contribution to Star Studies and Spanish Cultural and Film Studies based on theorized close readings which link the production of character and personality on- and off-screen to the social and psychic construction of masculinities. I took a decision early on in the project not to interview filmgoers or to ask the actors directly for their own opinions in interview, quite simply because I did not then consider myself theoretically equipped or sufficiently resourced (or resourceful) to write that sort of book. In the Conclusion I address in more detail the question of who and what is excluded: the Introduction offers a substantial explanation of the methodology and aims.

Film titles are given their official or festival English-language titles in italics, and films with significant profile in English-speaking regions (for example *Live Flesh*) are, after their first mention, referred to by their English titles. Where no official or festival title exists, a translation is given in brackets and in roman type.

In the Filmographies accompanying each main chapter the figures for audience and box office takings used throughout refer to Spanish territory only and are taken from the official data of the Ministerio de Educación, Cultura and Deporte, Instituto de Cine y Artes Audiovisuales (http://www.mcu.es/bases/spa/cine/CINE.html) as at 15 Feb. 2002.

Some source materials, mainly press cuttings and short reviews, were consulted in the library of the Filmoteca Nacional, Madrid, which since the early to mid-1990s has been able to keep meticulously referenced dossiers, now gradually being transferred to digital media. Before that time, however, its agencies' approaches to record-keeping and the transfer and copying of materials were less consistent and many items have no page references and some no attributions. Where this is the case, and where it has not been possible to consult the documents in other archives, items are marked FOA (Filmoteca Old Archive). Although the materials are catalogued and stored in numbered envelope files, readers are at liberty—which some appear to have taken—to return items in a different order and to different files; but for readers wishing to consult any of these items, the principle is roughly chronological, thus most of the early Banderas material is in files Banderas 1 to 4, and so on.

My thanks are due to the following for advice and encouragement in the course of writing and redrafting: Mark Allinson, Bruce Babington, Ann Davies, Santi Fouz, Jayne Hamilton, Marga Lobo and her colleagues at the Filmoteca Nacional (Madrid), Phil Powrie, Paul Julian Smith, Gustavo Subero.

The trustees and administrators of the Professorial Development Fund of the University of Newcastle not only facilitated the purchase of films on video specific to the project but also, crucially, were enlightened enough to pay for me to go regularly to the cinema in Madrid (and to consult the archives and stock of the Filmoteca Nacional and the Biblioteca Nacional).

A version of part of my discussion of Jorge Sanz (in Ch. 6) appeared in *Forum for Modern Language Studies* 37/1 (2000).

Contents

List of illustrations

Illustrations 2–5, 7, 9–11, and 13–16 were provided by the stills department of the Filmoteca Española (Madrid) and special thanks are due to Alicia Potes and her colleagues in the Archivo Gráfico.

Every reasonable effort has been made to trace those holding rights to the images reproduced and to acquire the relevant permissions.

Introduction

Spanish stars and doing Spanish Star Studies

The question of how far we can apply such a term as 'star' to actors in a relatively small and only intermittently global market such as that of Spanish cinema must be considered an open one, although, obviously, one of my intentions in this book is at least to half close it. The useful *Diccionario de las estrellas cinematográficas españolas de los años noventa* (Clemente 1998) (Dictionary of Spanish Film Stars of the 1990s) lists thirty-nine contemporary male stars, their names culled from magazine polls, awards, and nominations in the main Spanish festivals and ceremonies. Here I cover just six of these in detail: Imanol Arias, Antonio Banderas, Javier Bardem, Carmelo Gómez, Jordi Mollà, and Jorge Sanz who were all born between 1956 and 1970, and had their first big successes in major films of the post-Franco period, appearing with unusual frequency in co-starring roles together. I cover a further four younger men briefly in a single chapter, second-guessing to a certain extent their future careers. In the cases of the six main leading men, I look in some detail at their performances and the meanings arising from them—their embodiments of culture (McDonald 1998: 180)—in specific films of significant profile within Spain, Latin America, and, in some cases, beyond. In each chapter, too, there is presentation and analysis of the construction of star personae in print media and on the web. As the title of the book and the second half of this Introduction suggest I frame their performances and the production of their personae off screen in a double context: that of the general cultural field of masculinities acted out and represented; and that of certain productions of masculinity which are conformed by the tastes, aspirations, and fantasies (in so far as we can know them) of Spanish audiences across the period I cover.

As well as coming into that wide category of *estrella* as used in the dictionary mentioned above, all but the very youngest actors discussed here have in their early to mid-careers been labelled by the press, and sometimes by their own publicity machines, with another crucial term: *galán*. This is a nostalgic term looking back in time to an idealized eighteenth century, to the figure of the gallant gentleman, to later pre-cinema days when it signified 'handsome, elegant, and eligible', and then

to the more recent golden age of cinema. It is the term habitually associated in Spanish with Clark Gable, for example—but also with a long
list of Spanish names of the mid-twentieth century (Reboiras 1996 gives
a summary)—and its old connotations of leading man are carried over
into its usage in the 1980s and 1990s, where in many circumstances
it may also be overlaid with a sense of high-quality sex symbol status
(I trace something of this shift in my discussion of Arias's dislike of the
term in Ch. 1).[1]

Although the cultural importance of cinema in Spain has in at least
one significant case been implicitly belittled in relation to the United
Kingdom and France (Finney 1996: 53–63), I hope that what I have to
say in the chapters that follow will add to the many existing studies of
Spanish cinema that offer evidence of the centrality and vitality of all
aspects of cinema to contemporary Spanish cultural and everyday life.
Moreover, all the arguments adduced by Finney for France's ability to
sustain a star system (historically) now hold good in the case of Spain:
producers can rely on the values of actors' names to launch new projects; there is massive attention paid to films and actors at all levels of
the press (including at least six prestige glossy monthlies) and in casual
conversation; there are regular and many television magazine pro-
grammes on cinema (I wonder if it is true any more that 'France offers
more [of this type of programme] than any other European country');
and cinema has a prominent place in everyday life (ibid. 63). Finney's
claim that 'France is the only other European country [than the UK] which
has a star system' (63) may well be true in the literal studio-system
sense. However, the significance, resonance, and prominence of the best-
known Spanish actors means that there now exists a matrix of production and consumption of Spanish stars within Spain and beyond (of the
actors to be discussed Imanol Arias and Eduardo Noriega have been
significant presences in Argentina; Jordi Mollà—like Victoria Abril—in
France).[2] As with France in the period I am covering in this book, the

[1] Even Ricky Martin is only one generational step away from being a *galán* in this sense, being 'el
heredero de la tradición de galanes, intérpretes y artistas que dieron el salto al estrellato
universal' (the heir to a tradition of [Latin] leading men, interpreters, and performers that
rocketed to universal stardom): http://www.rickymartinmanagement.com/spanish_html and
english_html (28 Aug. 2001).

[2] Arias and Noriega have a name in Argentina: Arias for his roles in *Camila / Camila* (María Luisa
Bemberg, 1984) and *Buenos Aires me mata* (Beda Docampo Feijóo, 1997); Noriega for *Plata quemada / Burnt Money / Burning Money* (Marcelo Piñeyro, 2000). Noriega's role in Guillermo de Toro's
Mexican-Spanish co-pro *El espinazo del diablo / The Devil's Backbone* (2001) has brought him fame
in Mexico, Argentina, the US, and the UK. Mollà has played in the French/Belgian co-pro *Le Fusil
de bois / The Wooden Gun* (Pierre Delerive, 1994); the French-Spanish co-pro *La Cible / Romance
peligroso / The Target to Kill* (Pierre Courrège, 1996), in *A Dollar for the Dead* (Gene Quintano, 1999),

classic understanding of the 'star' as a product of consumer capitalism on a huge scale—linked to the Hollywood studio system or more recent agency-and-contract structures—clearly will not hold (Vincendeau 2000: 1–2), even if it is indeed true that the confluence in Spain of previously clearly demarcated star systems (film, theatre, television), market liberalization, and the advent of multimedia corporate enterprise had enormously enlarged the field of influence of Spanish stars even in the early 1990s (Maqua 1994: 31–3). But, again following Vincendeau, the number of active performers in demand by the industry, their filmographies (Vincendeau 2000: 1), their quickly consolidated careers, and the volume of printed and electronically mediatized coverage of their lives and roles (14–21), all argue if not for a Spanish star 'system' exactly, then certainly for a strong and specifically determined supporting matrix of image production, deals, outlets, tailored scripts, and simple star vehicles (Arias and Sanz in particular are as often as not to be found cruising along in these and looking somewhat disengaged).

Indeed, it is possible to argue that the Spanish State in the mid-1980s stood in as a kind of studio system, supporting certain genres and favouring certain actors (Caparrós Lera 1992: 57–109; Jordan and Morgan-Tamosunas 1998: 2–3, 32–5). By focusing on a very small pool of actors in prestige products, indeed, there were explicit attempts at creating a Spanish star system (Hopewell 1989: 421), partly to exploit a responsiveness in Spain to big star names in US productions which at the time was elsewhere out of fashion (418). Only in the second half of the 1990s had it become clear that there was a consistency, range, and density of performers, opportunities, and performances sufficient retrospectively to justify the use of the terminology of stardom—although P. Evans (1995b: 329) and Jordan and Morgan-Tamosunas (1998: 126) both set the start of the new Spanish star system earlier, in the mid-1980s, when a limited number of big reputations were being made.

One could, of course, go further back: a significant feature of Spanish media and leisure culture through the Franco years had always been a fixation on the female stars of stage and screen musicals with 'folkloric' emphases (Pineda Novo 1991; Labanyi 1997) and on indigenous feminine ideals or *femmes fatales* such as Ana Mariscal (who combines the two) (Martín-Márquez 1999: 85–111), Sara Montiel, and particularly Imperio Argentina (see also Morgan 1995b: 152–3). A fascination with

and in Ted Dem's *Blow* (2001), with Penelope Cruz (though credited sixth to her second). Sanz's international career is modest but runs from *Conan the Barbarian* (John Milius) in 1982 through *A Further Gesture* aka *The Break* (Robert Dornhelm, 1996) and *The Garden of Redemption* (Thomas Michael Donnelly, 1997) to the Mexican-Russian co-pro *En un claroscuro de la luna* (Moonlight Shadow) (Sergio Olhovich, 1999).

Hollywood cinema had also kept alive a culturally translated engagement with the notion of great screen stars. Of the men, Francisco Rabal, Fernando Fernán Gómez, José Luis López Vázquez, and (into the 1970s) José Sacristán were all actors with sufficient leading roles of presence to have had the label attached to them; so too, though at one remove from the nation, was Fernando Rey (on whom see P. Evans 1995a: 16–18). But in the wake of the Antonio Banderas phenomenon (one which as I write is starting to be matched in female stardom by Penelope Cruz) a culturally very widespread machinery of promotion of 'the new stars of Spanish cinema' has developed in Spain with the annual dossiers and multipage spreads in the main film magazines on the newest, the latest, the youngest, the most established, the sexiest, the cleverest actors (and directors and producers, but less so) becoming what would be an almost wearisome feature of life if it were not for the interest, optimism, and sheer brazen promotional confidence behind it. So, for instance, it was possible by 1997 in a piece on Jordi Mollà for the reporter to use the only slightly ironic term 'star system patrio' ('the fatherland's star system') as well as the sub-header 'Galán' (Ponga 1997: 40, 44).

Christine Gledhill (1991: p. xiv), looking back into the 1960s and 1970s characterized the field of work on stars then as having been 'largely the province of fandom [. . .] focused on personal biographies' on the one hand, and on the other, of sociology analysing 'stars as industrial marketing devices or social role models'. There is a pinch of both these old approaches in this book; and a substantial segment of academic work on film in Spain, as well as much high journalism, still has more than just a pinch of them.[3] But as is well known, in 1979 Richard Dyer's *Stars*, in its Cultural Studies-inflected combination of semiotics and sociology 'read' the star image as a construct of media, ideological, and cultural practices in a dynamic relation to social meanings and values (Dyer 1998). In particular Dyer paid attention there to the star's image, as 'a complex configuration of visual, verbal and aural signs [. . .] manifest not only in films but in all kinds of media text' (ibid. 34), the second of which set of sources he was able to go on to explore more fully in *Heavenly Bodies: Film Stars and Society* (Dyer 1986). This he did as part of the necessary positioning of the meanings of stars in 'the context of social beliefs

---

[3] The Ninth Congress of the Asociación de Historiadores de Cine (Association of Film Historians) (2001) held for the first time, amid minor scandal, a panel session on Haciendo Estudios Culturales (Doing Cultural Studies) which drew attention to the split between empirical film historians and 'textual' critics in Spain, and to the distance that both groups maintain between their work and theories of gender and sexuality, or of history as cultural process such as those that form the common currency of Anglo Saxon, Latin American, and—to a lesser degree—French perspectives on film and culture.

and conditions in which the star circulates', as McDonald (1998: 179) points out. Here I pay a substantial amount of attention to extra-filmic, although still cinema-oriented, materials in order to follow this lead, and to underpin my readings of specific coincidences between instances of fictional representations of masculinity and instances of the social performance of masculinities in real time and space. This approach, of course, allows no tight indexing of the actors' roles to social roles, or of screen masculinities to those constructed in reality; and it allows no more than the theoretical adumbration of the desires and reactions of real audiences and fans tempered and adjusted by attention to interviews, reports on broad reactions in urban audiences, to popular and middle-brow film criticism, academic histories, and critical accounts. I also spend some time on detailed investigations—readings—of the way these stars act and look and signify, focusing on the relationship between certain arrangements of voice and body to those tropes, stances, and images out of which masculinities build themselves elsewhere in cinema and beyond. In short, this is a 'metaphorical' investigation (Allen and Smith 1997: 20)[4] of a set of social constructs, of 'typicality and representativeness' (Dyer 1998: 47), and of performance, all set in particular relation to changing constructions of gender and sexual desire, to social and political changes in Spain in the period, and to a wide range of key films and telling sequences.

McDonald (1998: 194–200; 2000) has rightly drawn attention to an imbalance in Star Studies since Dyer: stars have tended to be looked at from the point of view of their reception and consumption more than from that of the film industry, its economics, modes of control, and production (indeed, even Gledhill 1991, despite its subtitle 'Industry of Desire', does not analyse the industry proper for much more than a quarter of its length). I am not, in this book, going to be able to redress that balance in the Spanish context and have not set out to do so. This is a decision I have come to partly out of faith that Spanish academic film criticism's (continuing) bias towards historical and empirical but often left-wing inspired analysis will itself eventually fill this gap, and partly out of necessity—and perhaps through a mistake—since this book is written solo where in retrospect a team might well have done a better job.[5] Finally, along with Babington (in relation to the British scene) I believe

---

[4] Allen and Smith use the term to draw particular attention to one of the errors they identify in 'Continentally influenced film theory of the recent past' (10), that of 'wed[ding] the critique of epistemology to the critique of modernity' using the premise of coercive representation (i.e. the apparatus, interpellation, and so on) (1997: 14–21).

[5] As in the exemplary case of Jo Labanyi's AHRB-funded project (1999–2004): 'An Oral History of Cinema-going in 1940s and 1950s Spain'.

that, ultimately restricting though the 'textual' analysis of star images might be if it never opens out to analyses of the pragmatics and economics of stardom and star production, nevertheless, 'suggesting a cessation of textuality is premature and misguided' (Babington 2001: 23). There is still very little of what Babington calls 'significant textual commentary', even on contemporary female Spanish stars (but see P. Evans 1996 on Maura; and on an earlier period, Martín-Márquez 1999). On the other hand it is one of my main concerns to ask how, by considering the 'circulation, reception and cultural currency' of stars, one can begin to track the ways they 'condense a number of ideological themes' (Cook 1995: 50), and how, to take it further, the stars might at least sometimes be read as 'embodying the nation' (Vincendeau 2000: 35–8).

This is a concern that is still not often accounted for in film criticism in Spanish other than thematically (by which I mean using the fact of an actor's representation of a historical person or social type immediately to remit to issues pertaining to the era or the ambience evoked). I have already implied that the intensity and volume of engagement by these actors in the Spanish film industry inclines me to think of them —already labelled in Spain as *estrellas* and *galanes*—as translatable as 'stars'. They exhibit various star qualities and affective functions, the fullest (if dispersed) list of which is that provided by Dyer (1998), and supplemented by the 'contexts' discussed by McDonald (1998: 180–200)—the star system and the labour of stardom, the body and society, acting, audiences, everyday life, subcultures, high-concept film-making. A brief anticipatory consideration of some of the longest established categories of such quality will indicate this book's planned dynamic, a movement between 'textuality'—decoding the effects of performance and screen presence—and cultural currency. The categories I want to use here are those of heightened ordinariness, charisma, sex appeal, and—underlying all these—openness to identification.

Hopewell (1989: 421–2) makes the exaggerated but none the less useful point that the best-known and best-loved actors of the Franco era owed their success not to charisma and special, gifted qualities but rather to their ability to incarnate specific types; not to an idealized, amplified individualism, but to their representation of weaknesses and failures easily recognized and identified with. Homeliness, accessibility, (albeit eccentric) typicality—qualities important to the success of a number of British screen personalities of the corresponding era (Macnab 2000: 104–40, 172–200)—are certainly inscribed in Fernando Fernán Gómez and Alfredo Landa, for example, and are carried through into the 1980s and 1990s in different modalities in Carmelo Gómez and Jorge Sanz. In the case of Arias and Sanz their very prominent roles in television series have allowed the familiarity and familiality (Morin 1960: 32) of their screen personalities there to cross over to their film stardom, allowing special fictive intimacies between them and their fans.

The paradoxical ordinariness of the stars, as recapitulated by Cook (1995: 52) and Ellis (1992: 93–7)—both available and not so; both like and quite unlike the viewer; a mix of presence and absence—is evident on- and off-screen: Jorge Sanz's come-hither look has the same comfortingly familiar and seemingly imitable vulgarity and neighbourhood quality to it in photo coverage and in, say, *La niña de tus ojos / The Girl of Your Dreams* (1998). Carmelo Gómez has built a career, it sometimes seems, by looking and speaking like your older brother, or your dad, or like a sensitive, reliable, if troubled partner. Javier Bardem is even now, in the face of his hyping as the new Banderas,[6] still able to resist any explicit association with glamour and in interview and many roles constructs the illusion of the sort of strong personality and memorable character you might meet late at night in any big Spanish city. All this, as Ellis (1992: 97–108) might point out, expands the realms and effects of desire in relation to these actors, making them thereby, and by the multiplication of their identities in circulation or exhibition, different in degree to mere players. There are signs in interview, too, of the ostentatious simplicity in self-presentation which Morin (1960: 52) links to stardom. The early days of Arias and Banderas are, in this way, rendered as true stories turned urban myths through the prompted recountings of destitute early days in the capital and of moments of sudden fortune at being spotted by the people who mattered (J. L. Rubio 1984; De la Fuente 1986). In the case of Sanz, coverage of his origins as child and teenage actor consistently favours admirable craft over prodigal giftedness. Gómez is represented as bringing to his performances nothing more extraordinary than his Northern-ness; Mollà as having studied his way to perfection. Of those I discuss, only Eduardo Noriega, one of the younger generation, has consistently been presented as first and foremost gifted with special sex appeal.

The Spanishness of these men, in fact, makes their ordinariness shade over into charismatic specialness. As Babington (2001: 10) observes, the stars of indigenous cinemas 'give to indigenous audiences something that Hollywood luminaries cannot, reflections of the known and close at hand, typologies of the contingent, intimate dramatizations of local myths and realities [making them] local stars—but no less meaningful for that'. If Banderas and Bardem are charismatic, if they generate a 'current of attraction between star and audience' (Griffith 1970: 23), it is in no small part because of this connection to the (relatively) local social imaginary. We

---

6 *Semana*, 17 Oct. 1990: 62–3, 63.

might look, for example, to the furious energies of *Átame / Tie Me Up; Tie Me Down* (1989) and *Jamón, jamón* (1992) to pinpoint the start of this in the bonding of these nascent stars to the explosive matter of, respectively, urban and rural/small town desires and frustrations. Charisma sometimes has to do with a certain glamorous seriousness—the seriousness one might expect of the godlike and heroic figures of Morin's gripping half-analysis, half-imaginings on the old-style stars (1960). Gómez, for one, has a strong emotional gravitational pull and in several roles exemplifies the 'mythology of the romantic stars [that] associates moral beauty with physical beauty' (Morin 1960: 47) or, at least, he has intriguing qualities of a moral kind that combine with an attractively interesting look (Gómez does not actually have the 'ideal body' that Morin is discussing). Arias, when he shifts from deliberately alienating chill into a more audience-involving austerity of manner also has gravitas. Even Sanz, who tends to play comedy roles, has a cheeky charisma that is not mere sex appeal since it offers a model of behaviour for men supposed to be living in a time of uncertainty or 'crisis', and for Spanish men consciously or unconsciously nostalgic for a more neatly patriarchal era. We shall be seeing that these men play men bound up in particular historical and contemporary social circumstances; they become epitomes, icons of states of affairs and states of emotion. They are all, in Molly Haskell's terms, quoted by Dyer (1998: 16), sources of imagery of 'intellectual and emotional power' and, crucially to their charismatic status according to Dyer, are temporally locked in to 'specific instabilities, ambiguities, and contradictions' in the culture that produces and consumes them (31). They have a 'structured polysemy' (92) in relation to the social themes represented in the course of their performances and in relation to the general circulation of their images, a polysemy that is enhanced by their cumulative, 'iconic, transtextual sameness beneath variations' (Babington 2001: 7), and by their special, and heightened, range of beautiful or impossibly manly looks.

What is also certainly true of all, however, is that for different constituencies, and for different micro-periods (for example Banderas starting out with Almodóvar: 1982–6; Bardem in the wake of *Segunda piel / Second Skin*, from 2000 onwards), they have or are deemed to have intense sex appeal. They are stocked in varying degrees with those 'psychological associations' necessary to 'galvanize both men and women', 'memories of mother, the protective instinct, the destructive instinct, the [. . .] need for comfort, reassurance [and] risk' (Griffith 1970: 36). They engage in a good deal of on-screen sex, their bodies are frequently on display, and many of their characters are enmeshed in erotic and emotional complexities of intriguing extremity. Morin (1960: 172) suggests that the star classically 'gives lessons in the techniques and exact rites of amorous communication', and if we take this group of actors as a whole, putting aside the blunting effects of occasional near-pornographic sensationalism brought about by cultural and commercial imperatives, for their male audiences they represent—as foils or leads for their equally beautiful and sexual female co-stars (and occasionally for each other)—a sophisticated schooling in erotic depth, in creating or catastrophically destroying emotional commitment. There are many potential instances of self-doubling projection-identification of the sort discussed by Morin (ibid. 95–102)—identifications with the star as if with a fantasy alter ego (95, 98). Men watching these actors, and the erotic particularities and successes of their roles, become manœuvred into wishing they were with, as well as in the place of, the actor (although Morin's 'virulent', idolatrous fantasy identifications and through-identifications of spectator with a godlike screen hero or heroine is more the stuff of the new Hollywood than of recent Spanish cinema). They all construct 'affective participation' (146) as part of their sex appeal. And since such participation is grounded in language as well as look, in geography as well as spaces in the spectatorial imagination, this sex appeal is Spanish in its interpellations. These stars are frequently tied to place: in obligatory mentions of birthplace, of location of early acting experience, of their place now on the urban Spanish scene. They are linked to current affairs and topical concerns, or just to Zeitgeist in loose journalistic commentary at all levels. Because of the dynamics of consumption and ideology central to the production of stars (9–32), the way they look in these static images in the press seems to become an oblique index of change. It can be identified with as a provisional way of making sense of the world.

There is a sexualized appeal in their frequent appearances in fashion shoots and in their responses in interviews on their private lives and tastes. As LaPlace (1987) suggests, much of this sort of material, central to the discourse of the star persona, is 'not only directed at women but written by them' (146), and in the Spanish case, particularly in the 1990s, there is often an erotically objectifying complicity between the female writers and readers, flirtatiousness in dialogue, innuendo or plain sexual compliment in reportage. The images of Banderas in leather jacket, Arias in once-cool slacks, Mollà in denim, Sanz in generously open button-down shirts form part of the social circulation of mimeses of look and clothing (166–76) and condense in classic form some of the imperatives of consumer capital in relation to the body (de Cordova 1990; Dyer 1998: 35–42). For Spanish men there is, then, opportunity for low-level narcissistic identification with these images; for women they signify variously a nostalgic reassurance of the persistence of unreconstructed, reliable, proper Spanish men (Arias, Gómez sometimes, Sanz perhaps) or glimpses of ideal, new men to replace the older images, as tokens of compensation (Dyer 1998: 28–9) and of hope.

Embodiments of Spanish Masculinities

Spanish stars, then, embed themselves in the imaginary and real social construct that is Spain and the world's view of Spain, to adapt Vincendeau's (2000: 31–40, 40) perspective on France. They do so in generic and industrial contexts that themselves have a bearing on the construct that is Spain. As Bruce Babington has put it, taking his cue from Dyer, 'the institutions of film stardom exhibit major constants running across different film cultures, but each national cinema produces different inflections of them': the crucial task is to pin down the '"specificities"' (Dyer's term) (Babington 2001: 4). In each chapter here I shall be building on the suggestion that such specificities can be located with some precision by focusing on the representations of masculinities that these stars and their roles attempt or are aligned with. They are to be seen mediated but animate in the faces, voices, bodies, and remembered images of these actors moving through roles that trace sometimes ideal, sometimes fatal trajectories through manhood. They are the qualities and quiddities of acting like a man in the institutional context of Spanish cinematic stardom and the socio-cultural contexts of the span of time I have chosen (from the end of the transition to democracy in Spain—1976–82—to, well, the last sensible moment).[7]

As its headline title implies, Dyer's (1986) second book on stars engaged with a major new current in critical theory in the humanities and social sciences: Body Theory. Bodies—ours and other peoples'—become in this view both material and construct; a body image, an imago, an idea to be worked up as much as an organism to be worked on, something subject to other people's dicta on decency, normality, appeal, behaviour, difference, limits, and even shape, as well as something which is also someone, a person subject to punishment, violence, control, pleasure, biology, life decisions. Since film stars are their looks, their sex appeal, their gestures and performance, their photogenic

---

[7] I have refrained from discussing, except in passing, films that I have not been able to view. This means, of course, that the last part of the period covered has some notable gaps (which correspond to periods when I have been unable to be in Spain to catch first runs, and the time-lag between exhibition and video or DVD release).

quality, and increasingly, their flesh, an emphasis on theorizing the body was always going to be promising for Star Studies. Dyer, then, analysed Marilyn Monroe in the context of 1950s ideas on sexuality, examining specifically her desirability (42–50), Paul Robeson in the context of representations of him as incarnation of blackness and sign variously of intense sexuality and classical beauty, and Judy Garland partly through the image of an androgynous Garland (168–77). This strand of thinking also influences Vincendeau (2000) in her study of French stars. Alain Delon's looks and body, his 'beauty and objectification by the camera', she suggests, 'bring to the fore the issue of accommodating an eroticized male figure in the context of mainstream cinema' (173–4) (an issue I address particularly in relation to Banderas and Sanz); Gérard Depardieu she sees making 'an expressionistic use of his body' (235), in his bingeing and dieting, and as the 'boisterous, larger than life amiable macho' (217) off-screen, while on-screen embodying class identities (219–20), 'providing the "evidence" of heterosexual virility' (221), and playing tormented manliness and vulnerability (223–30) off against his sheer size and presence.

I shall be looking at a number of similar examples of striking beauty (Banderas, Noriega), the use of body shape and massiveness (Bardem, Gómez), and expressionistic uses of the body (Mollà, Fele Martínez). José Arroyo has long since made the point that Spanish cinema of the 1980s and 1990s was unusually insistent, in comparison with European and North American cinemas, on the display of the male body and in its explorations of an eroticized masculinity.[8] The body of the Spanish male star is, inevitably, a key point of inflection of stardom, masculinities, and national specifics. It is, for example, telling that—although many of the female stars of Spanish cinema of the period boast extreme physical allure of various traditional kinds (Victoria Abril, Angela Molina, Carmen Maura, Penelope Cruz)—none of the Spanish male stars has been visibly encouraged to take the obvious route to better commodification of their bodies by becoming spectacularly quick, lithe, or muscled (even Banderas had to wait for the gyms of America to change that for a while). Nor are they liable to engage in strenuous stunts (Maura, in fact,

---

[8] Unpublished paper presented at the day-conference Masculinity and Cultural Change in Europe, at the Centre for Research into Film, University of Newcastle (11 Nov. 1999). The late 1980s in Spain also saw the start in the quality press of informed cultural interest in the meanings of the male body in various media representations: see Antón 2000: 210–12; Mir 1988; Rey 1994: 187–215; and a special feature in *El País* (*Temas de nuestra época*) 5 April 1988. For a reprise of cinematic erotic images of the period 1989–99 see 'Diez años de erotismo Made in Spain', special supplement to *Fotogramas*, 1,865 (1999), including provocative torso shots of Bardem, Botto, Mollà (surprisingly the most sexualized), Noriega, Rabal, and Sanz.

has recently proved more physical, being chased over the rooftops in *La comunidad* (Neighbours) (2000)). Gómez has done his share of chasing around and shooting out, and trained hard for his role in *El portero* (The Goalie) (1999), but is solid rather than dynamic. Sanz's image in the 1980s and until the mid-90s is one of smooth compactness (and tight trousers), and he has some of the most energetic sex scenes of them all, but his roles otherwise tend to involve more fetching looks and hanging around than go-getting; and his directors are less good than Cruise's at disguising his stature. Mollà is, or is constructed as, altogether too thoughtful and different. Arias has been both fugitive (as El Lute) and policeman (in the television series *Brigada central* (Police HQ)) but across his career his physique and his elaborate style lead more to images which invite audiences to have impressions of noirish, tormented interiority or of near psychopathic cunning rather than of orthodox, exhilarating (or terrifying) physicality, as a spectacle of action and presence (Willemen 1981). With the notable exception of Noriega in more recent roles (see Ch. 7) the generality of Hollywood buffed ideal is set aside in favour of sharper stabs at looking and acting like a Spanish—or perhaps a European—man. Bardem is probably the nearest to being the physically dominant screen male of twentieth-century Hollywood type (another type, the pretty and fine-feeling male I deal with in my last chapter). He is a hefty presence, is involved early on in his career in a famous fight scene (in *Jamón, jamón*), and has an admirable record of athletic sex scenes (and revelations of his buttocks). In *Carne trémula / Live Flesh* (1997) he and the younger actor Liberto Rabal (who was only really muscled for that film, it now seems) are both focused on while training and are locked into intense physical as well as emotional rivalry.

These stars are engaged in a dynamic organization of masculine behaviours, ideologies, and performances that is caught up in the interplay of gender, class, and race (Connell 1995: 76–86), and inflected by sexuality, nationality, and a wide range of emotional and intellectual factors (Berger, Wallis, and Watson 1995b: 3). Their different roles and body-images construct complex and slippery points of engagement and tension between the fans, the viewer, and the star in the processes of the identification and projection of different formations of masculinity. For the actors, there are tensions and engagements between the role and their own experience of images of men and of interacting with actual men. They work—act—in a space of consumption where on the one hand cross-cultural continuities of masculinity might be at work (as reprised in Gilmore 1990: 1–29 and *passim*)—global, European, Mediterranean—but where on the other the individual consumer of images is convinced that he or she is responding to a sense of gender identity that is bound up with a sense of localized self (Spanish, Basque, Andalusian, rural, urban, and so on). There are also points of tension and engagement explored in the chapters that follow between what Gilmore terms 'intrapsychic dynamics' (in this case the stuff of script and fiction, of mimesis and performative creativity) and 'the social organization of production' (3) (making and selling the image); between different forms of identification; and between acting and 'man-playing' (220); between image-perfection (actors working on their roles and working with the production of their public persona) and the situational accomplishment of masculinity (men constructing masculinities and negotiating power within social structures). Hence the use of the now common pluralization 'masculinities' in the title of this book.

The genealogy of ideas linking being an actor and acting like a man (or woman)—crystallized at one stage in the ultimately unsatisfactory notion of sexual roles—is too intricate to be usefully foregrounded here. Kristin Esterberg (1996) reminds us of long-standing ideas in sociology on identity as performance in Erving Goffman's work from the late 1950s into the 1970s which argued, fairly simply it seems to us today, for a dramaturgical approach based on a relationship between a true underlying identity (now, of course, challenged) and the performance of social roles. Symbolic interactionist theory of the 1970s with its emphases on 'meaning, process, "invented identities" and the cultural constructedness of communities' (Stein and Plummer 1996: 131) have a clear bearing on the making and the consumption of star images. Crucial too, if we take into account Western popular cinema's long-standing 'problem with women' and more recent preoccupation with 'male trouble' (Cohan and Hark 1993a; Cohan 1993; Solomon-Godeau 1995), are the issues concerning identity, identification, subjectivity, and sexuality that are opened up in the visual, fantasized, remembered, and recorded relationships of audiences and individual viewers with leading men. For if they look, in part, to Banderas or Bardem for ratifications of male experience, for psychic and social feedback, or for pointers to more efficacious romantic and sexual performances, they are not only looking inwards (checking themselves out)—and in 'looking inwards, consciously or not, male experience becomes decentred' (Frosh 1994: 90–1)—but outwards at a range of representations caught up in the process of representation, at a star accreting personae, acting a role and acting on our behalf, at subject positions being brought into being. They find themselves looking not only at performances that in their dreams but also on their Saturday nights out they might mimic, but at the real possibility of masculinity as masquerade—like femininity, a representation 'constructed primarily through masculine discourse, as the object of male fantasy' and although not necessarily ' "other" to the phallic order of the Symbolic' (86) always anxious to '[seek] confirmation [. . .], to shore up boundaries', engaged in a masquerade of domination and repudiation (87).

The intensity with which my chosen performers bind to some of the 'ideological themes' of Spanish culture in the period, their semiotic impact, and their embodiments of type seem to me to justify the adaptive use of the terminology of stardom in this Spanish context. The link to masculinities arises out of the extent of their mimetic and generic engagement with the role of leading man, co-star, or significant supporting actor, and the range of their stabilizing and destabilizing representations of male sex roles, their relaying of narratives of masculinity. It is not the mere fact of the locking in of these stars and their roles to widespread social and imagined paradigms—their agency in ideological reinforcements and displacements (Dyer 1998: 20–8)—that concerns me so much as the details of the fit, and more importantly, the approximations, and occasional lack of true fit. By looking at the linkages between performance detail and 'masculinity ideologies' (Gilmore 1990), between Spanish stars and Spanish cultural assumptions about and constructions of men on-screen and off, I hope to pin down what exactly is special, attractive, and sometimes disturbing in these highly mediated men.

Writing relatively early on in the British engagement with the 'critique of identity', Dyer in 1978/79 suggested that the then recently re-enlivened 'sense of crisis as to what a person is' could be seen 'to lie behind star charisma as a generalised phenomenon, in that stars speak centrally to this crisis and seem to embody it or to condense it within themselves' (Dyer 1998: 160–1); Spanish cinema and its deployment of its new stars has been no different to those other Western countries which for some thirty years have colloquially referred to a crisis of masculinity at the centre of their cultures. As Connell (1995: 84) has pointed out the term 'crisis' presupposes the existence of a coherent system, such as masculinity cannot in fact be, multiply configured and contradictory as it is. As 'a configuration of practice within a system of gender relations' which has a tendency towards crisis (84), rather, masculinity's relation to crisis is its relation to crisis tendencies in relations of power, production, and desire (or, more precisely, cathexis) (85). In Bigas Luna's *Jamón, jamón* and *Huevos de oro / Golden Balls*, for example, the connection between financial crisis, male sexual dysfunction, and a breakdown of patriarchal authority and self-authorization is made with grim jocularity using the body of Bardem as its mediation, as we shall be seeing in Ch. 3. At one stage or another in their careers all the stars with which this book concerns itself find themselves representing crisis at the intersection of gender, power, desire, and social process: but as I hope to show in Ch. 1, Imanol Arias could be thought of as exemplary in this regard, having covered the fullest imaginable range of male crises in his career (victimization and torture for being a rebel male, death for being a homosexual, disabling sexual jealousy as the rejected lover, chill dysfunction as the unwilling husband); and all, even the youngest (of those I discuss), have their brush with the tragic and melodramatic topoi of cinematic representations of masculinity.

However, comedy also (and perhaps not so surprisingly) proves a rich source of images of problematized masculinities even if not all of the very many Spanish films of the genre have learned to adapt the hidden subtleties of many of the great Hollywood romantic comedies as studied by Babington and Evans (1989) and on which in some measure they draw; but several have something of the old 'wit and playfulness, the ability to change perspectives' (183), and to interrogate gender differences with originality. In line with developments in 1980s US comedy, where 'it might be said that the enigma of masculinity rather than the traditional enigma of femininity [became] the central issue of many films' (280), the genre in Spain, in this particular inflection, has attracted all the actors I have been discussing here. Of them, the key comic actor is Sanz who has often taken on traditional generic roles in which the deception and mockery of the male runs the plot (ibid. 1–44, 179–226) or in which the audience is coaxed willingly into fond complicity with a dim young stud who is easily led into low-key crises of sexual confusion and loss of a mastery which he anyway never had. Fernando Trueba's *Belle Epoque* (1992) is a well-known key example: a young soldier deserter is light-heartedly infantilized and toyed with by a series of women in a variation on the old ambivalent theme of the lusty male made helpless by an excess of sexual attention. In *Tocando fondo* (Touching Rock Bottom) (José Luis Cuerda, 1993) the topos is that of the cocky but ineffectual young male (the typical mid-period Sanz role) with a perspicacious and successful girlfriend, here a vetinary surgeon whose routine castrations of tom-cats become a sister metaphor to that contained in the film's premise of recession biting into the lifestyles of thrusting entrepreneurs. In a different mode but within the same topos, Banderas's Carlos in the first half of Almodóvar's *Mujeres al borde de un ataque de nervios / Women on the Verge of a Nervous Breakdown* is weak, naïve (Allinson 2001: 85) and dominated both by mother and girlfriend, while later in the film, when the comedy turns less caricaturesque and its gender politics more complex, he ambiguously represents a flight from the patterns of 'victimising constructions of subjectivity' (P. Evans 1996:

40) embedded in patriarchy, and in particular in macho masculinity, into a soft, new, sensitive (but recidivistically seductive and ridiculous) masculinity. Even the austere Arias, who habitually keeps light tonality restricted to his television roles, several times in the 1990s abandoned tragic and heroic masculinities to take part in fond mockery. It is with him that I begin.

1 Imanol Arias (b. 1956)

'Novio de España' (Spain's Sweetheart)

Imanol Arias is described in *Cinerama*'s 'Diccionario de actores' (1995/6) as 'el galán más reputado de su generación' (the best regarded lead male of his generation), has appeared in some thirty feature films to date, and has an ongoing (if up and down) career in theatre (having joined the Centro Drámatico Nacional in his early twenties, encouraged by its director Adolfo Marsillach),[1] and in mass audience television drama series stretching from *Anillos de oro* (Gold Rings) (TVE 1983) to *Querido maestro* (Dear Teacher: third series, Tele 5 1998) and *Dime que me quieres* (Tell Me You Love Me) (Antena 3: 2001). In part because of his presence on television, in part because of the gossip-magazine appeal of his long relationship (from 1984) to actress and broadcaster Pastora Vega and their family life (González and Pasquín 1990),[2] of the actors discussed in this book Arias has the second most extensive press coverage (with Antonio Banderas a clear first, but with relatively little on the Spanish period). The looser designations of fame, such as the one I started with here, owe themselves as much to this undifferentiated bulk of received images as to closer appreciations of his development as a screen actor. However he is considered by some of the more analytical critical reviews in Spain as a sign of the changing contexts of that industry; and his career is of particular interest for its mixture of 'continuity of iconography [. . .] visual style [and] structure' (Dyer 1998: 62) with an ambitious, almost experimental range of projects and modes of representation at a time of considerable change in the industry. By the time the next most senior name of the era, Antonio Banderas, had begun to establish himself with the role of Ángel in Almodóvar's *Matador* (1986), with its famously disruptive 'sense of Spanish tradition [as] its most intriguing subject' (Hopewell 1986: 240), Arias already had significant roles with two key directors, in two distinct modes, engaging

---

[1] For example, a high-profile role in the Madrid García Lorca centenary homage event 'La Imagen del Espejo' (The Image in the Mirror) directed by Cristina Rota: with Juan Echanove, Juan Diego Botto, Ana Belén, Juan Diego, and Carlos Hipólito.

[2] Vega plays opposite Arias as El Lute's sister Esperanza in *El Lute II*; in less direct relation to his character, she plays Larissa in *Ilona llega con la lluvia* and Merche in *Todos los hombres sois iguales* (on both, see below); on television, opposite Arias she plays Eva in *Dime que me quieres*; and she co-stars (with Jorge Perugorría) in Arias's directorial debut, *Un asunto privado* (A Private Affair) (1996).

Fig. 1. Imanol Arias in *El Lute: Camina o revienta*.

with crucial plot elements in the national drama: the bleak comedy *Demonios en el jardín / Demons in the Garden* (Manuel Gutierréz Aragón, 1982) (Francoism, corruption, and family) and *La muerte de Mikel / The Death of Mikel* (Imanol Uribe, 1983) (Basque nationalist politics, religion, family, and homosexuality). The series *Anillos de oro* and these two films, perhaps along with the more obscure Catalan literary adaptation *Béarn, o la sala de las muñecas* (Bearn, or the Dolls' Room) (Jaime Chávarri, 1983), had 'automatically' made Arias 'el galán del momento' (the leading man of the moment) and established him as the most popular young actor in Spain (Aguilar and Genover 1996: 53).[3]

---

[3] This is supported by evidence in *¡Hola!* 17 Dec. 1983, with talk of a 'perfect career' and 'huge popularity'; *Semana*, 10 March 1984, with an interview ('Imanol Arias: Galán de hoy') and sexy pictures in sportswear and elegant suits (35–6); *Semana*, June 1984, with a four-part series of interviews and pieces 'Tras las huellas de Imanol Arias' (On the Trail of Imanol Arias). By 27 April 1984 *¡Hola!* was able to dub him 'el gran divo nacional' (the great male Spanish diva) (64), an epithet still being taken up (and mixed with *galán*) in *Diez Minutos*, 10 Feb. 1987 (FOA).

Fig. 2. Imanol Arias in *Fotogramas* pin-up calendar for 1988.

Part of the appeal constructed by the press, by that first television series, and by *Demonios en el jardín* (where his character is the object of desire of the two main screen beauties of the time, Angela Molina and Ana Belén), is sex appeal, and by extension the actor's claim to be a *galán*. This is, as is customary, exaggerated and adapted to readers' expectations by the press, as one reporter (writing at the higher end of the market) points out in a piece where, as early as 1984, Arias is already beginning to express worries about being thought of as mere *galán* (de la Fuente 1984: 7), which he clearly equates with sex-symbol.[4] The modern Spanish *galán*, in Arias's view, is the dumb hunk, the foil for the female star of the moment, there

---

[4] The theme continues in *Ya*, 19 Jan. 1985 (FOA); *Diario 16*, 19 Oct. 1986 (FOA); *Interviú*, 14 April 1987: 106–9; and *Imágenes de la actualidad*, 119, Nov.: 98–104, where Arias accepts that he always has ended up playing galanes but 'los transformo en otra cosa' (I change them into something else) (113).

for a year or two then gone (10); the challenge is, even if one has the physique of the *galán*, to measure up as an actor (10), choose roles carefully, plan for a career stretching into late middle age, mete out one's talent, not burn out (7). His references to the *galán* go against the usual understanding, as laid out in my Introduction, of the term referring to a type of actor-image distinctively not found in the immediate post-Franco years and which only José Sacristán—a far from shallow actor—could be said to have brought into the late 1970s (Arias's then recent past). In fact, that same late summer it had been pointed out that by publicizing the Argentine production *Camila* (María Luisa Bemberg, 1984) at the Buenos Aires Festival of Spanish Cinema Arias had become a symbol of Spain, an ideal, just as Sacristán had done in the late dictatorship years (J. L. Rubio 1984: 76):

> Imanol Arias es, de lejos, el actor joven que mayor partido le saca a la cámara, a las miradas, al silencio, a la presencia física. Y también [. . .] el único galán que ha surgido en España desde hace décadas [. . .] un galán que la gente joven [. . .] asocia consigo mismo.   (76)
>
> (Of all our young actors Imanol Arias is, by a long way, the one who best knows how to respond to the camera, and make looks and silences, sheer physical presence count. Moreover . . . he is the only real *galán* to have come out of Spain in decades . . . one whom young people . . . can relate to.)

Rubio takes this question of identification no further once he has raised it (despite writing in the relatively analytical magazine *Cambio 16*) but the implication that emerges from this long article's coverage of Arias's looks, intelligence, and character (friendly, well-mannered, open), and his ability to exploit astutely his gifts and looks (78), is that it depends as much on a generalized attraction, and on admiration of success, as on that unexplored issue of the need for actors who can serve as iconic national representatives for each generation. Francisco Umbral in a (characteristically) shorter piece for the middle-brow but radically minded *Interviú* takes a sharper angle. Arias's dark looks and strong build, and his sudden fame, make him like Bogart, but (because of his association with gay directors Almodóvar and Jaime Chávarri, and, presumably, because of his gay role in *La muerte de Mikel*) he is, rather, 'el Bogart ambiguo del nuevo cine madrileño' (the ambiguous Bogart of the new Madrid cinema) (Umbral 1985), 'dulce e indiferente' (gentle and indifferent) rather than hard and direct. As part of his mildly homophobic argument, and in anticipation of the second half of the piece, which judges Arias a poor actor and a chilly personality, Umbral suggests that 'antes que un joven actor, es un caso sociológico entre la juventud neonovísima' (more than a young actor he is an object of sociological interest for our gilded youth).[5] Young women like him because of his clean, new-manly appeal; gay directors ('unisex' Umbral mischievously calls them) are enamoured of him and literary types fascinated: but Umbral is not one to rest on such clichés and his mischievous, telling twist is this:

Las señoritas le llaman 'novio de España' [. . .] [Arias] es un chico foto-génico, con una fotogenia antigua [. . .] Lo que pasa es que las señoritas, como los espectadores de teatro, van con medio siglo de retraso por detrás de la vida. Lo de Imanol Arias es una bella involución. Involución, pero bella. (ibid.)

(Young ladies call him 'Spain's Sweetheart' . . . [Arias] is photogenic, photo-genic in an old-fashioned way . . . The thing is that young ladies, like theatregoers, live their lives with a half-century time delay. The Imanol Arias phenomenon is a beautiful involution. Involuted, but beautiful.)

Both the sensitive, possibly exciting, new man and the reliable, hand-some, possibly dull image from the past coexist in Arias. His career to date gives off that paradoxical special ordinariness that used to attach star value to Hollywood actresses. A full-page photograph in 1985 offers a sensitively moody, unshaven but softly groomed, 'modern' Arias in an unzipped leather jacket, with chest exposed; but it is a non-new-manly hairy chest, and the caption, advertising a very old-fashioned value, is 'Imanol Arias: la naturalidad en escena' (Imanol Arias: a natural on set).[6] While he has certainly professed interest in looking elegant (*Diez Minutos* 1987: 13) and, like Banderas and Bardem (in particular), has accepted a number of advertising contracts, his clothes in contexts bey-ond the photographer's studio are what middle-class Spanish mothers might consider to be in classic good taste and could never be thought exciting.

Similarly balanced—but between greater extremes—is his filmography. Although he has seen himself as having had generally poor judgement in the scripts he has taken up (Cristina Gil 1996: 53), the corpus of screen production—film and television together—is judiciously divided between roles that are disturbing, daring, perverse, and those that are reassuring, charming, humorously intended, in other words 'involuted, but beautiful'. In 1983, the series *Anillos de oro* (the gold rings of the title being wedding rings, albeit in the context of divorce) tends towards the

5 The term 'neonovísima' signals—in its reference back to a brand of effete, trendy, strenuously modern poetry, and a bohemian way of life, of the 1970s—a somewhat precious urban, intel-lectual subculture.
6 *La Vanguardia*, 5 May 1985 (FOA). A fashion shoot in *ABC (Los Domingos)*, 10 March 1985 (1, 5–8) implies the same, mixing lone-adventurer images on railtrack and roadside with cosy rural and domestic scenarios. Similarly, *Elle* (June 1987) quotes Arias on the fragility and vulnerability of men while picturing him in black, with sleeves rolled up, tie loose for action, and a purposeful look.

latter; in 1984 *La muerte de Mikel* tends to the former (though less in Arias's character than in the forces surrounding it: see below); in 1994, *La leyenda de Baltasar, el castrado* (Balthasar the Castrato) (Juan Miñón) to the former, and *Todos los hombres sois iguales / All Men Are the Same* (Manuel Gómez Pereira) to the latter. His more recent roles are balanced, with historical and classical dramatic ones, 'involuted' ones, in Umbral's sense, wrapping the actor in the useful coils of tradition.

Finally, Arias's personal life, as reported in the media, is marked by ambivalence. The relationship with Pastora Vega contributed much in the second half of the 1980s to the image that pleased Umbral's 'young ladies'; but with frank cynicism Arias saw it early on as useful in putting youthful sexual ambiguity behind him and recognized that 'la familia es más rentable' (family sells better) (*Diez Minutos* 1987: 11; also Cristina Gil 1996), and he was open about how the two weighed up competing offers for the rights to photos of their first baby (Ferrando 1987: 106). The couple, with first marriages in ruins behind them, must, however, have been far from being to the taste of the socially and culturally conservative. The nation's sweetheart has after all an edge to him.

Performing national histories

Notwithstanding the balance between the disruptive and the conventional referred to above, the mature Arias of cinema is most memorable for his representations of masculinity's relationships with crime, civil strife, war, and domestic and psychological abuse, and for how these are articulated about moments in the national drama. Looking back on the early part of his career and a commitment to acting influenced directly by 'the social democratic tendency' in the Communist Party of Spain, Arias suggests that 'pretendía, cuando era joven, no ser sólo actor, sino que quería estudiar y entender el mundo, y ser un actor que estuviera a la altura del contexto histórico de la transición' (I tried, when I was young, not just to be an actor but to fulfil my desire to study and understand the world and be an actor in tune with the historical context of the Transition) (Siminovich 1996: 405). Not all his early roles fit this scheme, although *Bearn, o la sala de las muñecas* and *Camila* do associate him with (nineteenth-century) political histories and personal struggles (as well as with the priesthood). His participation in three of the prestigious new adaptation projects arising out of the PSOE's cultural policies of the 1980s—an emphasis on recovering a partially obliterated past, and on rediscovering more or less forbidden texts and famous names (Jordan and Morgan-Tamosunas 1998: 34; Monterde 1987: 152–63)—does, however, clearly mark him as a historically self-contextualizing actor and, increasingly, public figure. These three films are: committed left-winger Mario Camus's version of Camilo José Cela's critical (though in its time centre-right) vision of urban Spain under Franco, *La colmena* / *The Beehive* (1982), Vicente Aranda's (curiously unsophisticated) adaptation of the modern classic by Luis Martín Santos, *Tiempo de silencio* / *The Time of Silence* (1986), and José Luis García Sánchez's version of Ramón del Valle Inclán's *Divinas palabras* / *Divine Words* (1987), a play that despite or because of its avant-garde obscurity and potential for sexual explicitness in 1980s Spain, became a favourite of the young leftist chattering (and studying) classes. His role as Riza in Almodóvar's *Laberinto de pasiones* / *Labyrinth of Passions* (1982) immediately associated him (if at first for a fairly small audience) with Almodóvar's early role in the process of 'refiguring' Spain historically and politically (Kinder 1997: 3–4), with the cultural shake-up which was the 'movida' in Madrid in the early 1980s, with a continuing exploration of the possibilities and impossibilities of a 'utopian rupture with the (heavily censored) cinema [of the immediate past]' (P. J. Smith 2000: 17), and with questions of gender and alternative sexuality (nicely, in film historical terms, encapsulated by the bringing together of the two real life, straight, close friends Arias and Antonio Banderas in a gay sex scene—a situation that was to be matched, or rather surpassed, by Javier Bardem and Jordi Mollá eighteen years later: see Chs. 4 and 5).

Arias is of particular film-historical interest for his connection with Aranda (Sartori 1993: 48–9) and (albeit only in two films, and not in starring roles) Almodóvar—two key figures representing different aspects of the reclaiming and reconfiguration of cultural memory in the post-Franco years. I shall be returning to the importance of the Arias / Almodóvar connection, but would like first to turn to Aranda—one of the prime movers in the 1980s boom of Spanish cinema and a brilliant manipulator of the violent motifs of crime and erotic melodrama (P. Evans 1999c), then to Basque film-maker Imanol Uribe, and then back to Aranda.

In *Tiempo de silencio* Arias plays the chilly and fastidious doctor, Pedro, whose research into genetics, virology, and oncology[7] and his need for human subjects for experimentation on infection get him involved with a family living in the Madrid slums. In the first part of the film Arias can be seen nicely portraying Pedro's aloofness from, and elegantly contained disgust for, the filth, deprivation, social and family dysfunction,

---

[7] These are a central source of metaphorical critique in the original novel but are evacuated of most meanings for the purposes of the film.

and undertow of violence that are sited in the slum; but when he
is called in to attempt to remedy a botched kitchen-table abortion
performed on one of the family's daughters, Pedro is pulled into a
spiral of deceit (the child is her father's), violent jealousy (she was loved
by the local knife-toting petty gangster), shame (supplied by his class-
conscious, intellectual-bashing, and good Francoist police interrogator),
and muted existential crisis (in an intrusive jailhouse voice-over that
attempts to re-enact the effects of the literary text in its references to
alienation, disempowerment, mass desensitization, and living in the
'time of silence'). Although this descent into crisis is meant to be read as
due to the horrors of social inequality, to man's inhumanity to man, to
the dissociation and invalidation of the intellectual class—to the violent
'silence' of an era, in short—there are aspects of Arias's performance that
draw attention, rather, to the contribution to this state of affairs of some
classic enactments of masculinity. Pedro's whole demeanour is conformed
by the highly visible and simplified social constructions of gender that
surround him, in his all-male (and little frequented) workplace, in the
genteel boarding house where he lives, and in his surprisingly roué-like
social life with a rich and idle friend (Juan Echanove). He is driven by
his work and exploits the cachet of his profession in his clumsy flirta-
tions with his landlady's granddaughter, Dorita (Victoria Abril); he is insistently coded by her as a gentleman, quietly controlled and kept in role
by her maternal attentions; but out at night, and drinking, he moves with
ease and normality through a world where—in the café—he looks at a
painter's proudly produced recent nudes and ogles a young woman
dressed in caricature French 1950s intellectual style, even grasping her
face intrusively as he mistakes her for the landlady's daughter. At the
brothel his friend takes him to, women are lined up on display while
Dorita becomes associated with them in his mind as just another object
of rather unsophisticated desire. Arias plays this combination of being
positioned by gender and class expectations and being the mobile
agent in a leisured urban and erotic adventure with inflections of cool
acquiescence, a cynical volte-face as the demands of drink and pleasure
oust the good manners of daytime, and signs of single-minded sexual
irresponsibility—a glassy drunken stare underpinning his thoughts of
Dorita, a moment of resolution as he halts at his own bedroom door and
turns towards hers, vehement and thoughtless sex with her, and the frigid
recourse next day to the excuse of drunkenness. The emptiness is, in this
film, not so much at the heart of society as embodied in certain ways
of being a man that are emphasized in features of Arias's style. In a
number of subsequent films the deployment of such features of look,
performance, and ambience is often returned to, suggesting that the code

is carried in the actor himself (and, of course, in the genres of the
films) and that it relates to a specific awareness of acting out some of
the problematics of masculinity as constructed by, enmeshed with, and
productive of restrictive social and political arrangements.
In Uribe's *La muerte de Mikel*—released two years earlier—this is
acutely apparent. The film makes Arias a point of intersection of
sexual and national(ist) politics as well as being of interest for its part
in an Oedipal drama with allegorical resonances in national and state
politics (Kinder 1993: 215–16; J. Evans 1999: 106–8; Stone 2002: 147). His
upbringing and education in the Basque country (in Ermua and Eibar),
as well as his activity in oppositional issue-based politics (anti-NATO
demonstrations; opposition to the damming and flooding of the Riaño
valley (his birthplace) in 1986–7) had at the time of the film's release
already started to prompt questions in interview on politics in general
and the issues of Basque nationalism and identity in particular, eliciting
well-informed, subtle responses (while on the other hand the photo-
graphic repertoire favours gross caricature of Basqueness, including
Arias juxtaposed with a venerable tree trunk, or with axe and logs).[8]
  The film combines an investigation of the connectedness of individual and collective identities (D'Lugo 1999; J. Evans 1999) with a degree
of national commercial success notable for a film whose agenda and
affiliations appear (though only appear: D'Lugo 1999: 196–200) to be
regional.[9] The film was part of a mini-boom in Basque-government
supported production. It marked a key moment in Uribe's own already
significant career as a politically engaged film-maker (Ángulo, Heredero,
and Rebordinos 1994; Hopewell 1986: 233–5; Jordan and Morgan-
Tamosunas 1998: 194–9). It is still a point of critical reference in 'todo
un período de producción fílmica cuya principal característica era el afán
por abordar sistemáticamente todos los temas prohibidos bajo el régimen
dictatorial' (Alfeo Álvarez 2001: 139) (a whole period of film production whose main characteristic was its enthusiasm for taking on one by
one all the themes that had been banned under the dictatorship); and
it is the eighth in a series of gay affirmative Spanish films of this period
(138–41). Arias's playing of Mikel—at the crux of a series of conflicts of
allegiance (D'Lugo 1999: 196, 203–4): affective, sexual, political, belief-
and loyalty-based—comes, then, at a moment of articulation where traditional representations are under considerable stress and new issues are

[8] *Panorama*, 27 June 1988: 10–11; and photographs in *ABC (Domingo)*, 10 March 1985: 1 and Diosdado,
1988: 77.
[9] The film grossed 231.7 million pesetas, and, as Jo Evans (1999: 101) reminds us, was reckoned
tenth most successful Spanish film in an important study of Spanish cinema in the period
1975–89 (Caparrós Lera 1992).

being opened out. The insistence on rituals of identity-assertion centring on Mikel's dead body in the funeral mass which is the framing narrative present of the film engages the spectator in 'a productive interrogation of the patterns of contemporary society' (ibid. 205); the character of Mikel is in many ways barely that at all, being more type and exemplar than a biographically and psychologically filled-out personality (Martínez Expósito 1995: 94–5); but Arias's nascent star persona itself is engaging as it here absorbs and represents issues of identity, change, and allegiance.

Mikel—living in a small town, his marriage collapsed, with a sternly religious and gossip-obsessed mother—traumatically discovers his homosexuality. By very (unbelievably) soon accepting it and then proudly affirming it he tears open already revealed fractures in the structures of family, community, and friendship, and outs a reactionary streak in old-left Basque Nationalist politics, his active commitment to which is abruptly terminated by the bearded, chunky-sweatered males in charge. The emotional, political, physical, and psychological discoveries that Mikel is put through and works through—always placing actions above words (ibid. 96)—make demands to which Arias's responses are something of an anticipatory compendium of his later range in non-comic roles. In two moments in the woodlands above the bay and the town—prior to his wife Begoña's return from a trial separation and tour of Northern Europe, and after his torture and interrogation by police and betrayal by his closest friend—he works with the camera to allow his large, dark eyes to register for his audience soulful authenticity and an attractive ambivalence in the significance of his gaze (J. Evans 1999). Is he, as the occasional narrowing of his eyes in the first scene implies, in charge of the scene he surveys, to the extent of being readied to abandon it for the freer life he speaks of to Begoña late in the film (and again out in the open)? Or is he, as a POV shot of passing clouds strongly indicates in the second scene, caught up—admirably and romantically—in a fantasy, bonded to the 'sanctuary' and 'camouflage' (108) that the place, nature, and communion with the self offer? If the latter, then the fantasy is strongly compensatory since he is excluded from all these in terms of the film's narrative framing (he is already dead) and (while alive) by the community's dominant belief systems—on left and right—by which he is always condemned.

These looks into the distance—affirming Mikel's heroic authenticity and difference in abstract mode—are matched by closer looks of defiance, decision, and self-knowledge shot in interiors that correspond to sites of limitation or oppression. With Begoña in the glassed-in balcony of the home of mutual friends (with nature painfully at one remove beyond the panes) Arias has Mikel show in facial gesture and look a grave remorse (he has sexually mutilated her, disinhibited by drink and distress), but also a controlled determination as the terms of their separation and the unknowability of the pattern of his new life reveal themselves. When Mikel hears from his one-time comrades of his elimination from the local election hustings, Arias presents disdain, anger, and moral superiority through a combination of folded arms, stonily averted and downward gaze to leftwards, a well-timed flash of a look to extreme right, brushing past his interlocutor, a quick shutting of the eyes, and the utterance, as he turns on his heels, of the words 'sois unos curas' (you're no better than the priests). With his mother, resorting to emotional blackmail and talk of honour in the drawing-room, his look is one of principled refusal to compromise. With police interrogators, it is of properly righteous defiance. In contrast to these are the non-heroic but strongly identificatory looks of relief, pleasure, and amusement in the quite other interior of the drag club which is the site of his first attraction to another man, the self-assured transvestite who performs pop versions of 1940s and 1950s torch-songs there (amusingly offsetting the macho, pub-based chanting of the old-left men back home): the soulful eyes are now twinkling ones, the stark greys and blues of the home-town in its elements replaced by the camp crimsons, soft furnishings, and blurred light and dark of the club interior, and the way the men are dressed there, in period smart casual (and in logical extension of Mikel's habitual elegant dark cardigans, clean-shavenness, fawn trousers, and light zipper jacket which are a minor scandal to hard left masculinity and small-town piety alike). All these stake out positions of personal-politically specific difference for the character and anticipate Arias the actor as, variously, outsider, sexually tormented, perversely fascinating, self-determined hero, pitiable, strong, and representative of alternative destinies.

There were the usual risks in taking on the role of the homosexual Mikel, in the by then well-publicized association with Almodóvar, and in the minor but memorable role as Riza, the son of the Prince of Tirana, 'cured' of serial homosexual encounters by sexual compulsive Sexilia in *Laberinto de pasiones*. One interviewer (De La Fuente 1984: 9) goes into this directly, suggesting that on the Madrid *movida* scene, which Arias was known to have frequented, he is 'considered' as 'giving the impression' of bisexuality and that perhaps he plays to this; and that, although *La muerte de Mikel* clearly is not autobiographical in any way, the fact that he was married young (to Socorro Amadón) and soon separated has a clear echo of Mikel's relation to Begoña in the film. Arias politely recognizes in the interview that his avoidance of traditionally masculine roles, the role of Mikel, and the current ethos—'el tinglado estético' (this whole new aesthetic set-up)—of acceptance of alternative sexualities might all lead to a perception by his audience of an 'ambiguous image', but he insists he does not cultivate one (9).

While maintaining his associations with outsiderdom, Arias is very much straightened out, and his relation to resistant histories made more direct, in his formative roles in Aranda's political-historical dramas *El Lute, camina o revienta / El Lute: Run for Your Life* (1987) and *El Lute II, mañana seré libre / El Lute II: Tomorrow I'll Be Free* (1988). The films are based on the autobiography of Eleuterio Sánchez, 'El Lute', forced by social deprivation into delinquency in the 1960s and elevated to folk hero by way of his resistance to authoritarian injustice and the demonization of travellers, the poor, and the dispossessed, and by dint of a famous last-minute reprieve by Franco of his death sentence. El Lute is the target of obsessive control and punishment out of all proportion to his original petty crimes: jailed (in the first film) for the theft of a chicken in an early, nomadic period of his life, he moves to the Madrid slum outskirts, becomes involved in a burglary and murder, is tortured for information ostensibly on the case but in fact on the source of a perceived wave of delinquent crime. The films link Arias to the politics of resistance, and to specific aspects of the Spanish imaginary in that El Lute represents the marginalized and feared other of Francoist society at a time—the 1960s into the early 1970s—when it is beginning to intuit the rate of acceleration of its entropy. His treatment reveals typical political manipulations and diversionary tactics (Jordan and Morgan Tamosunas 1998: 26); and he comes to represent the low-key heroism of banditry working on the side of the dispossessed. His representation on screen in the late 1980s is layered with complex pleasures and the (re)mobilizations of political engagement. The painstaking, naturalistic reconstructions of period and micro-cultural custom (Castro 1987: 20)—the community of tinkers and travellers; 1950s rural Spain; 1960s city slums—and the continuation of a wider Spanish cinematic project of historical re-enactment, rediscovery, and rehistoricization (Jordan and Morgan-Tamosunas 1998: 15–60) have their own satisfactions and produced their own box-office returns. For left-wing audiences, already weary of the governmental institutionalization and distortion of their politics, the retelling of the story of the possibilities of powerful individual responses to injustice, and the memory of public support for El Lute's cause, may well have reignited old enthusiasms; as might also the simple but convincing Marxist framings tentatively acknowledged by Aranda in an interview (Castro 1987: 24).

Arias builds with finesse and accuracy on the character and its underpinnings. The performance is well prepared and studied, and Arias found that, as for the Method actor, there were unconscious transitions in gesture and behaviour between the role and private, non-screen life (C. Arroyo 1987). He engaged in periods of fieldwork studying the argot and behaviour of socially excluded micro-communities, and the accent of the Andalusian/Extremaduran borderland, which for both films added depth, to the characterization.[10] Boyero (1989) attributes to Arias and Victoria Abril, who plays Concha, his woman, as much as to Aranda as a strong director of actors, the success of the two films (subsequently screened as five episodes on television) in recreating 'dos personajes de la mitología popular' (two characters out of popular myth) and offering a convincing and undistorted snapshot of a period.

The first film, on which I want to concentrate here, owes at least as much of its power to convince to its exploitation of raw physicality as to verisimilitude, mimicry, and careful dramatic and cinematographic composition. Arias's body, as his character goes through flight, change of circumstance, hiding, stress, and duress, is as memorable as the story here. On the road, and with Concha in rough lovemaking, he is early on in the film feral and energetic in movements and looks; fleeing capture across country he wordlessly constructs gaunt fear but lean purpose; holed up in his slum home, placed in a shadowy corner bed by Aranda and his team, and contrastively lit, his eyes barely visible, and with a three-day beard, the image of the body in itself projects the illusion of full characterization. The film's torture scenes explicate the regime's discourse of control not just through the humiliations of insult and nakedness, or even through the repertoire of intense pain inflicted through bondage in chains, wrenchings, stretchings, canings, and insertions, but in the framing of the interrogation as an encounter between the normal and normative corpus of authority and decency and a subject interpellated as deviant. El Lute is 'quinque de mierda' (shitty little delinquent), Concha is referred to as blousy, buxom tart, a whole social type is drawn up and written off. El Lute is bestialized, made to shuffle across the floor on a leash tied to his testicles. Above all, the language comes back constantly and punitively to homosexuality. El Lute's submission that at the crime scene he had his back to the rest of the men cues this strain of talk from the interrogators: 'los maricones siempre están de espaldas por lo que les puede caer' (queers always have their backs to things in hope of what they might get that way); the size and quality of his buttocks are commented on in a caning session and the torturer observes that 'a los maricones les gusta este trato [. . .] este muchacho es un gran maricón' (queers like this sort of treatment; this boy is a *big* queer). Arias's body is lit from intense low and high angles in these various scenarios, brown

---

[10] *El Independiente*, 14 Nov. 1987: 39; *Ya* (*Fin de semana*), 20 Nov. 1987 (FOA).

and bloodied against the black and occasional white of part of an interrogator's profile and it takes to itself art-historical codings of martyrdom.

The perverse Arias

To be associated habitually with Aranda is not simply to be written
into the refiguring of Spanish history but also to be associated with
melodramatic intensities, forms of evil, and erotic convolutions of, usually, tragic outcome. However, Aranda's use of Arias in another literary
adaptation, *El amante bilingüe / The Bilingual Lover* (1993) (after the
novel by Juan Marsé), takes the actor in a slightly different direction. Its
engagement with history—the normalization of the Catalan language and
the re-establishment of Catalonia as a strong national other—is clearly
marked, if ambiguously effected. Despite its support from the Generalitat
de Catalunya the film frames Catalanization comically, associates popular Catalan culture with racism—anti-immigrant sentiments and presuppositions rule the streets—and portrays Norma, the woman who is
the intellectual driving force behind the Generalitat's policies of lin-
guistic change, as a spoilt, sexually obsessive, overdressed snob with an
absurdly rich family background. The focus is, rather, on masculinity,
its vicissitudes and its performance. Arias plays ex-ventriloquist and
street musician Juan Marès, whose failed marriage with Norma (Ornella
Muti), and consequent, or causal, crisis of masculinity, leads to his
descent into semi-indigence. The crisis is exacerbated by the disfiguring
injuries caused by a Molotov cocktail thrown at him by an ultra-rightist
objecting to his ill-advised playing of traditional Catalan melodies on his
accordion just after a nearby attack on a pro-Catalan language street stall.
His loss of an eye and the skin and hair of his entire scalp thus becomes
an absurd and unnecessary mark of alignment with the cause most
associated with his perfidious wife. Getting her back becomes entangled
with getting one back on her, and obsessive love with the overriding need
to possess her sexually once more. Marès decides to take on the persona—
an alter ego who addresses him in the filth and gloom of the ex-marital
home—of a hypermasculine and emphatically non-Catalan Juan Farneca,
with a strong, deep Murcian accent (mapping on, perhaps, to Texan or
Geordie in implication), with a pencil moustache, sharp sideburns, and
eye-patch. By playing this coarse cinematic Romeo, Marès is able to prove
to himself that he is still a man, and gets Norma to bed. The practising
of the self-consciously virile voice in front of the mirror, the mimicry of
the fictional type and social caricature, and the utter dependence on a

newly scripted self all draw attention to the fact of Arias performing Marès performing Farneca, and to the constructedness of the roles of husband, male sexual outcast, sexual predator, male as possessor and writer of his own story. The wobbliness of the performance (the film does not escape the overblown qualities, thin characterizations, and inherent simplistic sexual politics of the novel) is of interest not least because of how it points up this layered construction. The more Marès appears in his cloak and wide-brimmed hat, with his wounded scalp and scarred eye socket, and the more he perfects Farneca, the more visible Arias becomes as the audience strains to find the familiar features under the grotesque make-up and disguises. In a way he stands in for some of the grotesqueries of a masculine self-image constructed of notions of shame and honour, around the need for sexual predominance, and based on outmoded forms of seduction. Oddly, Arias came to see the role as a turning point and as some kind of therapeutic exit from two years of relative inactivity (Sartori 1993: 47), partly because of a coincidence in stories—his first failed marriage to a rich girl, his humble origins—and partly (reading between the lines of the interview (48)) because of the potential it released for inner dialogue in the process of developing new characters, and the impetus it gave for an exploration of alternative registers (48).

Released in the same year as *El amante bilingüe*, Aranda's *Intruso / Intruder* (1993) is, after *Amantes / Lovers* (1991) (see Ch. 6), his second psychological thriller with Pedro Costa Musté as producer. It has the same composer for its score (José Nieto: also for *El amante bilingüe*) much of the visual atmosphere, and several of the narrative twists on exacerbated passions of that earlier film. The camera has a fondness for darkened bedrooms, intense two-shots, winter light, anguish; the film concerns an impossible love triangle that ends in murder, and also uses Victoria Abril in characteristically disturbing (or would-be disturbing) mode. Here Abril plays a middle-class wife, Luisa (the same name as her character in *Amantes*), with a mystical and, eventually, deranged streak. Having married one of two close friends from adolescence, Ángel (Arias), she realizes that it was the other, Ramiro (Antonio Valero), whom she was meant for. Ángel accedes, moves abroad, and is wishfully presumed by Ramiro to be dead after ten years; but one winter day he is seen by Luisa destitute and ill on the 1990s Santander streets (Arias, none the less, making a handsome and noble down-and-out, with stubble accentuating his bone structure and his dark black hair more sexy in its unruliness than it is messy). Luisa takes him in, increasingly convincing herself (and telling Ramiro and Ángel) that 'destiny' (another echo of *Amantes*, as we shall see) has reunited them. Soon it becomes clear that Ángel is not only mentally unbalanced—and Arias plays the line between sane and unhinged with acuteness, especially in relation to the couple's children whom he spellbinds with his offbeat stories and his directness—but seriously, terminally ill. He has fits, foaming at the mouth; he coughs up blood on the way back from the beach (a re-enactment of a scene from his adolescent past with Luisa and Ramiro) with the children; and finally he is bedridden, in severe pain, and sporadically comatose. Arias brings to the character of Ángel a quietly powerful and sinister presence, despite an overwrought performance from Abril, and despite music that points to melodrama where plain intense drama is indicated. He carefully calibrates the escalation from understated hatred of Ramiro (with his successful medico-dental career) and mild mental disturbance through bitterly triumphant repossession of his right to sex with Luisa on the grounds of his imminent death, through to the film's crisis where he wrenches from Ramiro's grasp the hypodermic with its overdose of anaesthetic, kills him, and staggers, moments from dying himself, to the marital bed and Luisa. He is a victim of the same script as Abril, of course, and finds himself having to say to Ramiro, after some blood has been taken for analysis, 'yes, that's right: walk the streets of our childhood with the blood of your best friend in your coat pocket'; but two key scenes opposite Valero as Ramiro cut through this falsity to a subtle and dangerous area of masculine alliance and rivalry, and they do so by action and look more than words.

In one scene the two men are in Ramiro's consulting room. The drama is heightened by strong white light from the voiled windows behind Arias in turtleneck sweater and with hair unbrushed and, in the reverse shots, by the formality of Ramiro, in white shirt, suit, and tie. Ángel tells him directly of his hatred for him, of the 'atrocious tortures' he has imagined for him in the ten years of absence. Ramiro takes a step towards him and, equally directly, gives his version of 'the painful truth', that Luisa made a mistake in marrying Ángel and corrected it by marrying Ramiro; the white light on his face in close-up heightens his chilly candour. The reverse shot to Ángel shows him now with tears and intensity on his face. The two men swap positions, and Ángel ranges around as his rage and desperation increase. Again they are face to face: closer now than before. Violently he grasps Ramiro by the arms and, to the words 'sigo amándola . . . locamente' (I still love her . . . I'm mad for her), kisses him ferociously first on one cheek, then on the other in a bitter parody of the conventional Spanish token of friendship. He then crosses a line, and with an ambiguous intensity, with eyes closed, kisses him on the lips. Arias invests this moment with two possibilities, underlying the pure vengeful intent (his kiss is dangerous: his disease is respiratory; and the clinch is violent): one, more plainly, is that Ramiro is being forced into being a momentary fantasy substitution for Luisa; the other, and connected with this, is that a homoerotic undercurrent from the intense years of the adolescent triangle is being avowed. Ramiro's reaction is a caricaturesque manly threat—arm drawn back, eyes challenging, one hand at his rival's throat—and seems to recognize this latter possibility. So too do his words: 'si lo vuelves a hacer, te deshago la cara a puñetazos' (if you do that again I'll punch your face in): the mention of repetition of such an extraordinary action, and its naming, itself allows its established currency. The scene carries the classic violence of homosocial rivalry over into the arena of male rape, and yet it allows a violent tenderness, not between Ángel and Ramiro now, but between Ángel and what he has lost.

From this moment the relationship between them would be unsustainable but for the final prognosis for Ángel—steady and agonizing decline, with no more than months to live—which forces Ramiro into feeling he must allow him to stay. And this notwithstanding Ángel's triumphant, vehement, and sensually charged confession to him on the way back from the clinic on the day of the news: that he has slept with Luisa again. Ramiro's response is a bizarre form of gentlemanly agreement —'aguantaré el tipo' (I'll put up with this for form's sake)—a mixture of misplaced loyalty, emotional dysfunction, and self-interest, all conformed by codes of male friendship. There is a sense in which Ramiro acts as he does—bringing on his family the tragedy of the double murder —because he simply does not understand his wife or the situation (Villalobos 1993), but that lack of understanding is one that is actively produced by such codes. It is one of Arias's particular fascinations that his roles so often act as catalysts for the splitting open of such shells of wilful, created ignorance; for the demystification of masculinity. Another is his gift for representing by means of the conventional look of the *galán* what ought to be unsuitable variations on perversity and moral evil.

In *La leyenda de Baltasar, el castrado* (Balthasar the Castrato: Juan Miñón, 1994) Arias proves adept at representing subtle perversity, sadism, and decadent masculine sexuality. As the Duque de Arcos at the end of the Spanish viceroyalty in seventeenth-century Naples, Arias is the proud, cruel, handsome libertine. Balthasar the castrato (Coque Malla), whose voice the Duke's dead wife bought at the time of his castration, soon finds his body is also the Duke's possession. During a night of feasting he is cross-dressed and brought to the Duke whom Arias intricately represents, as he rises from between the thighs of one of his many women, moving from astonishment through fascination, then making little movements of soon-conquered self-disgust (a swallowing, a twitch of the sensual lips), lust, and cruel deliberation as he takes, kisses, and snuffles obscenely at the boy's hand. At confession the next day it is clear from Balthasar that he was then stripped and caressed and more. But as he is displayed to the Neapolitans—singing the eponymous role from Alessandro Stradella's oratorio San Giovanni Battista—to the visibly sensual pleasure of the Duke in the audience, and introduced into aristocratic society, and as he continues to be subject to the Duke's intense attentions, it becomes clear that he is feeding masochistically what was from the start an erotic attraction for the handsome and potent figure Arias cuts. Finally what is monstrous in the Duke transfers itself, augmented by the lust for fame, to Balthasar. Unhinged by the discovery that the Duke has long since consorted with María de Loffredo (Aitana Sánchez-Gijón), the woman with whom he has had a lifelong obsession, he arranges to have him violently killed (intercut with his performance that night of Dido's lament from Purcell's *Dido and Aeneas*) and strung up, with dramatic irony, next to the fighting cocks' cages in the palace outhouses. Suddenly, out of the matrix of star roles, that earlier image of Arias strung up, as El Lute in the torture scene, comes into view. Whereas there patriarchy set out to punish the socially deviant male, here the sexually deviant male is punished by the monster that his own pride and concupiscence have created. One castration leads to another, at once more symbolic and more definitive in effect. Arias's body once more displays the effects of an archetypal story of masculinity's destructive play with power.

War and Adventure

Three years later, in *Territorio comanche / Comanche Territory* (Gerardo Herrero, 1996) Arias plays Mikel, a war reporter working in Sarajevo during the Balkan conflict with cameraman José (Carmelo Gómez). Mikel is driven by adventure, neglects (like José) his emotional life, and files reports constructed from a consistently event- and action-oriented point of view. Laura (Cecilia Dopazo)—who has got herself assigned through her father's financial interests in a TV station, punctiliously critiques and challenges this and sets out to tell the more 'human' stories of the war, refusing—as she says in a phone-call to Madrid—to compete 'con ellos' (with the men). Mikel and José at first relish their being in Western-style 'Comanche territory', two men alone, in the calm before the storm; as a British reporter remarks, the two of them are bonded by their competitiveness, by their need to get the most vivid story out of the most dangerous circumstances. Of the two, Mikel is the more silent, the closest to the need to avoid the symbolic threat posed by language—with its embedded signs of lack and otherness—'to the image of the self as totally enclosed, self-sufficient, omnipotent' (Neale 1993: 13), but the two end up pacted in a silence that is a dramatically effective reaction to the unspeakable horrors the two have seen and recorded. It is also a vindication of their competitiveness as something vital and good, better than the war, somehow not merely a microcosm of war's own motivational force but instead the mark of their participation in adventure as a phantasy, as Graham Dawson (1994) has suggested, that is part of the cultural imaginary, part of the ideal of masculinity and the myth of nationhood (1–24, 48). It has been José's personal and professional obsession to get the perfect shot of a bridge exploding; with charges laid on a strategic bridge the two men crouch together—José wounded—on the river bank downstream, to watch. Mikel's look is intense, and José asks him what he is thinking about: 'en tu puta puente' (your fucking bridge) he replies; the two men part, but with half a torn banknote each as a token of their determination to be reunited. The explosion—as in so many war films—brings the two men together, both releasing and dispelling unspoken emotion; and we see Arias, as the film draws to its end, with the image of another man's emotional needs in his eyes, the token of their bondedness in his hand, but nothing except silence in the space where there might have been exploration through words of the meanings attaching to the making and breaking of bridges. Together they reforge the classic, damaging, and hegemonic code of complicity of the quiet man at war (Donald 1992: 130–2), soldiers by proxy.

The role of an officer, Paco, with NATO Allied Forces in Almodóvar's *La flor de mi secreto* / *The Flower of My Secret* (1995) had also associated Arias with armed conflict and defensive silences. The break-up of Paco's marriage with romantic fiction writer Leo (Marisa Paredes) is described in the dialogue between the two of them in the scant ten minutes he is on screen in terms of war and battle in what we might suppose (although in fact it does not matter) to be a deliberately trite, if realistic, dramatic strategy. The banality of the clichéd exchange underlines step by step the dismaying predictability of Paco's reactions to emotional challenge (coldness, procrastination, impatience: all accurately embodied by Arias), and it is seen in retrospect when his (again predictable) infidelity is revealed, also to have underlined the lack of imagination involved in sleeping with your wife's best friend because she is a good listener. Leo has the best (if scandalous) line here, accusing Paco—who says he has to leave for Split at once—of using 'those poor Bosnians' as a pretext for avoiding her; he, already more an infrequent voice on the telephone than a presence on-screen, has little to say outside this language of skirmish, and when he puts off her sexual advances by saying he has something to tell her, it is not the truth he tells, but a lie about the unexpected foreshortening of his leave. At the door he declares 'estoy bloqueado, no puedo hablar' (I'm blocked, I can't speak). This silence, though, is not the simple, psychoanalytically prescribed silence of the undifferentiated male but rather a sociologically particular response to Leo's amplification of an already assigned and constructed gender role for modern Western women, that of being articulate in matters of emotional intelligence. As is pointed out—more-or-less reliably and more-or-less fairly—by the psychologist friend Betty, with whom Paco has been having the affair, his silence has been of Leo's making.

This strand of his on-screen persona—a time-honoured mélange of silent, sinister, devious, and deviant—is further developed, though with much less emphasis on the heroic, in the Colombian-Italian-Spanish co-production *Ilona llega con la lluvia* / *Ilona Arrives with the Rain* (Sergio Cabrera, 1996) and—with Arias as a thief of religious paintings—in the ambitious made-for-TV three-parter *El camino de Santiago* (The Road to Santiago) (Antena 3: February 2001), with its large international cast. In the rather too densely structured *Ilona . . .* , Arias is the Lebanese Abdul, a roving, semi-piratical opportunist fresh out of jail in Ceuta and seeking to buy his own boat to make his fortune and rejoin the love triangle composed of Ilona (a high-class, globe-trotting club-owner turned fortune-hunter and Madame) and Maqroll (another seafaring adventurer).[11] Ilona and Maqroll have settled temporarily in lush and dirty-money-strewn Panamá and set up an elaborately themed brothel to generate funds for the boat. The film cuts backwards and forwards between the two locations and sets of stories, and each time it does so it augments the contrast between the frivolity and luxury of the brothel in a Panamá swimming in rain and money and Abdul's operations in Ceuta. Arias plays him with an eerie mix of austerity, quiet bitterness, and glowering rage and purpose. He builds powerfully on some classic tropes and scenarios of crime and intrigue, squaring up to the double-crossing arms dealer who had originally framed him with displays of manly pride and thieves' honour, stolidly maintaining by letter and telegraph the homosocial bonds with Maqroll across the obstacle of oceans, time, and adversity, and intimidating morally and physically the corrupt customs chief in port who stands in the way of his getting the licence on the boat he wants to buy. In a memorable and wholly masculine scene in a Turkish bath Abdul's and Arias's strong, sinewy, and tanned body

11 Maqroll is the pseudonym of novelist and poet Álvaro Mutis. The film is based on Mutis's *Tríptico de mar y tierra* (1993).

emerges from the steam and sits down next to the customs chief (an acute cameo from director José Luis Borau) who is plump, white, startled, with a towel wrapped around his head, and spectacles fogged. Arias projects contained menace, and the camera is encouraged to pick up the gleam of sweat and the high contrast of white of eye and blackness of pupil to make them tokens of the edginess of the encounter. His exit is marked by a richly nuanced, cruel, sardonic smile, his whole body in frame, standing dominating the left middle plane while the defeat and pettiness of Borau's character is magnified by his seated proximity to the camera front right. This is a typical moment of quiet menace for Arias, with the edge of desperation that informs the role in *Intruso*.

Arias as comic actor

Arias's smile is not, however, invariably unsettling. By sharp contrast, his first significant comic role was that of the sexually confused absconding son of the Prince of Tirana in *Labyrinth of Passions*; roles in the comedies *Tierno verano de lujurias y azoteas* (Tender Summer of Lust on the Rooftops) (Jaime Chávarri, 1993), *Todos los hombres sois iguales / All Men Are the Same* (Manuel Gómez Pereira, 1994), *Sálvate si puedes* (Save Yourself if You Can) (Joaquín Trincado, 1994), and his presence in television light drama (*Querido Maestro*), link Arias to Jorge Sanz in the business of (reasonably) high comic deflations yet reaffirmations of stereotypes, fantasies, and prohibitions (Jordan and Morgan-Tamosunas 1998: 86), in particular in relation to heterosexual masculinities of early middle age.

In Gerardo Vera's *Una mujer bajo la lluvia / A Woman in the Rain* (1992) Arias plays alongside Banderas in a remake of Edgar Neville's play, and subsequently film script, *La vida en un hilo* (Life on a Thread) (1945) which carries forward faithfully its classic Hollywood premise with more than a touch of Lubitsch—especially with its mildly supernatural framing. In the outer narrative frame of the film a stage medium/magician tells two intercut alternative tales of the life of a glamorous woman (Angela Molina) from the moment she is caught in a rainstorm after shopping at a smart department store (in a Madrid that looks like 1950s New York). In one version she is picked up by a rich but painfully gauche Basque businessman (Arias), and in the other by a poor but strikingly handsome artist (Banderas). Stock contrasts between masculinities conformed by class, age, money, and different urban milieux are keyed into nicely by Arias's playing to physical type (distinguished and conventional) and Banderas's recapitulation of his customary 1980s roles as sexy young rebel.

Pratfalls, an interest in golf and old school friends, conversation limited
to work or short-lived lifestyle caprices (Tantric yoga; Japanese food; exercise routines) wrap Arias's character round with disabling boorishness
framed by empty consumerist ambitions, a conservative family, an over-
bearing mother, and traditionalist micro-societies (that of the Japanese
businessmen to whom he is exporting recordings of baroque music, and
that of mercantile Bilbao).

   Todos los hombres sois iguales explores a different sort of male, in the
milieu now of Madrid, and uses the three-divorced-men-sharing-a-flat
situation, with their rules (no same woman two nights running, no
falling in love), their childishness (joky comparisons of penis size,
domestic helplessness, spying on each other's adventures), and a sexy,
capable cleaning woman, functioning theoretically as the usual token
of exchange in a homosocial economy, but none the less out for all
she can materially get. Arias co-stars with Antonio Resines and Juanjo
Puigcorbé—'trio de oro de nuestro cine' (the three golden boys of
Spanish cinema) as one reviewer put it (Albert 1994)—and plays Juan José
who, although he has (we are regularly reminded) the smallest penis, gets
the most and the sexiest women. It is Arias whose body is in the best
shape and is most shown off (he strips off his sweatshirt during his
exercise routine, inviting the cleaner to put some sunscreen on his
back) and he exploits his earlier image as sex symbol, using it smilingly
as a substitute for the superior, easy comic talent of Resines. Arias has
good, but slow, timing generally and—perhaps to his credit—rarely if ever
unbends into demotic expression in this genre, nor would his elegant
physique and ironic eyes easily allow it.

   There is a certain unease to the performance here. The ill-intentioned
might see a telling crossover with his stated 'real life' views on home life—
liking to be served at table, occasionally cooking for friends but never
washing up (González and Pasquín 1990: 92)—and perhaps the extreme
caricature of just that kind of man in this film is designed both to disavow and to reaffirm them. *Todos los hombres sois iguales*, with its
only just subversively self-aware misogyny and realistically reproduced
homophobia (*maricón*—sissy—is the favoured insult used by the women
when deriding the men), with its dependency on bipolar gender stereo-
typing and only provisional ironic deflation of it, aligns Arias with the
wider phenomenon in Western European and North American cinema
of a type of comedy that functions 'at one and the same time to express
a problematic male identity and to alleviate male apprehension in
laughter' (Powrie 1997: 146). As I have been trying to show, Arias is more
usually involved in the first of these functions, sometimes alleviating male
apprehension through naturalization of the problematics, sometimes,
through perverse representation, simply accentuating the apprehension,

and tying it painfully, necessarily to male identity. It is, in short, his tragic timing and his serious or sinister looks that are the better.

An update

In the period following Arias's self-imposed rest from filming in 1997–9 (possibly a repeat of the 'crisis' that preceded *El amante bilingüe*) there seems to be a pattern of re-emerging seriousness. *Una casa con vistas al mar* (A House with a View of the Sea) (Alberto Arvelo, 2001) is, reportedly,[12] a return to actorly seriousness of an emphatically cinematic nature, as too is the intense, short *Quiero morir* (I Want to Die: Toni Meca, 2000) with its extreme moral dilemma—should the cop whose life has been ruined by a psychopathic killer, now paraplegic and in agony in a hospital bed, help him to die; can euthanasia be done by revenge killing? In *La voz de su amo* (His Master's Voice) (Emilio Martínez Lázaro, 2001), he plays a corrupt right-wing policeman in a film set in the Basque country in the 1980s, exploring—like *Yoyes* (Helena Taberna, 1999), *El viaje de Arián* (Arián's Journey) (Eduard Bosch, 2001), *La muerte de Mikel*, and *Días contados / Numbered Days* (see Ch. 3)—terrorism, authority, nation, and personal commitment.

As a public figure, throughout the 1990s Arias's involvement across the industry has grown, with the presidency of the Asociación de Intérpretes, Sociedad de Gestión (the government-recognized association for the management of intellectual property rights of performers), a first feature film as director of *Un asunto privado* (A Private Affair) (1996, starring Jorge Perugorría and Pastora Vega), and with his entry into production with *Rigor Mortis* (Koldo Azkarreta, 1997) (in which he also stars, but which very few watched). His prominence in the 23 January 2000 antiterrorism demonstration in Madrid (reading out, in place of indisposed philosopher Fernando Savater, a manifesto against violence and ending with the cry, in Basque and Castilian, 'ETA out!'), and as signatory of the Artists' and Intellectuals' Manifesto against the Partido Popular in March of that year (of this book's actors only Arias and Botto signed up), appears to signal fidelity to the principles of oppositional political commitment formed by Arias as a young actor and stands in productive contrast to the continuing domestication and sanitizing of his image—particularly on television—as the dependable, neighbourhood *novio de España*.

---

12 It premiered at the Huelva Film Festival 2001, but I have been unable to view it. See http://www.festicinehuelva.com/27edicion/vistasalmar.html (28 Dec. 2001).

TABLE 1. *Filmography*

Year	Title	English title(s) (official in italics; literal in roman)	Director	Billing	Audience figures and takings	Other information
1982	*Demonios en el jardín*	*Demons in the Garden*	Manuel Gutiérrez Aragón	4th	983,381 €1,331,756	
1982	*La colmena*	*The Beehive*	Mario Camus	Minor	1,493,139 €2,054,360	
1982	*Laberinto de pasiones*	*Labyrinth of Passions*	Pedro Almodóvar	2nd	357,900 €596,782	
1983	*Bearn, o la sala de las muñecas*	*Bearn, or the Dolls' Room*	Jaime Chávarri	4th	477,624 €715,089	
1985	*Fuego Eterno*	*Everlasting Fire*	José Ángel Rebolledo	2nd	119,487 €198,904	
1984	*La muerte de Mikel*	*The Death of Mikel / Michael's Death*	Imanol Uribe	Top	1,169,376 €1,702,311	
1985	*Lulu de Noche*	*Lulu By Night*	Emilio Martínez Lázaro	Top	326,599 €551,676	
1986	*Bandera Negra*	*The Black Flag*	Pedro Olea	Top	159,868 €283,353	
1986	*Tiempo de silencio*	*Time of Silence*	Vicente Aranda	Top	433,149 €757,981	
1987	*Divinas palabras*	*Divine Words*	José Luis García Sánchez	3rd	573,603 €1,062,477	

Year	Spanish title	English title	Director	Rank	Figures	Notes
1987	El Lute, camina o revienta	El Lute, Forge on or Die / Run for Your Life	Vicente Aranda	Top	1,422,188 €2,586,728	These figures, left, ignore the considerable television exposure of the film
1988	El Lute II: mañana seré libre	El Lute II: Tomorrow I'll be Free	Vicente Aranda	2nd	382,764 €681,131	See note above, for El Lute, camina o revienta
1990	A solas contigo	Alone Together	Eduardo Campoy	2nd	232,583 €533,229	
1992	Una mujer bajo la lluvia	A Woman in the Rain	Gerardo Vera	3rd	234,239 €611,528	
1993	El amante bilingüe	The Bilingual Lover	Vicente Aranda	Top	273,218 €738,397	
1993	Tierno verano de lujurias y azoteas	Tender Summer of Lust on the Rooftops	Jaime Chávarri	3rd	190,223 €495,346	
1993	Intruso	Intruder	Vicente Aranda	Top	843,839 €2,492,906	
1995	La leyenda de Baltasar, el castrado	The Legend of Balthasar the Castrato	Juan Miñón	Top	44,666 €121,764	
1994	Sálvate si puedes	Save Yourself if You Can	Joaquín Trincado	Top	73,495 €209,568	
1994	Todos los hombres sois iguales	All Men Are the Same	Manuel Gómez Pereira	Top	843,839 €2,492,906	
1995	Africa	Africa	Alfonso Ungría	Top	66,902 €189,526	
1995	La flor de mi secreto	The Flower of my Secret	Pedro Almodóvar	4th	981,688 €3,196,909	
1996	A tres bandas	The Cue-Master	Enrico Coletti	4th	23,841 €87,479	Co-pro Spain, Italy

TABLE 1. (*continued*)

Year	Title	English title(s) (official in italics; literal in roman)	Director	Billing	Audience figures and takings	Other information
1996	*En brazos de la mujer madura*	*In Praise of Older Women*	Manuel Lombardero	Minor	92,104 €303,333	
1996	*Ilona llega con la lluvia*	*Ilona Arrives with the Rain*	Sergio Cabrera	2nd	39,781 €116,787	Co-pro Colombia, Italy, Spain
1997	*Rigor mortis*		Koldo Azkarreta	Top	429 €1,531	
1997	*Territorio comanche*	*Comanche Territory*	Gerardo Herrero	Top	196,528 €665,770	Co-pro Spain, France, Germany
2000	*La voz de su amo*	His Master's Voice	Emilio Martínez Lázaro	2nd	67,159 €300,507	
2001	*Una casa con vistas al mar*	A House with a View of the Sea	Alberto Arvelo	Top	No figures available: festival release only as at 6 Feb. 2002	Co-pro Venezuela, Spain, Canada
2001	*Salvajes*	Savages	Carlos Molinero Valera	Top	16,939 €67,390	

Shorts

Quiero morir (I Want to Die) (Toni Meca, 2000)

Television series

Anillos de oro (Rings of Gold) TVE, 1983/1984
Brigada central (Police HQ) TVE, 1988
El conde Arnau TV3, 1994
Querido maestro (Dear Teacher) Tele5, 1996/1997 (Fotogramas de Plata 1997 for Best
TV Actor; and gaining, for example, a larger audience—5.4 million—on Monday
2 June 1996 than the previous weekend's Zaragossa–Atlético Madrid match—
4 million: http://www.el-mundo.es/1997/06/04/television/04N0128.html (2 Feb.
2002)).
Dime que me quieres (Tell Me You Love Me) Antena 3, 2000/2001
Cuéntame (Tell Me Something) TVE, 2001 (top audience ratings for series in Spain
in 2001, overtaking *Periodistas,* Tele5, and *Compañeros,* Antena 3)
Severo Ochoa TVE, 2001/2002

Films for television

Lazos (Bonds) (Alfonso Ungría, 1996)

Fig. 3. Antonio Banderas, Ana Belén (left), and Mari Carmen Ramírez (right) in *La corte de Faraón*.

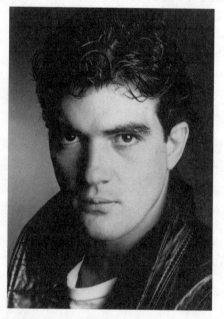

Fig. 4. Antonio Banderas, publicity photo.

2 Antonio Banderas (b. 1960)

Identifying the early Spanish Banderas

With his move to Los Angeles in 1991 and the shooting of *The Mambo Kings* (Arnold Glimcher), a shift into English-speaking roles, and his assumption into the hyperbolic imaginary of US show business, Antonio Banderas began for a time to be the most famous of twentieth-century Spanish actors. Simultaneously he became no longer Spanish but 'Hispanic'. *Interview with a Vampire* (Neil Jordan, 1993) denationalized Banderas and translated his adventurous representations of sexuality and his prior associations with contemporary Spanish drug, crime, and youth culture, into a higher perversity. *Miami Rhapsody* (David Frankel, 1994) placed him as Miami Cuban—in some ways doubly dispossessed —and playing opposite Mia Farrow's seduced older woman instead of Carmen Maura's, as in *Bâton Rouge* (discussed below). Two Latin-American sourced and themed films, *The House of the Spirits* (Billie August, 1993) and *Of Love and Shadows* (Betty Kaplan, 1994), took two familiar role types from the Spanish years, those of oppressed rebel and political idealist, and cast them in broadly Latin terms.

This chapter, however, focuses on Banderas's career ending, effectively,[1] with two Spanish films of limited success, *Una mujer bajo la lluvia* (see Ch. 1) and *¡Dispara! / Shoot! / Outrage* (Carlos Saura, 1993), whose shooting schedule was interwoven with that of *Philadelphia* (Jonathan Demme, 1992). As is widely acknowledged, especially by Banderas himself (Oliva and Fernández 1995: 134; and in countless interviews) it was that part of the actor's career spent working with Pedro Almodóvar (and with Carmen Maura and Victoria Abril) which formed and gave substance to his image,[2] and this will necessarily be central to what I have to say in this chapter. However, I shall also be wanting to give emphasis to the argument that the complex pleasures of negotiating a place for ourselves

---

[1] At the time of writing, although Banderas and Griffiths are resident in Spain (Marbella) during the summers Banderas's acting career in Spain still belongs to the past.

[2] Most brief accounts, reviews, and portraits of the early Hollywood Banderas make dutiful but usually uninformative reference to the Almodóvar years as seminal: Heredero 1992; *El Mundo*, 29 March 1992; *Fotogramas*, May 1992; *Cinerama*, March 1995; Narváez (1989).

in the dramas of so strong and so auteurist a director as Almodóvar (Allinson 2001: 122–5; J. Arroyo 1996; P. J. Smith 2000: 1–6) are enhanced and better analysed if we give due weight to what the actors bring to the œuvre by way of structures of identification and meaning, as is proved by P. Evans's (1996) study of Carmen Maura and Allinson's (2001) useful emphases on Almodóvar's actors. To do this I want to pay particular attention to an Antonio Banderas becoming an identificatory object and building up a distinctive personality prior to and in parallel with his involvement in the Almodóvar phenomenon, and his independent elaboration of his intuitive style, magnetism, and quickness to learn and empathize (Borau 1998: 112).

When in Carlos Saura's Los Zancos (Love on Stilts) (1984) Banderas's character—a gentle, earnest, belated hippy type—turns an enthusiastic and long-haired look towards veteran actor Fernando Fernán Gómez's character and at their first meeting tells the older man (soon to be his rival in love) 'soy actor' (I am an actor), the significance of the moment far exceeds the intentions and possibilities of the film. The open-air theatre company he fronts puts on a play on stilts that is an amalgam of old Spanish folk and ballad tradition, and Banderas strides up out of it and into the beginnings of the making of him as a typically Spanish actor, soon to be the far-fetched chico Almodóvar (one of the Almodóvar gang) on the one hand, and developing a repertoire of more realistic types of Spanish youth on the other. Furthermore, of all those considered in this book Banderas has the most connection with the popular notions of how the story of becoming an actor unfolds, and is the one whose development of talent, of 'skill [. . .] at being a certain sort of person or image' (Dyer 1998: 17), is the most vividly displayed. Before coming to the extra-filmic aspects of the actor's story, I shall focus for a while on how a Spanish cinema enthusiast could trace through the 1980s the prototypes of Banderas that are transferred to and developed in the three key Almodóvar-Banderas films Matador (1986), La ley del deseo / Law of Desire (1987), and Mujeres al borde de un ataque de nervios / Women on the Verge of a Nervous Breakdown (1988).

Taking form as Banderas types in these years are: the young male whose body is used as much for violence as for sex, suggested obliquely in the attractive young terrorist Sadec in Almodóvar's Laberinto de pasiones / Labyrinth of Passions (1982), but developed fully in El placer de matar / The Pleasure of Killing (Félix Rotaeta, 1987); the young tough living on the margins, in 27 horas (27 Hours) (Montxo Armendáriz, 1986); the feckless but counter-culturally idealistic innocent of Los zancos; a bewildered virgin with a vow of chastity who ripens into the object of female desire, both sexual and maternal, in the role of a friar turned stand-in actor in the show movie *La corte de Faraón* (Pharaoh's Court) (José Luis García Sánchez, 1985). This film, at one level, safely anchored Banderas in the Spanish light-operatic tradition of *zarzuela*—no more risqué and no less nostalgically nationalist than Gilbert and Sullivan—and in the deep, wide terrain of the popular canonical, while in the same year his role as the peasant activist Paco in Francesc Beltriú's adaptation of Camilo Jose Cela's short novel (and secondary-school text) *Réquiem por un campesino español (Mosén Millán) / Requiem for a Spanish Peasant* again formed a bond with the recognizably Spanish, and, in this case, with the literary canon (and a future Nobel Literature Prize winner, in Cela). However, these examples of cultural grounding (themselves containing substantial elements of trouble and subversion) are hedged about not only by the images of violence and sex already alluded to but by a more specific image accruing to Banderas as the 1980s progress, that of the disturbed hustler whose body is the focus of pleasurable attention intra- and extra-diagetically but which is the locus of betrayal and self-destruction. In 'El informe' (The Report) (episode 4 of *Delirios de amor* produced for television by Fernán Gómez: Félix Rotaeta, 1986) Banderas plays what turns out to be an in-the-closet undercover policeman who allows himself to be seduced by a high-class male drug trafficker, discovering that the role he has adopted is really an unstable identity, that he enjoys man-on-man sex (graphically, especially for television in those days), and that he has a destructive bisexual streak which leads to his betraying both his wife and his rich, new male lover. In *Bâton Rouge* (Rafael Moleón, 1988) he is again enmeshed by his body—narcissistically displayed, costumed, caressed, and preened throughout—in a narrative of two-way pull and betrayal, though here it has a twist. Hitting on an apparently rich divorcee (Carmen Maura) whom his character Antonio identifies, guiltily, with his own absent mother, he finds that the sexual energy generated for the initial plan is diverted into a more sinister and more emphatically criminal area by his attraction to a supposed psychoanalyst (Victoria Abril, in bad girl mode *par excellence*); her guile far exceeds his wit, she exploits and destroys him, as too—it turns out—does Maura, involved as she is, in fact, with Abril. Like *Los Zancos* the film has a crucial moment of inscription of Banderas into the pantheon of Spanish film acting: early in the first reel Maura (with six Almodóvar films already behind her and a very considerable filmography as supporting actress) picks up Banderas and asks '¿Quién eres?' (Who are you?), getting the multiply resonant answer, 'Me llaman Antonio' (They call me Antonio). Unlike the sweet, naïve actor of that earlier film, now 'Antonio' has begun to signify confusion and complexity.

Off-screen considerable effort went into disavowing the particular emphasis on disturbance, psychic splitting, sexual ambiguity, and mother-fixation to point up less challenging Antonios for certain important sectors of the public. As a fantasy projection of the image consumer's own dreams for the future and as role model, and imitation (Dyer 1998: 17–19), Banderas worked well for his interviewers and for staff reporters in need of quick archetypal narratives and catchlines in these early years (as still). The type of image constructed here is reassuring, if shifting—after all, the emerging star persona is acting, as Metz (1983: 67) reminds us, 'the best of his parts'; and 'inconsistency, change and fluctuation are characteristic of star images' (Mayne 1993: 128). A young, pretty but verging on hunky Andalusian drama student from the provincial (though mildly exotic) Mediterranean city of Málaga makes the classic journey to the capital city, 'con 15.000 ptas y sin conocer a nadie' (with 15,000 pesetas in his pocket and knowing nobody) (Abelleira Briz 1986), rings a fellow *malagueño* who has made it in theatre direction, Luis Balaguer, gets a bit part in a play, works as an usher and understudy, is noticed by big shot Lluis Pasqual, gets another small part (in a classic drama, *La hija del aire*, watched one night by Almodóvar), then has a lucky break when actor Juan Geo hurts his ankle and Banderas temporarily takes on the role of Gaveston in *Eduardo II: Rey de Inglaterra* (seen one night by Carlos Saura) (T. Rubio 1985; Oliva and Fernández 1995: 89–103). This is a story that is widely taken up again at the time of Banderas's entry into Hollywood (for example, in Alameda 1992: 23; Heredero 1992), and there are three main hooks: Banderas's sexual-romantic availability, the image of the loner, and his openness to all career possibilities (an openness that loops back onto the first of my hooks). The magazine *Semana* asks him straight out in November 1985: '"¿Tienes novia?"' (Do you have a girlfriend?) (Fergo 1985); *El Periódico* in December photographs him looking rather alone, and rather appealing, against the clay-tiled rooftops of a traditional, old-town Madrid: '"¿Te has convertido en un personaje popular?"; "A mí la gente no me para por la calle, no me conoce"'(Do you think people have started to see you as something of a personality?; Nobody stops me in the street, no one knows me) (T. Rubio 1985: 54): but this response barely suppresses its 'yet' and the interview is one marked as much by lively, appealing ambition as by the equally calculated, languid rooftop romance of the images. The interview's catchline is in fact 'Quiero ser el Butragueño del cine' (I want to be the Butragueño of the film world). Banderas's fantasy self-alignment with the Real Madrid player of 1980s myth is the beginning of his development as an icon of modern Madrid, and as a masculine sex symbol (it may or may not have been in the actor's mind that what the footballer was popularly famous for, as well as his prowess, was the size of his penis):[3] much of the affiliative identification with Banderas at the popular level involves loyalty to a great city in the process, in the mid-1980s, of rejuvenation and realignment, and it involves too a fascination with what in the Spanish cultural and popular press are always called the 'protagonists' of social and cultural life, the celebrities. The scandalous carnal interest of Banderas (in the minor role of Sadec) having sex with Imanol Arias in *Laberinto de pasiones* was in the end less significant for him than was the film's immediate positioning of its cast, and his body, in the field of intense energies that formed the youth and pop-art culture scene in Madrid, the *movida madrileña*, in the first half of the 1980s, and at the start of the creation of a new shared cinematic sensibility, initially around the programming at the Alphaville cinema (P. J. Smith 2000: 33), and subsequently around the cinema of Almodóvar. Banderas became part of the bricolage and radical camp aesthetic of the *movida* (on which see Allinson 2001: 15–18), his look a facet of a national/urban exhibition of 'glittery *Zeitgeist*' (34; also Stone 2002: 185–6), and soon to become an icon of a moment of social and cultural change. This, intertwined with his simple actor's story, is as important to his emerging career as the not inconsiderable potency of the look in his eyes and the sheen on the denim, leather, dark hair, and flesh which make up the typical Banderas of the 1980s.

The muscular, athletic associations of the footballing reference just mentioned were not to come fully into view until, perhaps, *Desperado* (Robert Rodriguez, 1995); but the associations of celebrity through the training and exhibition of the body in movement were to do so at once (indeed, at the end of the 'Butragueño' interview, the photographer is reported to have tried to persuade Banderas to do some gymnastic moves on the railings of the rooftop terrace location). In *Matador*, of course, one key element in Ángel's complex of deferred desires is the lure of the arena, the need to engage the body in the drama and choreography of the bullfight as, perhaps, a means of sublimating the desire to penetrate and be penetrated. His psychosomatically strategic fainting at the sight of blood and his visions only serve to corral him in a behavioural and representational space where—as with his mother, though more subtly—prohibition amplifies, diverts, and perverts what we might call lust. The more he is unable to perform—as fighter, heterosexual lover, amateur detective, and, wishfully and metonymically, killer—the more

---

[3] I am grateful to members of the audience at the conference 'Almodóvar 20 Years On' (Institute for Romance Studies, London, 25 Nov. 2000) who first pointed this out to me.

we focus in on his body as the site and producer of a series of truncated narratives of desire. Truncated partly through what P. J. Smith (2000: 71) recognizes as the 'constellation of disavowals which go beyond his character to contaminate the film as a whole', partly through a faulty identification mechanism in Ángel (sparking out incoherently in the direction of all the main characters, male, female, motherly, brotherly, passive, active, and in between), and partly—a flaw identified by José Enrique Monterde (1987: 11) in regard to *Law of Desire*—through insufficient or non-existent development of motivation for his character. In the absence of this in Ángel we just, though not simply, identify with Banderas.

Looking at Banderas

As we have already begun to see, spread across several films of varied quality and commercial duration, and across the pages of the glossy and cultural supplement press, are stimuli to admiration, envy, excitement, and to speculative fantasies about meeting, caressing, submitting to, or somehow being the people Antonio Banderas represents, and these have power that perhaps outweighs, perhaps compensates for, the perceived weaknesses of 'character' in Banderas's early Almodóvar roles. Young men could perhaps identify with his burgeoning control as a personality over the narrative of his life and could have an attachment, an affinity, with his cockiness and glamour both lived out and acted; young women could identify if not with Banderas alone (although he sports sufficient markers of rebel-biker, borrowed masculinity for a butch lesbian knowingly to do so) then certainly with the romantic configuration Banderas-plus-one, and could again have affinity with the glamour; while both young and older women (and perhaps older gay men) might have warmed to his vulnerability and found themselves stimulated into albeit wryly aware tenderness.

Clearly, at this stage I am beginning to move on from identification understood as reaction across a single vector to human figures on screen, sympathy with characters played, simple recognition of gendered sameness (as summarized by Mayne 1993: 26; and Turner 1988: 132–3). I have anyway been stressing, in my first section, more the interplay of the actor, the nascent star persona, and the viewer and fan (following Cook 1980 and McDonald 1998: 187–93). There is also the still important question of how the cinematic institution and apparatus position me 'long before I have "identified" with a favourite actor or character'

(Mayne 1993: 27, after Baudry and Metz). As Metz suggested, I see the actor—his human form, his story, constructed on screen—I apprehend 'this perceived imaginary' and yet 'I am myself the place' where meanings accrue, where the imagined, projected personality takes shape, and the story begins to build (Metz 1983: 48–9). The question of my subject position, of where I might be, is tied up with this (though not, as later commentators have been quick to point out, to the exclusion of alternative positions). The identification turns inward—'the spectator identifies with himself [. . .] as pure act of perception' (49)—and away from the actor/character in a diffusion of attention, with the object of identification both present and absent, 'distributed over the whole surface of the screen'. My presence, which is also an absence—I am not on-screen, I was not there—'hover[s] ready to catch on preferentially to some motif' (54). However, if I ask if my desire to know about, see, possess the image Antonio Banderas—on- and off-screen—fixes me or disperses me (that is, aligns me with others imagined and real), I begin to explore the possibility of a provisional stability of identity structured around the shared and repeated experience of the images of stars. Being a Banderas enthusiast—especially when being so takes me out of the cinema and its (possible) entrapments, onto the streets, onto the phone, talking with the like-minded, watching favourite scenes on video with them, swapping pictures—gives me at least a notion of a subject position supplementary to, and at best free of, the identificatory processes implicated in the gaze as thought of in '1975 Film Theory' (Bordwell 1996: 15–17). In going to the cinema (or watching a video) with others as part of a shared urge to see Banderas, I take up who I am, am not, or could be one day, in relation not just to the processes of subject formation, narrative, *mise en scène*, performance, and so on, but in relation to other individuals identifying variously with an unpredictably structured series of images of Banderas and Banderas personalities.

Of course, Banderas—along with the Jorge Sanz of the 1980s (see Ch. 6)—is especially interesting to look at in the light of the turn in spectatorship theory, in that same decade, away from a concern with mainstream cinema's 'assumption of a male norm, perspective and look' (Neale 1993: 19; originally 1983) towards issues which, as Cohan and Hark (1993*b*: 3) suggest, 'film theory ha[d] repeatedly linked to the feminine and not to the masculine: spectacle, masochism, passivity, masquerade' and the body as a signifier of ('gendered, racial, class, and generational') difference. The desired, objectified, masochistic, and entrapped Banderas is spectacularly ubiquitous in these years and although his body very emphatically marks generational and class differences at a time of exceptional social and cultural change in Spain—marks an epoch, that is, in an immediately recognizable way for young audiences at the time—it also evokes the pleasures and anxieties in seeing, in the terms both of '1975 Theory' and the 1980s turn to looking at the male, the eroticized and objectified male body in the place of the female body (for a review of this binary differential position and its later critiques, see Lehman 1993: 1–36). A scene of voyeurism and self-mortification from early on in *La corte de Faraón*—which was to be given a more disturbing edge in *Matador*—is of interest in this regard. In the film Banderas plays a chaste young friar who, seconded to a theatre company by the censor's office, has got himself involved in the performance of the eponymous operetta in the mirror role of El casto José, Chaste Young Joseph, the Egyptian slave. To this purpose his habit has had to be abandoned; and the outer narrative frame of the film has him sitting bare-chested, decorated, and be-loinclothed throughout a farcical police enquiry into the morality of the show. In much of the film he is the inno-cent male tutored by the sexually experienced woman, a type prefigur-ing obliquely elements of the roles both of Antonio in *Law of Desire* and Carlos in *Women on the Verge of a Nervous Breakdown*. He is very much on display as object and as love interest, as the fantasy malleable and available male. In a key scene, on a stage laden with Ancient Egyptian kitsch, his semi-naked body is pulled this way and that by two women vying for his affection—the Queen of Egypt and the Babylonian Princess (played by a startlingly erotic Ana Belén, who more or less sold the film single-handed). He is toyed with, bemused, and in comical, mock-shocking mode has his penis revealed: when he falls off the back of the stage and falls akimbo on a pile of drapes passing women note with astonishment its size, and invite the spectator to share with them their delight in it as a farcical sign of the incongruity of José's desirability and his chastity on-stage and off.

Anecdotally and in the press, it was commonplace in the 1980s to use this *destape* (naked moment)[4] as a metonym for the actor's promise, just as in the 1990s, Madonna's Hollywood gaze at him and his appearance in *Playgirl* indicated the American future for him. The film has another anticipatory and formative moment for Banderas. Recently arrived at the digs used by the troupe, the young monk, given the room used by Ana Belén's character Mari Pili, cannot resist looking through the chest of drawers. In the intimacy of the room the camera stays at first at the level of the seated Banderas's head as he looks at what he finds, and takes

[4] His first full-frontal nude scene in fact comes in *Pestañas postizas* (False Eyelashes: Enrique Belloch, 1982), but very few saw it: the film was an utter commercial failure (see Filmography).

several angles of him as he moves around the room; but from another, high angle Mari Pili is looking in from a window set into the partition wall. This POV shot allows a shared delight (hers and ours) in spying on the chaste and handsome monk engaged in his own surveillance activities, and preparing to remove that cassock. This view, though the common currency of farce, can only with difficulty be separated in the Spanish filmgoer's mind from one equally impelled by the ridicule of the emasculated male, in Buñuel's *Cet obscur objet du désir* (1977) as Fernando Rey peers down into a bedroom from the light above a door to see Conchita and we are invited very forcibly to remember that 'any idea that the gaze is always inevitably male in Western art [. . .] loses much of its credibility', as P. Evans (1995a: 128) observes of this scene in relation to traditional spectatorship theory.

What, from our vantage-point and non-male POV, we next see Banderas as the young monk do is tighten a thick belt around his waist to fight against the potential for lust-driven thoughts that lies in the drawers, the room, and the house; and this has a clear, inverted, match in Almodóvar's *Matador*. There, the young Ángel is under anxious surveillance by his widowed mother, an Opus Dei fanatic, herself a user and abuser of self-mortification which in part she hopes will ward off by proxy the impurities of thought of her disturbingly alluring and pseudo-mystically disturbed, sexually confused son. In the well-known sequences, discussed by P. J. Smith (2000: 68) among others, Ángel spies on his neighbour Eva in her bathroom, and subsequently attempts to rape her, motivated by homosexual panic and a compounded desire to prove himself to and identify with his bullfight trainer (71). He is then himself spied on naked in the bathroom by his mother as he attempts to wash away the memory of the attack; immediately after she is seen pulling a cilice tight around her upper thigh, as she attempts to remove the sins of his father which she sees visited on herself and her son. These sequences are crucial to the film's 'fantastic abolition of sexual difference' and its 'graphic code of contagion or reversibility' (70) and place Banderas at this stage in his career in a role with connotations of extreme subjective and erotic versatility. His character's misdirected identifications with heroic, violent, impetuous masculinity; the approximation of his body in performance to 'the fetishized, feminine object of narrative cinema' (72); the overlap of his character's libidinally fuelled and luridly portrayed, swooning, visionary powers with the superstitious religiosity of the mother; his soft, virginal, and passive look; and yet his anchoring charisma: all create a 'disturbance in representation' (72) not only in terms of gender and the psychic apparatus of the gaze but also in terms of the young actor's career.

The habit, the belt, and the loincloth in Garcí Sánchez's musical comedy, and the apparatus of inherited patriarchal oppressions and repressions in Almodóvar's hybrid thriller/melodrama, all, in their different modalities, draw excessive attention to a body supposed to be virginal and by extension to a career supposed, in its extra-filmic manifestations, to be typical and cycling steadily through the standard youth roles. Such attention soon reveals that moodiness shades alarmingly often into confusion: the young Banderas alternates between being dreamily open to and violently drawn to sexual experimentation, to non-standard masculinities, and to reversibility. As Ángel, he is the perfect illustration of 'a masculinity in crisis' (Allinson 2001: 83); as the doubly undercover policeman of 'El informe', he is as uncertain as Ángel of the reality of what he feels, shifting from observer to observed and stained with guilt; as Antonio in *Bâton Rouge* he moves from the position of the in-control gigolo to that of the passive accomplice in murder and that of the used man. As yet another Antonio, in *Law of Desire*, he desires of course both the 'burden of sexual objectification'—as Lehman (1993: 6) argues is surprisingly true of so many represented men on film—and the weight of another man's body.

With which Antonio is it possible and desirable to identify? As a refuge from such 'vicissitudes of identification' as are produced by the early Banderas, and his indeterminacies of pleasure (scopophiliac or narcissistic) and anxieties (the residue of pre-Oedipal relations) (Rodowick 1991: 11), again the filmgoer on the street could turn to the press for more reassuring identifications. During 1986 Banderas seemed to start to get a feel for self-presentation in accord with the preferences of different publications' readerships, taking up some reassuringly normalized positions. In April he told *La Vanguardia* (1986: 6) 'no creo excesivamente en la pareja' (I don't believe too much in coupledom) in a fashion photo shoot (plus topless shaving scene) in a smart hotel, the transient, promiscuous status of which location is disingenuously and in clichéd terms spelled out by the text itself ('porque la vida de un actor transcurre siempre de hotel en hotel' (an actor's life is always spent moving from hotel room to hotel room) (6). In December, however, he backtracked, telling *La Revista del Mundo* (Álvarez 1986) 'me gustaría encontrarme con una mujer fija [. . .] con la futura madre de mis hijos' (I'd like to have a steady woman [. . .] I'd like to meet the future mother of my children). The statement runs somewhat counter to the lead photo image of him here in zipped-down leather jacket and no shirt, and with very undomesticated hair, though it is more or less in line with the final photo of him in same jacket but leaning on a decorator's ladder, provocatively but possibly with the purpose of getting in some practice for that future nursery bedroom (though it is Melanie Griffith who nowadays does—or at least oversees—the decorating at the Marbella home).[5] This, then, is a sensible show of acceptable adaptability against the mildly perverse and oddly varied background of the roles.

Disavowals

In his discussion of disavowal in *Matador,* P. J. Smith (2000: 71–4) makes and illustrates the point that 'the question of homosexuality is constantly reasserted in the film, only to receive equally vehement denials' (71), that it is 'allowed to enter consciousness only on condition that repression be maintained' (73). He is referring not simply to scripted dialogue but to matches and manipulations at the level of image and staging, to patterns of behaviour emerging from performance, and to an underlying impulse towards an impossible/ideal bisexuality in Ángel, part of a fantastic abolition or suspension of sexual difference sustained in the three main characters of the film. Similarly, the generally gay affirmative *Law of Desire* has a much-discussed sexual-political indeterminacy (summarized in Fouz-Hernández and Perriam 2000: 97–9), involving, for example, the assertion for dramatic purposes of the inevitability and even the acceptability of internalized homophobia, and of extreme bad faith as a good engine for narrative and emotional movement.

The straight-identified Antonio engages in a cascading sequence of disavowing moves in relation to film director Pablo whom he wishes to seduce. The film's second prelude, in which he masturbates in the cinema toilets moaning 'fuck me, fuck me', as a substitute for seeing the première of Pablo's film (which he could not get in to), deploys the classic male trick of getting straight to the point in order to avoid the issue (of commitment, tenderness, proper lovemaking). When he can no longer bypass sexual contact and has penetrated Pablo's home, his kisses are too fierce, he is graceless and clueless in bed, both enthusiastic for and averse to anal sex (ibid. 85), and—in a telling repetition of those other Banderas roles of the 1980s just discussed—he is quick to displace his somewhat intermittent lust onto his fascination with Pablo's life, belongings, and writing as he roams the flat on the first night. The passage from surly straight-acting boy, to fussy househusband, then to jealous husband, is rapid, and it shows Antonio's

[5] Interview by Concha García Company, Telecinco, 'La gran ilusión', 14 Oct. 2000.

entrapment in reactionary mores at every turn. A traditional clean-cut masculinity inhabits his demeanour and dress. He is not only 'indifferent to camp' (ibid. 85), but adapts what could easily have been one of its signs—a colourful, satin shirt, a copy of one favoured by Pablo—to vengeful purpose, and finally burns it, in a toilet bowl, in his parent's home, in an act of displaced, anal-fixated erotophobia. In his relationship with Pablo he mimics the manners and assumptions of his parent's straight, conservative world and applies the binary codings of traditional masculinity. Furthermore he wilfully ignores—as does the film as a whole, in its gestures of 'straightening out' (J. Arroyo 1992)—the potential in gay lifestyles for escaping from coupledom, possessiveness, and the assumption of compulsory heterosexuality's preferred pattern of monogamy.

Regarding homosexuality—both imputed to him personally and as a defining feature of his film-making—Almodóvar's own strategic ambivalence, increasing over time, is well documented (P. J. Smith 1992: 162–71; 2000: 79–85; Fouz-Hernández and Perriam 2000: 97), as are the complexities of the director's representations of homosexuality and their relation to lesbian and gay culture on the one hand, and heterosexual cultural models on the other (J. Arroyo 1992; Mandrell 1995). Not surprisingly, Banderas soon became nervous of association with the former and took up ambivalent positions on the latter. Looking back on the early Almodóvar years, from the perspective of May 1989, and under the futile tag line 'No despierto el morbo' (I don't arouse sexual thoughts) (Narváez 1989), he notes that if in 1989 people have a persistent image of him as a policeman—following the success of the crude comedy *Bajarse al moro* (Going South Shopping) (Fernando Colomo, 1988)—only a few years earlier there had been a different obsession, 'el morbo consistía en descubrir si era mariquita o no' (people took a perverse interest in finding out whether or not I was queer) (4). Whatever may or may not have come to pass between the actor and the director or his friends and entourage, it seems incredible that features as classically disposed to incite homoerotic attraction as those of the young Banderas should not have played their part in the Almodóvar-Banderas dynamic. Thus, when Oliva and Fernández (1995: 89) suggest ironically that Almodóvar, seeing Banderas perform in *La hija del aire* in 1983, 'se queda maravillado por las piernas del malagueño' (is left marvelling at the legs of this young man from Malaga), they are recycling an open secret. Banderas has always been firm about the professional nature of the bond between actor and director, and, indeed, between actors: in order to get over their 'timidity' about the 'delicate moments' of *Law of Desire* he and Eusebio Poncela had to spend a fortnight together in Mallorca getting to know one another, he tells the middle-age targeted women's magazine *Garbo*, but 'una cosa debe quedar clara: yo no soy homosexual. Jamás he tenido relaciones de ese tipo. Simplemente se trata de una interpretación en una película' (one thing has to be made clear: I'm not homosexual. I've never had sexual relations of that sort) (Siles 1987: 29). His perspective on homosexuality is similarly naïve and markedly unreconstructed in declarations such as 'hago de gay como puedo hacer otro tipo de persona' (I play gays just as I play any other type of person) (*Tiempo* 1988: 130) or 'hice de gai como podía haber hecho de cartero' (I played gay like I might have played a postman) (Narváez 1989). On the one hand this is the familiar discourse of liberals in normalizing denial, on the other it seems to be looking back far beyond the liberal *movida* and the beginnings in Spain of serious critical discourse on homosexuality (P. J. Smith 1992: 5–10; Mira 1999: 153–5, 267–8) to earlier simplifying typologies including that of the homosexual as dangerously chameleonic (liable, say, to resume his street-wandering occupation at any time in any guise). There is more than a little haziness in Banderas's equivalence of gayness and postal delivery, but more definite in ideological precedence is the caveat 'además, nunca he hecho de maricón, ni de loca, he hecho papeles de tíos que tienen relaciones con tíos' (what's more, I've never played actual gays or effeminate queens, I've always done roles with regular guys who have sex with regular guys) (*Tiempo* 1988: 130); similarly, asked yet again on another occasion whether his gay roles worry him, his response is 'en absoluto [. . .] en el sentido que su homosexualidad es lo que menos importa. Son personajes normales que simplemente tienen otras preferencias sexuales' (not at all [. . .] in the sense that homosexuality is actually the least important thing about them. These are normal people who simply happen to have different sexual preferences) (Parrondo 1994: 100). This discourse and its terminology is that of 'la tradición circunmediterránea' (Spain, Portugal, and by complex extension Latin America and the Phillipines) in relation to sex between men (Fernández-Alemany and Sciolla 1999: 69–87; also Mira 1999: 486–8). The *macho* is that precisely because he is penetrative and thus he always remains *hombre* in relation to the *loca* (the supposedly, or mimetically, effeminate male partner; or, in heterosexual relations, the woman); and in his wider performance of his masculinity the *macho* differs from the *maricón* in his constant self-differentiation from femininity. It was either the many questions begged by Banderas's forceful self-alignment with the language of this particular Latino tradition or a bland, familiar statement about having a lot of gay friends that forced a possibly flustered reporter to have the interview in this case move hastily on to the next question, 'you're married, aren't you?' (131).[6]

Banderas as rebel

One way out of such ambiguities—although straight into the arms of others—came in a series of rebel roles, either after the manner of the anti-heroes (like Bogart, and Clift) 'reflecting the anguished sensitivity of the audience' or calling on a common cause (like James Dean) in rebellious uncertainty (Walker 1970: 332). In *Bajarse al moro*, mentioned above, he plays Alberto, a young policeman comfortably involved in the drug-running scheme operated from the flat he shares, a place of hip sensual pleasures (sex and smoking to the backing of the band Pata Negra, playing on the balcony opposite). His character here festively represents a laid-back disregard for authority (the police, and mother-hood: Chus Lampreave here playing the polar opposite of the mother in *Matador*). More seriously, in the role of disaffected working-class Mario in Bilbao-set *La Blanca Paloma* (The White Dove) (Juan Miñón, 1989) Banderas, like Imanol Arias before him, finds his image embedded in some of the outline discourses of Basque nationalism, and in particular the struggle *grosso modo* between the young, Basque left and the old, Spanish (here Andalusian) right. Mario—an outsider linguistically and by migration from the South—is fatherless, has lost his activist brother to the troubles, bonds (though in a conflicted way) with his male peer group of Basque-Spanish bilingual young activists (and players of Jai-Alai) but falls for Rocío, daughter of the owner of the Andalusian-themed bar La Blanca Paloma, Domingo (Francisco Rabal). This father is the figure of an old Spanish masculinity of the traditional right: worshipping the Virgin of Rocío (whose popular nickname gives the bar its name), but flirting with spitting images of 1950s singers of *coplas* and other popular song forms which had been sanctioned as part of Franco's Spanish cultural politics (Labanyi 1997). He favours *paso dobles* as the music to dance to in his religiously named but paganistically decorated establishment, turning a blind eye to the pimping (by her own brother) of a female prostitute on the premises, running the bar despotically, neglecting a critically

---

[6] The whole question comes up again in the Spanish press with the release of *Interview with a Vampire* (1994), with a new twist: 'no soy homosexual, pero no creo que un homosexual sea muy diferente a mí' (I'm not a homosexual, but I don't believe a homosexual is all that different from me) (Uruena 1994).

depressed wife and taking patriarchal power to one of its extremes by having sex with his daughter—the virgin's namesake—whether drunk (which he often is) or not.

Banderas plays the moody, taut, rebellious, and slightly ambiguous young male icon here, contrasted with the gruff, manly, brutish, Heston-like presence of Rabal. Rabal's star persona brings with it memories of caddish handsomeness (from Buñuel's *Viridiana* of 1961), the lubricious but arrestingly charismatic or fascinatingly ugly older man, and, specifically, an earlier father–daughter incest role in *Tiempo de silencio* (see Ch. 1).[7] The contrast between the physical presences of these actors heightens the oppositional tensions of the film but also draws the eye to similarities based on flaws in the performance of masculinity in each. Rabal is shot and costumed in ways that emphasize a certain shabbiness in clothing and haircut, and he has a face which in medium shot at once reveals signs of guilt and regret through actorly technique and make-up (a set of jaw, pouches under the eyes, a yellow-greyness). He never leaves the environs of the bar. Banderas represents in Mario the male in action and at large (hurling stones at the police in the opening sequence; running to his hideaway; driving round the city delivering crates of bottles). His body is eroticized and given a basic repertoire of variations. His face is alternately coded with soft romantic appeal in sad little close-up moments of loneliness, or set in a rough-boy look, with leather jacket extending his shoulder width and underpinning the face with forcefulness in medium shots. Alone on the beach near the film's crisis the turned-up jacket collar and loose body movements conjure up a classically directionless, lost mood while the same collar and jacket moments later in the context of gestures of sudden determination signal toughness, action, and decisiveness. Tight jeans and the jacket are dwelt on by the camera throughout, the actor's body brought forward for admiration as Mario's body is routinely admired by his delivery-round partner. She surprises him fresh from the shower one day, caresses his flank, and grabs his crotch once the jeans have been prised over it; but as part of her failed seduction in this scene, she remarks that his pony-tail would be best snipped off—condensing in this observation a perception of masculine sexuality wrongly directed.

In a way she is wrong (for all that she, like the viewer, has seen the odd, homosocial glances between Mario and the Basque boys at play, full understanding of whom is unobtainable to him). Mario's erotic

[7] See *Fotogramas*, Oct. 2001: 158–62, for a homage to Rabal, who died on 29 Aug. 2001. Also available, in part, at http://www.fotogramas.navegalia.com/fotogram/01oct/homenaje.shtml (12 Nov. 2001).

encounters with Rocío are nothing if not forcefully masculine, even if she initiates physical contact on the first encounter, and even if subsequently he glowers rather than charms her into sex. Their first penetrative sex is quick, unsophisticated, passionate, and in the dark, and is echoed immediately upon her return home by an equally rapid, but more brutal, man-on-top forced intercourse with Domingo, her father, again in the dark. Their last sex act is marked again with urgent passion and, this time, blood, taking place as it does in a hospital after a knife fight between Mario and Domingo. Mario and Domingo become overlaid, their ways of relating to the impossibility that is Rocío made similar. From their entirely different social positions they are figures of the same destructive and perverted masculinity of classic screen representation: both possessive, weak-willed, yet magnetically attractive, both lone males at the stressful pivot of disintegrated families, and full not so much of the anger of their clan as with their own frustration at never quite belonging (Domingo is geographically cut off from his origins, Mario an outsider to his immediate milieu). Despite the dramatic and vivid staging of the finale of the film—in which Mario sets fire to the bar, not realizing that Rocío has returned to her father and is inside—Banderas plays Mario's horrifying realization that he has killed Rocío somewhat too blankly for the full constellation of meanings of the fire and explosion of the scene, and of the end of love, to be registered through performance. However, in a more generalized, thematic way Mario's hatred of Domingo as both the representative of the enemy, fighting against whom his brother was killed (nationalistic Spaniards), and as a sexual rival allows Banderas to perform key facets of masculinity under stress, reflecting questions of generational, political, and national difference as well as the disturbing similarities and overlaps with Domingo's sexual preference and socially marginalized position. The often noted 'ambiguity' of the young Banderas's physical appearance points the audience in this film not only towards this basic, visual dichotomy in him as a presence on screen and, intradiagetically, to the simple love dilemma and tale of confused youth, but more interestingly to the uncertainties of being fatherless, being in the interstices of two possible fatherlands ('Spain' and Euskadi), lacking a brother, and being a rebel but being at an oblique angle to the cause.

In the following year, in *Átame* / *Tie Me Up! Tie Me Down!* (Pedro Almodóvar, 1990), Banderas's Ricki again allows him to play an interstitial role in the sense that the many transitions of his mentally disturbed character in relation to the actress he kidnaps and restrains demolish fixed emotional positions and leave Banderas representing an impossible psychic space between tough and vulnerable. It is true that Ricki, partly under pressure from the film's abrupt movements between genres (horror, comedy, romantic melodrama) 'lurches wildly between romantic courtship, domestic banter, and violence' (Morgan 1995*a*: 115), and his character might even be read as a classic sadistic subjectivity in action, mixing tenderness with restrictive cruelty. However, Banderas's performance of these modes mingles and blurs them through its very excessiveness, and, as Stone (2002: 188) neatly observes, he plays a man 'so straight he [is] (literally) crazy'. Ricki's manic donning of a long rock-star-cum-apeman wig when first he tracks down Marina (Victoria Abril) in the studios; the Latin-style false moustache used for disguise when he is obliged to go with her to her doctor friend for painkillers; his dressing in cosier, less raunchy jeans and light green T-shirt—rather than the vivid red jersey of the first reel—for the false domestic interlude of the kidnap: all these make a pantomime of masculine roles, just as the 're-enactment of rituals [. . .] and grotesque parodies of marital routines and bonds' insist on the socially constructed nature of heterosexual convention (Morgan 1995*a*: 120). So too do Banderas's own renditions of the extremities of mood by the undercutting and cross-cutting of them, emptying them out parodically but filling them with greater resonance for an audience fascinated by his perceived affective and erotic ambiguity (Stone 2002: 185–8). In particular to the fore is the Banderas on-screen persona of the outsider intruder who fools or rehearses himself into feeling an attachment for the person he is duping, coercing, or betraying (as in *Bâton Rouge* and the episode 'El informe').

In the later stages of the drama, when Marina has been captured by his looks, sexual prowess, the pathos of his orphanhood, and (in a low-key variant of the Stockholm syndrome) his status as jailer and psychological torturer, Ricki reveals to her a diagram of his original plans. It is a cartoon narrative running from his feigned recovery of mental stability and release from the psychiatric unit to locating her and forcing the 'discovery' of her reciprocal love. It might productively and immediately be read as a chillingly traditional story of male narcissistic goal-oriented dominance, as a representation of heterosexual models of male power (Morgan 1995*a*: 120). It underscores the parodic element in the film's and its actors' look (P. J. Smith 2000: 109). It is also in part a deployment of crowd-pleasing masculine archetypicality mixed with the thrill of the bad. The speech of intent that is prelude to the first tying-up and which Marina will repeat back to her sister when the kidnapping is over points blatantly and comically to the social constructedness of masculinity in its appeal to the spirit of self-determining adventure and its reliance on basic, heterosexual, procreative expectations: 'tengo veinticinco años y cincuenta mil pesetas, y estoy solo en el mundo.

Intentaré ser un buen marido para tí y un buen padre para tus hijos' ('I'm 25 years old, I've got 50,000 pesetas, and I'm all alone in the world: I'll try to be a good husband to you, and a good father to your children'). All this rudimentary (if ironic) attention to masculine behaviours, looks, and narratives is given the necessary spin through also being reflexive upon the nascent star's career. It calls up the Banderas of interviews, as discussed above, the Banderas who sets out on his Madrid adventures with 15,000 pesetas in his pocket and no contacts; it calls up the persistent image of Banderas's body deployed self-interestedly, as an instrument of escape, fulfilment, direction; and it forcibly reminds the audience and fan base of the ways in which elements in the performance of gender crossmatch the star and his characterizations, the life story, and the back histories on-screen.

In one direction (back across the Almodóvar œuvre) there are connections to be made in the audience's mind between Ricki and Ángel, through the violations that inaugurate and encapsulate the flawed working through of their fantasies, and in their madnesses, their frenzies (P. J. Smith's observations on Ángel in *Matador* can extend to Ricki, whose impossible positioning is that of not an ideal bisexuality but of an even more unrealizable combination of wilful, sadistic protagonist and decentred, vulnerable symbol of innocence and inexperience). In another direction, looking to the chronologically neighbouring *La Blanca Paloma*, the dynamics of generational and sexual rivalry springing from the Rabal and Banderas roles in that film have echoes here. Rabal now plays a director of lightly pornographic horror films (on the intricacies and implications of which structural feature see Morgan 1995a: 115–16; P. J. Smith 2000: 111–13); he is a post-stroke wheel-chair user but, as he tells a naïve interviewer, is more 'excited' than he has ever felt in his life before, and lewdly, pathetically fixated on Marina as sex object, undressing her with his eyes and literally for the camera. Ricki has no such fixations, remarking almost politely on her beauty when he first sees her naked, looking away at other times; and, as Morgan points out (116), Ricki is emphatically not involved by camera-work or in playing the character in such regimes of voyeurism as have Máximo in thrall. None the less he is crossmatched with Rabal's Máximo in so far as both, as Smith observes (110), are 'bound [. . .] to the image of Marina'. They are joined by their having been damaged (one by physical illness, the other by abandonment; both by paradigms of masculinity); and they are linked by their fascination for Marina, in particular by a sequential juxtaposition of a brief romantic-obsessive monologue recorded onto Marina's answering machine by Máximo and a shot of Ricki talking to Marina (and to himself) of his desires as she sleeps. Like Domingo and

Mario in the earlier film, Máximo and Ricki lose themselves to the same machinery of desire, prohibition, and disinhibition; Máximo's protestations to the contrary suggest the reality of his sense of emasculation by illness, and Ricki—beaten up by and on the orders of a (female) drug dealer he has assaulted (for the sake of Marina's drug habit), and reduced to tears by Marina's mid-film refusal to give in—has had his role as controller and aggressor turned back on him and is 'feminized by the abject nature of his love' (115). The Banderas image, then, again accrues perversities and forms of regret and shame not consonant with sexy male youthfulness, giving edge to the ambiguity and morbid fascination of that body, not only in *Átame*'s second half 'attractively blemished by [cuts and] bruises' and pitched obliquely into the masochist's physical and psychic space (115; 114–15), but through the 1980s and into the early 1990s marked by psychosexual dangers and uncertainties.

The role as Juan, sexually attracted to his sister (played by Emma Suárez) in Francisco Periñán's *Contra el viento / Against the Wind* in the same year, again associated Banderas with a certain perversity, though this time in a film whose dull way with narrative and visual structuring only accidentally contributes meaningfully to the discomfiting atmosphere. A disused quarry complex in a bleak (and windy) landscape in the Cabo de Gata area of Almería province is being exploited as a nuclear dump: Juan has escaped Madrid, his incestuous fascination for his sister Ana (Emma Suárez), and an alcoholic father, and is now working at the plant (adding a new range of costume to the Banderas repertoire: soiled tight vests, hard hat, and boiler suit). An early conversation with a fellow worker links the feared contamination of the village semi-jocularly with Madrid as a source of vice and moral and venereal contamination. From Madrid, and on a day when the wind is getting up and pushing open the shutters of Juan's cabin home, Ana arrives and states her intention of sharing the cabin with Juan, a scene whose simple tensions between sexual temptation and self-disgust Banderas plays efficiently, with rueful, downward glances, sitting at 90 degrees to her. He springs up with relief to escape this sit-down stand-off and secure the shutters against the gale, as well as his emotions against the clumsily exposed sub-text of Ana's deviously excitable 'I like this wind'. By the end of the film—when Ana's affair with American company boss, Nick, has led to a jealous brawl with Juan and Nick's accidental death—the quarry depths and a waste container are used to dispose of Nick's body and the contamination and disruptive wind motifs find closure (but fail to compensate for a somewhat tedious getting-rid-of-the-body nareme). The act of violence is also, in a cod-psychological way, the logical end to the emotional and sexual containment forced on Juan: while Emma Suárez is even more than usually hypersexualized in her performance (alternating tense, brooding obstinacy with conventionally fiery desire) Banderas is framed as the incapacitated male. In one sex scene, disturbingly erotic close-ups show the flushed, dishevelled faces and hair of both, with Juan looking more hot and bothered before sex than after; afterwards he strikes a post-card, soft-porn pose, shirtless in jeans, elbow up against the window frame looking mournfully out at the moonlight, and more like Banderas in a photo shoot than the supposedly down to earth Juan. In a second sex scene their bodies are filmed in such a way as to emphasize the sweaty and sinewy, the intensity of Ana's lust in her open eyes being set against a mechanical and desperate thrusting by Juan, whose eyes are closed or, after sex, looking out defiantly at the camera from a head resting on the pillow, turned again at 90 degrees away from Ana who is looking down, insistently, from above. During sex and after he will not speak; and he silences her attempts at developing a narrative of her dreams (to be with him, to go to the nearby coast and hear the waves) with an oppressive and self-repressive 'Cállate . . . es mejor si no dices nada' (Don't: it's better if you say nothing). With local girl Rosario, who tells him of her romantic and erotic thoughts on a significantly wind-free night, the problem is the same. So Banderas here becomes the weak and silent type, in thrall to a *femme fatale* who is also family, no doubt echoing for older audiences the images of emasculated and infantilized manhood in a famous, earlier incest-themed film, José Luis Borau's *Furtivos / Poachers* (on which see Kinder 1993: 232–5; P. Evans 1999*b*).

In *¡Dispara!* there seems at first to be a reassuring reprise of the slightly geeky look of Carlos in *Women on the Verge of a Nervous Break-down* in the role of Mario, an earnest, bespectacled journalist at *El País* who falls for the exotic circus performer Ana (Francesca Neri) whose act (shooting at targets while performing acrobatics on horseback) is one feature that gives the film its title. The other feature, her reluctant trans-formation into a revenge killer and fugitive following a brutal gang rape (with fresh-faced Coque Malla cast very much against type as one of the rapists), leads quickly to the translation of Mario from the plane of objective reporting to that of impassioned involvement. With Ana run to ground in a distant farmhouse and holding a family hostage, Mario— on the trail of the story and still in love with her—is allowed by the police surrounding the house to go in and negotiate with her. As with Pablo and Antonio in Almodóvar's *Law of Desire*, there is a desperate and poignant rehearsal of what might have been, the scene is bathed in blue light, and on the soundtrack, instead of the bolero 'Bésame mucho' in *Law of Desire*, we have the sentimental power of the 1959 Italian hit 'Sinno me moro' (with its familiar refrain 'Amore, amore, amore, amore mio . . .'). When Ana is picked off by a marksman, there is another half-match to the well-known Almodóvar love–death scene as Ana dies in Mario's arms, and prior to the police—their audience in suspense outside —rushing in. So Banderas finds himself in a classic, older Hollywood position as the man who should never have tangled with the fascinating, dangerous woman and who finds his life and career perverted; he also finds himself playing a scene of highly wrought melodramatic intensity, at the focus of emotional interest, an object of pity, and a victim of desire.

The comedy and action roles of later, Hollywood years went some way towards erasing or at least flattening out the perverse and excessive notes in Banderas's first career (although *Interview with a Vampire* dares to play with them to good effect) as too did the practised disavowal of that quality of *morbo* in interviews of the late 1980s, discussed at the start of this chapter. But increasing attention to him at the turn into the 1990s as sex object, athletic body, Spain's best-looking actor, Spain's, and then the world's sexiest man,[8] while usefully reinforcing his appeal as ideal male positioned just on the right side of narcissism, also simultaneously threatened the masculine ideal through the destabilizing objectification that went with it. Banderas began to show the usual symptoms of professional anxiety, especially with regard to the sexual emphases of the terms increasingly applied to him, *galán*, and—in the wake of *The Mambo Kings* and his presentation of the 1992 Oscars—Latin lover.[9] Fear of not being taken seriously is the tenor of a number of interviews of this time, and Banderas specifically insists on the importance of laughing off the attribution of sex symbol and of avoiding playing up to the new image and its risks of typecasting (López 1992: 62; and unattributed interviews quoted in Oliva and Fernández 1995: 180). By 1995 personal integrity was also recognized as under threat. To a gay audience Banderas emphasizes that he is 'a worker', a 'regular [. . .] happy

[8] First in *In Bed with Madonna* (Alex Keshishian, 1991), then at the 1992 Oscar award ceremony when introduced by Billy Crystal. Prior to that, *Diez Minutos* (4 Aug. 1989) reports on his winning the Golden Playboy award in Mallorca and the photo coverage is poolside and provocative; *Semana* (14 Feb. 1990) is interested in his gym-going, as is Alameda 1992: 24; *La Gente* (21 Jan. 1991) dubs him iconically 'Guapo de cine' (translatable as 'screen idol'); in the *Diari de Barcelona* (22 Sept. 1991) he is simply tagged 'aquest guapo actor malagueny' (that handsome actor from Malaga); and so on.

[9] As *galán*, for example, in *El tiempo* (4 July 1988); *El Independiente* (1 Nov. 1989); *Semana* (7 June 1990) (reporting on a TV appearance alongside Imanol Arias); *Viva* (22 Oct. 1990). The phrase 'Latin lover' is used in *El Mundo* (29 March 1992), *El Semanal* (Madrid) (6 March 1994), and López 1992: 62; and—at the start of a long tradition soon to be translated into the Hollywood context—there are a great many images of Banderas topless or be-vested and smouldering: for example, *Viva* (5 Jan. 1992) and Alameda 1992. *Fotogramas* 1994a has a full verbal and pictorial resumé of the image. Also, in an interesting variation, as *capricho español*, in Alameda 1992: front page and 18–31; and as 'L'Últim Valentino' ('the latest Valentino') in *Diari de Barcelona* (22 Sept. 1991).

guy' who does not ask himself 'too many times' who he is (Rebello 1995: 24); but on the same page there is a counterpoint to these declarations, a strong illustration of the very process that is being denied: yet another image of Banderas shines out at the reader, one of him embracing the chunky bonnet of a glossy, black, antique car, with a tousle-haired blond boy in soft focus in the background with his vest straps fortuitously hooked back over his shoulder-blades halter-style, his sculpted chest exposed, and with a provocative look direct to camera, matching Banderas's own, linking them in a nice fetishistic triptych for a male audience. And even later in his career the threat of the adoring gaze still had to be addressed, and still ambivalently so: on the one hand, in a Dutch film magazine in 1999, family and married life (anyway much featured in the photo-journalism of the Melanie Griffith years) are preferred to being mobbed by women, while on the other Banderas admits (obviously enough) to using his sexual attraction, referring without apparent irony to the feeling of power that men have during sex, and (more playfully) suggesting he could certainly rival Ricky Martin if ever he broke into singing professionally (van der Sanden 2000). As Marta Belluscio (1996) rightly implies (in an otherwise rather loosely written set of sketches), Banderas is complicit—even in his ambivalence—with the publicity machine throughout the 1990s: the vogue in the USA for 'Latin' music and images, a new prominence in publicity and advertising materials of the male sex object, and growth (perhaps more accurately a rebirth) in the film magazine market allowed 'la muestra jactanciosa de su carnalidad' (the proud display of his sensuality) and '[una] transgresión banderiana' (a transgressive style proper to Banderas) which surpasses Valentino's daring and updates the old myth of the Latin lover (ibid. 52). As the actress Assumpta Serna also saw it, after all, he had no choice; that particular image always sells, and he was destined to exploit it (Oliva and Fernández 1995: 179).

TABLE 2. *Filmography (of Spanish-language productions only)*

Year	Title	English title(s) (official in italics; literal in Roman)	Director	Billing	Audience figures and takings	Other information
1982	*Laberinto de pasiones*	*Labyrinth of Passions*	Pedro Almodóvar	Minor	357,900 / €596,782	
1982	*Pestañas postizas*	False Eyelashes	Enrique Belloch	3rd	348 / €285	
1984	*El caso Almería*	The Almería Case	Pedro Costa	7th	968,793 / €1,233,921	
1984	*El Señor Galíndez*	Señor Galíndez	Rodolfo Kuhn	3rd	46,872 / €64,182	
1984	*Los Zancos*	Love on Stilts	Carlos Saura	3rd	56,789 / €92,607	
1985	*La corte de Faraón*	Pharaoh's Court	José Luis García Sánchez	3rd	889,023 / €1,552,565	
1985	*Réquiem por un campesino español (Mosén Millán)*	Requiem for a Spanish Peasant	Francesc Betriú	2nd	369,019 / €624,108	
1985	*Caso cerrado*	Case Closed	Juan Cano Arecha	Minor	182,310 / €278,436	
1986	*Matador*		Pedro Almodóvar	2nd	415,912 / €712,809	
1986	*Puzzle*		Jose Luis Comerón	Minor	53,956 / €90,379	
1986	*27 (Veintisiete) horas*	*27 Hours*	Montxo Armendariz	8th	278,930 / €506,668	
1986	*Delirios de amor: Delirio IV (El informe)*	The Frenzies of Love: IV (The Report)	Félix Rotaeta	5th	116,931 / €211,836	Billing is for the whole set of episodes (each with a different director); Banderas has the lead role in episode 4
1987	*Así como habían sido (Trio)*	Just the Way They Were	Andrés Linares	3rd	14,504 / €23,567	
1987	*La ley del deseo*	*Law of Desire*	Pedro Almodóvar	3rd	780,211 / €1,446,007	

TABLE 2. (*continued*)

Year	Title	English title(s) (official in italics; literal in Roman)	Director	Billing	Audience figures and takings	Other information
1988	*Mujeres al borde de un ataque de nervios*	*Women on the Verge of a Nervous Breakdown*	Pedro Almodóvar	2nd	3,344,640 / €7,004,796	
1988	*El placer de matar*	*The Pleasure of Killing*	Félix Rotaeta	Top	97,870 / €197,467	
1988	*Bâton Rouge*		Rafael Moleón	3rd	202,444 / €408,874	
1989	*Bajarse al moro*	Going South Shopping	Fernando Colomo	2nd	414,737 / €830,828	
1989	*Si te dicen que caí*	*If They Tell You I Fell*	Vicente Aranda	3rd	340,702 / €700,184	
1989	*La Blanca Paloma*	*The White Dove*	Juan Miñón	2nd	110,923 / €225,297	Valladolid Film Festival: Best Actor
1989	*El acto*	The Act	Hector Faver	5th	230 / €691	Made 1987; not released until 1989
1990	*Átame*	*Tie Me Up! Tie Me Down!*	Pedro Almodóvar	2nd	1,351,650 / €3,124,876	
1990	*Contra el viento*	Against the Wind	Paco (Francisco) Periñán	Top	81,558 / €183,390	
1992	*Una mujer bajo la lluvia*	A Woman in the Rain	Gerardo Vera	2nd	234,239 / €611,528	
1993	*¡Dispara!*	*Shoot!* / *Outrage* (US title)	Carlos Saura	2nd	169,814 / €410,448	Co-pro Spain, Italy

Film for television

Fragmentos de interior (Fragments of an Interior) (Pedro Abad, 1984)

Fig. 5. Carmelo Gómez and Silvia Munt in *Secretos del corazón*.

Fig. 6. Carmelo Gómez and Emma Suárez in *El perro del hortelano*.

3 Carmelo Gómez (b. 1962)

Still waters

It is tempting to begin by suggesting that Carmelo Gómez is arguably the closest of the actors under discussion to the classic model as interpreted by Walker (1970: 362) of the leading man 'repeating his personality in film after film'. He appears, in many roles, to line up with an older type of Hollywood star, a 1930s hero, in whom the combined impression of 'still waters [and] deep roots' (300) offered a manly and reassuring route to emotional identification with a perceived national destiny, who offered women a fantasy man ideal for his reliability rather than his capacity to thrill and to hurt, and offered men a fantasy role model. Here is a Spanish actor who very markedly incarnates for his audiences a solid yet sensitive virility: his intellectual and philosophically inflected performance style constructs intense effects, variously, of closeness to land and region, of plain, magnetic manliness, and of a psyche and identity troubled by doubt and desires but able to overcome the former and to fulfil the latter.

Outside Spain he is most likely to be connected in cinema-goers' and video-buyers' minds with the three mythogenetic and mythographic films of Julio Medem, *Vacas* / *Cows*, *La ardilla roja* / *The Red Squirrel*, and *Tierra* (1992, 1993, and 1995).[1] These films (and much of what has been written on them) have associated his characters, in varying degrees, with the non-rational, the unpragmatic, and, in *Tierra*, with a drifting and passive turn: with bondedness to the earth, a special relationship with death and love, a mind and body caught up in and radiating emotional and psychological intensity. When in *Mararía* (Antonio José Betancor, 1998) vivid associations were made between his character's pent-up desires and the volcanic landscapes, vents, and hot spots of Lanzarote the same qualities of connection were being exploited and built upon. In his foundational period, in the mid-1990s, then, Gómez

---

[1] *The Red Squirrel* and *Tierra* have UK exposure through Tartan Video, and in the US through Vanguard and Connoisseur/Meridian respectively. *The Red Squirrel* was broadcast in the UK by Channel 4 on 9 Oct. 2001.

Fig. 7. Carmelo Gómez in *Mararía*.

came to embody cross-linked values relating to masculinity and to belonging: rootedness both to natural and to constructed environments, and allegiance to what Anderson has famously called 'imagined community'—to 'being Spanish' at a number of different levels.

However, P. J. Smith (2000), who mistrusts the connections sketched out above, has already identified some pitfalls in seeing Gómez's character Ángel in *Tierra*, for example, as a simple set of codings that relate to issues of nationality (149), suggesting instead that we think of Ángel as a new subjectivity emerging at the end of the film free from the violent inner troubles caused by his split personality, his 'lethal self-absorption' (152), and free from embedded dichotomies and false connections (earthly versus spiritual; interiorized self versus the external world of others; land and nationality; Medem and Basque cinema). But it can also be argued that Gómez is most often placed so as to confirm precisely those dichotomies and pat attributions and connections of ideas that Smith is so rightly chary of in the particular context of Medem's peculiarly intense, equivocal, and evasive cinematic practice; and that it is this positioning which gives, paradoxically, both directness and subtlety to his performances. Even in *Vacas* Gómez is associated with, enriches, and embeds stock images of masculinity in spite of the film's strong flight away from the sociological into the anthropological and mystical, and in spite of its urge to be ambiguous. His playing of the three male

Irigibel family members across the generations marks him with strong allegiances to forest and (Basque) homeland, and inscribe him in a psychological as well as a social scheme where masculinity is constantly defining itself in terms of strife and competition between males, where prowess is (as is repeatedly said) carried in the bloodline from father to son. Although patriarchal power, as Santaolalla (1999) argues, is circumscribed by and subsumed into a semi-mystical matriarchal structure, and although in this film (as in *Tierra*) it is women who give access to and can conjure the earthly powers, the men played by Gómez are never completely displaced from the central arenas of masculine activity as traditionally represented (even if the other two key males are unhinged by guilt and failure).

In the three time-frames of the film Gómez is the soldier and survivor (in the Carlist wars), the champion logger and potent lover, the smooth professional returned from America to chronicle on camera war among the natives (in 1936). Although the many narrative blurrings through repetition and other devices (ibid. 323) problematize notions of sameness and difference, Gómez's presence reinstalls dichotomies that other textures of the film might wish to veil and mingle. The reappearance in the narrative of his same strong facial features allows a masculine line of continuity to compete with the feminine; his narrative rebirthings punctuate the undifferentiated temporal zone of the place (homesteads, trees, a mysterious smouldering pit representing death, fertility, and imagination) making the man the reference point. If he is not in touch with the earth he is nevertheless the one to give it shape in time. Even his last manifestation as Peru—the photographer who has shifted away from the older masculine world and who is played with toned-down manliness by a Gómez contriving to appear less physically substantial than he is as the father (ibid. 321)—is there to impose narrative and visual order on the chaos of a skirmishing war, on nature, and on the impressions and memories of the place; and he is there to whisk his old love away on the back of a horse.

This exaggeration of dichotomies and entrenching of conventional masculinities is, in all probability, intentional on Medem's part and parodic in purpose, but it is not in the early Gómez's range or solid presence to activate in his own screen image the deconstructive energies at work around him. The character of Félix in *La ardilla roja* veers from one spookily played film type—the man with a supernaturally strong mental hold over his woman—into another manically played film type—the man who diverts his sexual competitiveness into driving fast and dangerously. The character of Ángel in *Tierra* acts as a catalyst of male rivalry, and his love objects respond to stereotypes of pure and lubricious women; his spiritual troubles—a tension between and blurring of earthly and angelic voices—and his status as outsider (a towny technician in a rural environment) appear to pitch his character at more intense levels of complexity of reference. There seems to be more at work in the character here than simply masculinity staking out rough old territories (some men hunt down others, some are hunted; some women are like our mothers, some are sensual others). Yet here again the deconstruction of such mythical and misogynistic discourses, it can be argued, goes on around and not in the figure of Gómez who ends up being iconic, strongly ambivalent—moody and dependable; sensitive and intrusive; philosophical and lust-driven—but not polysemic enough to move beyond these binaries or to match up the representation of Ángel's character with the undecidability of the film.

This is not a problem of acting; more a given, a look exploited in a relatively limited range of roles contributing to a star image of considerable consistency. Gómez's particular fascination is that for all that he is the perfect, inscrutable front for alternative subjectivities, of intricate new states of mind, and for all that he is habitually asked to play roles of psychological and dramatic extremity, he always looks ordinary, modestly heroic, humorous, handsome, and prone only to sudden and delimited losses of control (although these are as characteristic as his imperturbability, and I shall be returning to them soon). His star persona in the press is built around references to earthiness, solidity, and Northern-ness, and in interview he has reminded—or perhaps been prompted to remind—readers of a continuing link to the land, helping his dad to 'cultivar la tierra' (work the land) (Cortijo 1997: 54); or declaring himself 'hombre de campo' (a country man) in contrast, in this particular case, to director Gonzalo Suárez's implied superior intelligence and 'cultura urbana' (city culture) (*Diario de León* 1994). Paloma Leyra (1994), evoking his presence at interview, compares his large, tanned hands to polished wood, and allows the hobby of woodwork to arise as a topic of conversation; and her first (though far from original) impression is of '[un] chicarrón del norte [. . .] Hombre de tierra' (a strapping Northern lad [. . .] a man of the fields). Rosa María Echevarría (1996: 42) declares to her readers in *Blanco y negro* that 'su hermosa y cálida voz parece brotar de las entrañas de la tierra' (his warm, beautiful voice seems to well up out of the depths of the earth) and uses a quotation in her subtitle that suggests that Gómez would be out there now sowing corn were it not for his lucky break in films. His face, for Cecilia García (1996: 30) in *Cinerama*, is 'curtido y algo asilvestrado' (weather-beaten and somewhat wild): 'tiene la fuerza telúrica de los que están familiarizados con la tierra' (he has that telluric strength about him that you associate with people who are used to living on the land).

The first two sets of shots of him in *Secretos del corazón / Secrets of the Heart* (Montxo Armendáriz, 1997) confirm this amply and in cultural short-hand affirm a deep Spain far from the territories of the Latin lover or the frantic time of the ultramodern urban present such as is traversed by Antonio Banderas in his early career. The film narrates the coming of age in Franco's 1960s of 9-year-old Javi, living for part of the year with his maiden aunts in town but for the school holidays with his widowed mother and his uncle in a farmstead in a remote village: one of the secrets of the film is the traditional open secret of the power of sentimental nostalgia for simpler, non-urban living and for childhood innocence. However, not only does he discover—spying on a smarter but spooky house on the town's periphery—sex, and extramarital sex at that, but also the truth about his father's death (suicide) and his mother's relationship to the dead man's brother (sexual). This discovery comes bit by bit, by reading through the stubborn silences of his grandfather (which are also politically charged: he is an atheist, and clearly one of the losers under Franco) and the domestic prohibitions imposed by mother and uncle. It is against this revelation that the safe and wholesome aspects of Gómez's look and calm dealings with his character stand as protection. The first of these sets of shots is of Gómez with his arm round little Javi's shoulders in the stable, the two males filling the screen with their faces in close up as they watch a spider in its web approach its prey, in a curi-ous reflection of their own bonding (and one of the film's many signals that experience is about to creep up on innocence). The second shows him appearing in long shot, preceded by cowbells on the soundtrack, walking steadily towards the camera, herding and gently stroking and embracing his few cows as they all move down a green, misty path in rural Northern Spain into a simple two-shot scene before a modest hut and into dialogue with the inhabitant on issues of mutual support, fam-ily, and community. It was this image (with obvious visual echoes of *Vacas*) of the simple man of the earth and of the people, a hero seen through a young boy's eyes, that must in no small part have led to the huge suc-cess of this rural heritage and lost innocence film (for two years in the Spanish box office top ten). However, there is more to his character than meets the eye here, as we shall later see; moreover Gómez's star history when it begins to accelerate does so in two apparently distinct directions.

Conflicting identities

Although the groundedness with which art cinema and foreign audiences associate this actor might lead to an expectation of a more intuitive, 'deep', empathic, artistic, or indeed irrational approach to his roles and inhabiting them, Gómez is meticulous, strategic, and cerebral as an actor. We read in the pages of *Cinerama* of an actor who is 'minucioso y obsesivo' (meticulous and obsessive); 'explora los territorios más oscuros de sus personajes para atrapar toda su luz' (he explores the darkest areas in his characters in order to capture their particular gleam) (García 1996: 28); he says of himself (as have, in other languages and in so many words, many big screen stars of the second half of the twentieth century) 'tengo que ahondar en su psicología y entrar dentro de su alma [. . .] meterme en la piel del que estoy interpretando para creérmelo y luego creerme en pantalla' (I have to dig deep in the psychological make up and get into the soul [. . .] and under the skin of the person I am playing in order to believe him and to have belief in myself there on the screen) (30), and one can see the intellectual effort written large on expression, movement, and above all in most of the scripts he takes up (his register is rarely simple). Moreover, Gómez has often been cast as the thinking man of action or of purposeful enquiry: as intelligent hired killer, freedom fighter, policeman, detective, war reporter, and, on television, as the driven, tormented schemer of all time, Don Fermín de Pas in the serialized version of the nineteenth-century classic novel *La Regenta*. With emphatic frequency he is cast—or chooses roles—as a mediator in or victim of the interplay of good and evil, health and disease, truth and lies. Few of his roles, moreover, fail to place this set of dramas in the wider national historical drama, and as much as Depardieu is France, Carlyle is Scotland / Northern England, Gómez is Northern Spain. Imanol Uribe's *Días contados / Numbered Days* (1994) casts him in the role of Antonio, an idealistic ETA terrorist, and converts the customary solidity of this actor into hardened, forward-looking, iconoclastic purpose rather than groundedness in place and tradition. He appears, in the opening credit, not beside a cow wandering down a green track but at the wheel of a car on a rural motorway, with intense drumbeat-dominated incidental music, signalling, with his intent stare ahead, thickset head, and crisply macho stubble, the classic mix of dangerous and beautiful of the male antagonist of the morally bipolar action movie.

Antonio's thoughtful activism and constant questioning of his own motivations—sentimental and erotic as well as political—and, as Brooksbank Jones (forthcoming) suggests, emblematic both of ETA's own crisis and Uribe's commitment to (aspects of) the cause of nationalism—associate Gómez with problems of identity both personal and national that were, arguably at least, more immediate for cinema-goers of the mid-1990s than those of the more-or-less unglamorized rural past. When the film's title comes up large over a panorama of Madrid at dawn, followed by establishing shots of Antonio walking through the lonely streets, it is clear that Gómez is going to be concerned to portray versions of urban masculinity. One version, and part of his character's complex of dilemmas, is that of the young male to whom urban space offers a series of erotic possibilities and for whom—in the representation—women become objects of the gaze. The first interior scene involves a shocking encounter with this version as his new neighbour Charo (Ruth Gabriel), locked out of her flat and in need of a bathroom (to shoot up, vomit, and finally to take a bath) displays her naked body to him, invites him in, draws attention to how nice her breasts are, and explains that she likes to be looked at (a possibly, but probably not, two-edged sexual politics that owes itself as much to the original novel by Juan Madrid as to the script and attitudes of Uribe and his team). Antonio's cover is, naturally enough for these purposes, that of a professional photographer, and the camera itself is used to conflate sexual, national, and oppositional politics (treated in depth by Brooksbank Jones): after a second encounter in a bar with a smoulderingly flirtatious Charo, Antonio comes across a grotesque street performance—with a sparse audience, grey skies, and grimy buildings—of the famous seduction song, the *habanera*, from Bizet's *Carmen* (which has an echo later when Charo dances semi-naked to an old *bolero* for a bloated shopkeeper). The national *femme fatale* is performed, and made pornographically sexual, by a masculine-looking woman in a bright, cheap imitation Andalusian dress to a not very proficiently wheelchair-using Don José in the damp open daylight. Turning from the performance, Uribe's camera and Antonio's line up on the garage doors of a central Madrid police headquarters, the place in which at the end of the film Antonio will violently die, partly for the love of Charo, and partly for his cause. An early bar encounter with Charo (and a junkie acquaintance, Lisardo, played by Javier Bardem) partly corresponds to the tavern scene of the opera and its film version, and the closing sequence is set both in opera's symbolic arena of a crisis in erotic and patriotic desires and in the political arena of terrorist action. Antonio fails to reconcile the demands of heroic activism with those of romantic decisiveness, and the state continues to be unable to reconcile distinct visions of nationalism.

Although Gómez is presented as sexual—especially when away for an erotic break with Charo in Granada, where they spend their time in the Andalusian city naked—a characteristically dispassionate facial disposition is employed by him and Uribe (Gómez's face in close-up and medium close-up is a key marker) throughout the film to signify his character's metaphorical bilocation, in the real and ideal worlds, and in the bodily and the cerebral, giving rise, as Brooksbank Jones observes, to an 'oddly ambiguous performance' partly through 'a potent mix of sexual reticence and obsessiveness'. Indeed, in the Granada hotel room a news report of a car bomb in Madrid, linked to him, blows his cover with Charo and interconnects the erotic and the political quests in a way that prompts a sudden switch from sensuality into the programmed moves of the undercover man, as he seeks Charo out in the suite with pistol in hand (although he is able to use her self-administered high dose of heroin—her reaction to the news—as an excuse to back down from shooting her). His face, in encounters with the junkie police informer Lisardo, reveals a chill conviction of moral superiority that demonstrates impatience of weakness, degeneracy, and lack of purpose, and it perversely mirrors the very authoritarianism against which his organization sees itself as pitted. Furthermore, the association of Charo not only with drug use, prostitution, and (socially enforced) aimlessness but also with the archetype of the *femme fatale* sets up a binary of goal-driven, heroic virility versus distracting, emasculating femininity that—despite the existence in the film of Antonio's ex, who is part of the terrorist cell, and a strong, wronged woman—imprints itself on that typically Gómez look as inflected in this film.

This look reappears, tellingly, in the final moments and signifies a specific, fatal crisis in the character's masculinity. In the street where the performance of the pseudo-Carmen had taken place before, Antonio sets up a car bomb which is to be rolled down into the garage beneath the police headquarters; simultaneously, though, Charo arrives having been picked up by the police for questioning as a result of Lisardo's informing. Just as she is bundled into the building the car's brake is released. Antonio races off after it and her, and with the now familiar expression of absolute conviction and impassioned purpose on his face plunges into the building at the moment of explosion and the start of the final credits. Gómez's *hermetismo* (Molina Foix 1994) (hermeticism) encloses, conflates, and magnifies the conflicts of love and the conflicts of what amounts to war, two ways in which a male might make a man of himself in film narrative; and it echoes that of Arias in Uribe's earlier *The Death of Mikel* (as discussed in Ch. 1). In both actors' faces the look suggestively represses and therefore reveals the acknowledgement of anticipated crisis where hegemonic masculinities—working within Antonio, and outside Mikel—destroy their subjects but in so doing are destructively critiqued themselves. This is not to say that Uribe's film does not leave us with an uneasy after-image of the voyeuristic look on Gómez's face, nor that it does not problematically subsume Charo —who is supposed to be central—into its fascination with Antonio, and men. But it is to say that Gómez, like Arias, is positioned there in that problematic and problematizing discursive space, an image of contradictory manhood on screen, much less unidirectionally iconic than usual.

Tu nombre envenena mis sueños (Your Name Poisons my Dreams) (Pilar Miró, 1996) very explicitly inscribes on the body signs of conflict psychic and political, on the quietly expressive face of the star, and on the love affair his character plays out. In the manner of the great movies of intrigue set in war or cold war times, in other contexts, this (though at a much more modest level of achievement) bonds political and personal dramas and revelations (Allinson 1999: 39). The killing in the immediate post-civil war period of a fascist fifth columnist arouses the professional curiosities of policeman Ángel Barciela and sets him against not only his superiors, under pressure from 'los de arriba' to get a quick and clean plausible solution to the crime, but also from a sinister Falangist, Montilla, determined to find out who has murdered his colleague. To the element of principled rebellion of his character is soon added that of the professional who finds his emotions intervening in work. In the course of his investigations he falls in love with Julia—left-wing sympathizing daughter of decent right-wing folks who had in the war thought it their duty to offer a safe house to the dead man and his fascist colleagues. It turns out that she has committed the murder, in revenge for the brutal killing of her previous boyfriend (the once glamorous Toni Cantó rather improbably in the role of a member of *juventudes socialistas* (socialist youth)). It further transpires that within her calm and lovely non-private persona she (Emma Suárez) enfolds a violence the very hatred of which has by classic reversal of same and other constructed itself in her. And so too does Gómez's Barciela come to uncover brutal violence as much in himself as in the gruesome band whose history he studies. Again this is counter to appearances in character, and here, more pertinently to my particular focus, against the grain of earthiness and goodness in star persona.

Although the film's title sequence abruptly inserts the history of conflict into the filmgoer's experience and into its narrative by anticipating a moment of terrorist violence—a drive-by shooting of innocent Republicans off-duty at a bar—the main focus of the first seven or eight minutes is on placidity, solidity, the meditative, in other words the characteristically Carmelo-Gómez-ian. In the narrative outer frame, some years on, Julia is returning from her enforced exile to bury her now dead father, and Ángel is no longer a policeman but a maths teacher. An interior monologue ensues which, along with the name Ángel, uses the star persona of Gómez to bridge back one year in cinema history to *Tierra* and its monologues. Although Ángel Barciela is even more cerebral now than he was even as an investigative policeman, and formal too, he has the smell of that slightly earlier earth about him: and his thoughts are elegiac, slightly mesmerizing in their delivery, and casting Gómez's character- istic spell. The monologue invokes the past and cancels out the temporal distance (so many years, and there you stand) in gentle, powerful words and in long-distance reverse shots, from one part of the cemetery to another, with Gómez standing centre-frame against a background of greenery, and Julia's face turned 45 degrees away from the grave. When Julia turns back to the grave, bends her head, and removes her dark glasses and looks back the sequence is cut as if her eye contact were a direct product of the look of intensifying emotion on Barciela's face and of the sound of this male voice. Gómez's suited and bespectacled seriousness in the role of Barciela at this point, his stare, and the intensity of the mem- ories and feelings evoked in the monologue, seduce us into a grave and melancholy world. When this time-line and monologue are taken up again in the last minutes of the film the mood is seen partly to belong to the poet Luis Cernuda (1902–63), a famous two lines of whose—quoted at the end of the monologue—give the film, and Joaquín Leguina's novel on which it is based, their title.[2] The monologue mingles—like Cernuda's poems—narratives of personal and national loss, war, passion, and commitment.[3]

For much of the film Gómez and his character inhabit fairly straight- forwardly delimited liminal zones: between professional and private and between Spanish (in dutifully recorded specifics of the post-Civil War days) and a glamorous otherness which is markedly American Romantic. At a tea dance with Julia, once Barciela has made the transition from investigator to suitor, Gómez takes on the role of *galán* seductively, moving elegantly around the floor to the strains of 'Ramona', and allowing the passionate and vulnerable to slide in under the controlled persona of the competent professional. Swirling dissolves and, close-up, two shots of the gently swaying couple assist this; as a counterpoint Gómez manages in a look a virile mix of professional determination (asking why she has kept back important details relating to the case) and sensual assertiveness (injecting into the first question another more insistent one to do with her erotic restraint). However, the permeability thus built up between the professional and private in the fashion of film noir betrays both the quest for truth and the quest for love, bricking masculine subjectivity up into a restricted imaginative space. The romance of the dance is soon displaced by unwelcome revelations. Around a kitchen table,

---

[2] For an analysis of the adaptation, see Allinson (1999: 38–44).

[3] The poem, 'Un español habla de su tierra' (A Spaniard Tells of his Land) is part of the first collection written and published in exile, *Las nubes (The Clouds)* and is in part an indictment of the moral and cultural disasters of the Civil War and the victory of Franco's troops.

with Barciela's emotional vulnerability signalled by wide smiles, an open shirt front, and Gómez's easy leaning back in the chair, Julia makes a damaging double confession. She is involved with another man; and she is anyway emotionally disabled by a deep emptiness, something unidentifiable, lying beyond her grasp, but linked to death. She uses the word *desolación* (desolation) of her state of mind, and is thus made to invoke Cernuda who becomes once more shorthand for the connectedness of national and personal disasters. Gómez has Barciela take this with a terrible (if stock) stoicism, a single gulp, a quick nod of the head, and—reaching out to hold her chin—manly acceptance. But something of Julia's turbulent emotional darkness subsequently maps itself onto Barciela whose own narrative has already had attributed to it an abiding emptiness (Allinson 1999: 42). Tormented by the news that their affair is over, he becomes unable to stay calmly at the threshold of professional and personal life. Indeed, the barrier between his private life and the world of crime and politics is anyway false, and it now becomes impossible for him to distinguish between his anger at his broken love and his rage at the sinister and vengeful events unfolding around him. Gómez has him veer into instability in a well-paced sequence back in Barciela's home. Seated in an armchair under a single standard lamp, hedged in by the telephone he will not answer on one side and a bottle of brandy he is drinking fast on the other, he goes from immobile weeping, to apparent recovery (fingers to temples, pulling himself together), to suddenly standing, being still for ten seconds, then smashing the brandy glass against the floor, and trashing the room.

The typical still waters of this actor are even more radically disturbed later in a classic pattern of representation of dangerous masculinity in which strong emotion breaks though into extremity of deed, and erotic frustration is unleashed as man on man violence. Barciela lures Montilla into a train depot, and Miró—after the manner of her notorious *El crimen de Cuenca* (The Crime at Cuenca) (1979)—has Gómez explore the chillier reaches of sadism. He shoots Montilla, strings him up upside down, and, circling, fires bullet after bullet into the twisting corpse. Julia's frozenness and emptiness have been stamped on Barciela here, the violence of war and revenge become unusually associated with the gentle Gómez. So around a series of fairly basic dichotomies and connections—Barciela as kind and intelligent but desperate and ruthless; a doomed love affair, a doomed republican nation—which are not particularly deconstructed or problematized here, a more sophisticated and looser set of links is made through performance between ideas of masculinity and the concept of destructive emptiness, between calm solidity and primitive instincts lying in secret.

Secretos del corazón, of course, constructs a series of secrets nesting in secrets (in memories, relationships, a house, a village, a landscape, a school, a town, a nation) like the famous *El espíritu de la colmena / The Spirit of the Beehive* with which it shares brilliantly the premise of the child's-eye view. Although with top billing, Gómez here is a less prominent and has less screen time and active presence than the child actors and the women (Silvia Munt, Charo López, and Vicky Peña). As we have seen, as Tío he is the reliable, masculine, earth figure, apparently contained within his role as the man of the house (the figure of the grandfather having through grief abdicated power). But he is also a stand-in for a dead brother and disqualified from the exercise of patriarchal power by the transgressive sexual relationship he has with the dead man's widow, Javi's mother. It is Javi who is the prime mover of the narrative and is involved in the quest for discovery, for active participation in a world of complexity, while Tío is left impotent with guilt. Tío's silence marks him not necessarily as strong but, like his stubbornly taciturn and self-incarcerating father, harmed. When one night at the kitchen table, Javi offers his version of why he is so quiet and why there is tension in the house—because, in his newly learned words, 'por la noche vas al cuarto de mamá a chingar' (at night you go to Mum's room to screw)—he activates the repressed signs of a particularly masculine set of interlocked dramas. Tío's assumed fatherly authority is challenged; his honour is stained, both by the accusation and by the grandfather's immediate comment that the whole village anyway already knows; and, as Javi runs off past the much highlighted blue-glassed door behind which his father had died at his own hands, there is a rekindling of the guilt-inducing memory. The narrative of fratricide familiar in Spanish culture since at least as far back as the Generation of 1898—in the poet Antonio Machado's image, 'la sombra de Caín' (the shadow of Cain) stalking the landscape —sits aslant the film both in the figure of the grandfather as the loser in a struggle that pitted brother against brother in the war, and in the indirect connection between de facto adultery in the present and the suicide in the past. Gómez's role here is again both simply performed and rich in connotation. He is unchallengingly archetypal, a familiar movie figure in a familiar domestic dilemma and in a roughly rural, nostalgic setting; and he is simultaneously a set of suggestions of psychological troubles that lie far beyond his stolid characterization. His character participates in the regime of silence embodied by the grandfather, that tragic mirror image of the loss of innocence that the film tracks as its central motif in the boy Javi. Gómez makes the quietness of his gestural and vocal delivery more and more of an amplification chamber for the repressed; and he makes his reliable, comfortable physical presence the very sign of things that unsettle: taboos, secrets and lies, lack of communication, guilt, death, and sorrow.

Similarly, in *Extraños* (Strangers) (Imanol Uribe, 1998) emptiness and yet also a poignant exploration of its effects, is a major theme. This is a film whose inspiration and flavour come from Juan José Millás's novel *La soledad era esto* of the same year,[4] and Gómez plays the private detective Goyo Lamarca, hired initially by a Madrid architect who is suspicious of the apparent indifference of his wife Sofía (María Casal)—a professional musician—to her mother's suicide and of long absences from home which do not always coincide with rehearsal, performance, and touring. The investigation, in a film of considerable narrative and conceptual complexity, becomes strangely entangled with the dramatic unravelling of Lamarca's mind, prey to intense depressive episodes that border on the schizophrenic, and to images of death that in the final reel are revealed to have been accurately premonitory. The connotations and micro-structures of classic private-eye roles of Hollywood and European cinema accrete to the professional persona of Lamarca—the voyeur, the guardian, the seer—and early on in the film there is a strong reinforcement of the psychological implications of the investigation of domestic misdemeanour. Sofía, having discovered that she is being followed by Lamarca anonymously hires him to follow her on her own behalf and stages the infidelity of which she is in fact wrongly suspected. In playing out her fantasy of erotic adventure—in which she is paying to be watched—she stumbles on that which 'explains' her behavioural strangeness: an emptiness only partly due to the paralysis of grief and incomprehension attaching to the suicide of her mother. Seeing this, and seeing her visit again and again the site of the suicide—the now empty flat from whose window the mother threw herself—Lamarca becomes witness and accomplice to trauma and he himself discovers, in his dreams and in his investigations, the compelling images of his own death and emptiness.

Thus Gómez plays here not only the man of thoughtful action uncovering the causes of betrayal and self-betrayal but also, in his relationship with his client, a therapist insisting on the revelation of sites of emotional damage and—inextricably, by projection—the damaged and hypersensitized subject caught up in a complex of *incomunicación* (failure to communicate). Just as the classic film detective, from one perspective, and the classic neurotic-psychotic, from another, act as ciphers for non-subjective malaise (the social problems and readjustments

---

[4] About to come out, as I write, in a version closer to the text and with the original title: by Argentinian director Sergio Renán.

of post-Depression America, post-war Europe, or the excesses of late capitalism) so too does Gómez's Lamarca indicate specific and social disease. There is something frozen at the heart of wealthy middle-class Madrid—an architect's dream house is both the shiny stage for cruel silences between him and his wife Sofía and its elaborate garden pool is the place of Lamarca's eventual death; Sofía's gift of music (aimed at a middle-class audience: she is a cellist for a symphony orchestra) becomes reduced to mere rehearsal, mere repetition. Lamarca's increasingly mentally disturbed life on his own, and in the company of his also divorced colleague, suggests—like many Spanish narratives of the 1980s and 1990s—that solitude is a major and particular threat in a society that superficially at least places value on gregariousness, on the community of family, and on talking. His premonitions of his death point to a crisis not his alone.

Heritage, and jealousy

In the same year as *Tu nombre envenena mis sueños*, and with the same director and co-star (Emma Suárez), there was a different reminder of Gómez's ease of connection with the common ground of the national imaginary, and a reminder too of his early commitment to classical theatre (Leyra 1994). This came in his playing of Teodoro in Miró's and Rafael Pérez Sierra's screen version of the Lope de Vega Golden Age comedy *El perro del hortelano* (*The Dog in the Manger*). The film was number nine in box-office returns on Spanish-produced films in 1996, gained Gómez the Fotogramas de Plata award for best actor (in the same year as his Unión de Actores award in the same category), and itself won seven Goyas, including make-up, costume design, and cinematography, with the award for best leading actress going to Emma Suárez (who had also played key roles in the three Medem films mentioned above, is a passionate foil to Gómez's represented complexities, and a crucial figure in the development of his career: see Conclusion). The film's title, and the play's, refers to a proverb whose topic is jealousy, particularly that of 'el perro del hortelano que ni come ni deja comer' (the gardener's dog which will neither eat nor let others eat). The Countess Diana, in her sumptuously blue-tiled palace, is in love with her secretary Teodoro but is, of course, above him, and knows him to be involved with one of her maidservants, Marcela. For most of the drama the Countess will neither say outright what she feels nor allow Teodoro to continue his courtship of Marcela. The atmosphere of tightly restrained emotion works well for Gómez's habitual growing star persona; but the film also moves his image in other directions, linking him strongly with a development in the mainstream of the Spanish industry, the emergence of a modest Spanish Heritage Cinema.

In Spain this classical subspecies of the genre, it has been argued, started with this film, against a background of scepticism among financial backers and relegation from the official section of the San Sebastián festival in 1996, but with the positive outcome indicated in the prizes mentioned at the start of this section (and the top prize at the 1996 Mar de Plata festival in Argentina (Fernández-Santos 1997)). For the purpose, Gómez is allotted a look which is like that of Depardieu in *Cyrano de Bergerac* (Jean-Paul Rappeneau, 1990), with long hair, beard, and period costume making him handsome, and Lope de Vega's (lightly adapted) witty words adding the aura of age-old savoir faire. His brisk movement about the colourful monumental interiors and exteriors—made sumptuous by the Goya award-winning camera work of Javier Aguirresarobe— add to the sense of the actor's facility with the material, and although some of the monologues and asides ring flat, the verbal fencing matches with Emma Suárez as the Countess Diana, involving many a false confidence and jealous subtext, associate Gómez with skills of dexterity and high comic timing that are only very infrequently apparent in his earlier filmography. (They also fail to re-emerge with any consistency later in *La gran vida / Living It Up* (Antonio Cuadrí, 2000), the darker comic potential of which—a penniless, suicidal bus driver is offered 100 million pesetas which he must spend in a week, but then agree to die— is somewhat flattened by Gómez's overuse of the register of happy incredulity, the script's dependence on the clichéd satirization of the fatuity of the world of the very rich, and by the poor match of the passable handsomeness of Gómez to the high-pressure allure of Salma Hayek in a *Pretty Woman*-style role).[5]

When, in the Miró film, Gómez as Teodoro leans love-lorn over the balustrades above the gardens, or when he all but winks to camera in the execution of some piece of gently duplicitous business, the effect is 'mannerist and postmodern' in the sense that, like the film itself, he is 'highly aware of retracing earlier grounds' (Vincendeau 2001: p. xviii), taking part not just in an adaptation of Lope but in an adaptation of costume drama, taking a place, that is, in the twentieth-century generic context of the heritage film. Miró had seen Kenneth Branagh's *Much Ado*

---

[5] Torreiro (2000) sees the contrast differently, noting a welcome reappearance (after *El Portero*: discussed below) of Gómez's control of register and range and the inability of Hayek to engage with her character.

About Nothing (1993) (as well as *Henry* V (1988), and *Hamlet* (1996)) and *Cyrano de Bergerac* and made a conscious decision to translate the trend into the Spanish context (Nieva de la Paz 1997). Her film, in line with Vincendeau's characterization of the genre, 'showcase[s] acting skills' and has 'theatrical settings, scintillating dialogue and flattering costume' (ibid. p. xxiv); its equally typical exploitation of the cultural capital (p. xxii) of the famous playwright not only creates a marketable high concept but elevates its actors. Usually in the genre already big stars are matched to and augment characters similarly already legendary in the public imagination (p. xiv), but unlike the case of Catherine Deneuve, 'conferring patronage on the films she appears in' (Romney 2001: 42), for example, Emma Suárez and Gómez are not so much reaffirmed as national icons for the middle-aged, middle- to upper-class audience for heritage cinema as suddenly transcribed from another subcultural sphere, one where students and graduate 20-to-30 somethings went to see Suárez and Banderas in *La Blanca Paloma / The White Dove*, and Gómez and Suárez in the Medem films. Now they were associated with a cultural product whose sophistication was owing not to its novelty but its vintage, although Allinson (1999) may also be right in suggesting that the film's success is owing to its almost complete abandonment of the traditional heritage movie in questions of structure and technique (34–9).

In the scene in Act Two of the play which contains the lines that first refer to the eponymous proverb, a hurt Countess, who has seen Teodoro seem to get back together with Marcela, plays hard to get and cruelly reminds Teodoro of his lower status and consequently low expectations of success in love with her. Gómez, standing in front of her raised seat, sets his face and body in such a way as to signal contained irritation and barely held-back tears; he uses a three-step movement to one side and back to change emotional gear; and breaks into measured anger, making each word of the well-known words count as he flings at her the accusation 'Mas viénele bien el cuento / del perro del hortelano' (But how well the tale of the gardener's dog becomes you!), 'Pues coma o deje comer; / porque yo no me sustento / de esperanzas tan cansadas; / que si no, desde aquí vuelvo / a querer donde me quieren' (Well either eat or let others eat: I for one can't live on such meagre hopes; either that, or I'll go back now to where at least I know I'm loved).

In *Mararía* (José Antonio Betancor, 1998) it is Gómez who plays the jealous one who will not eat or allow another to eat, and, although given much scope for acting handsome, soulful, and familiar, he ends up representing a more disturbing narrative of masculinity destroyed by forces coded as irrational other (the eponymous woman; strong emotion itself;

and the primitive, natural order as figured in rocks, sky, and sea). The arrival at Lanzarote of a new village doctor from the Basque country, Fermín (Gómez's character) allows the actor to establish at once a certain measured nobility as he stands at the prow of the ferryboat. He plays being out of place in the van that transports him through the arresting landscape to the village where he is to practise; and he adjusts his body coding from its usual signalling of calm to that of aloneness as he wanders through the doctor's ample house with its patio and look-out tower. From the tower, unwinding, and in vest and trousers (in the manner of many an English gentleman in desert movies old and new), he sees in one direction the dry lands and mountains, and close down below—in classic movie style—a beautiful young servant splashing her face, and her invitingly revealed neck and shoulders. She, Mararía (Goya Toledo) immediately captivates the doctor but becomes associated with his growing perturbation. Not only is he increasingly troubled by the harsh and hot landscape, especially on an excursion to the volcano (recalling the trip to the Marabar Caves in David Lean's *A Passage to India*, though with camels not elephants) but also by the arrival of tall, blond, arrogant representative of the Royal Geographic Society of Great Britain, Bertrand (Iain Glenn), one of several radical alterations to the original novel by Rafael Arozarena (1973).

The arrestingly photographed landscapes, their geological complexity and solidity, and their sombre colour range become counterpoints and reflections of Gómez's acting style: on the one hand he manifests a vulnerable sensitivity—frequently raising a hand to his brow, wincing at the heat, looking longingly at Mararía—and on the other hand he signals his character's Northern phlegmatism, his teetotalism, and his stoicism in the face of the tedium of life on the island. This is in contrast to Bertrand, who is more pioneering, intrepid in proximity to the volcanic vents, flirtatious with both the women in Fermín's life, who drinks, swims naked, and dares to dance at the tavern where Fermín does not, has sex with Mararía on the wave-beaten beach, makes her pregnant and appears, at least, to become formally her fiancé. In fact the usual roles of cold Englishman and fiery foreigner are nicely reversed.

As Fermín, in the role of the honourable man, confronts the caddish Bertrand at his makeshift scientific site on the volcano slopes, and hears that he plans to abandon Mararía and his child, Gómez has his character display an intense, beautiful, and contained indignation, enhanced by medium close-up side views of his face in half profile against the yellow, rocky landscape. As the camera takes up a low angle—with Fermín's pure white suit and hat filling the screen—he looks down with intensity, and there is a sudden turn into savagery. Fermín takes a pick, plunges it into Bertrand's neck as he stoops to adjust instruments, and, again from a low angle, flies screaming around the encampment tearing it down, clothes now bloodied, and tipping all the equipment, and then the body, into one of the nearby vents. There is no such event in the novel, instead an Arabic travelling salesman who has captured Mararía's heart is set upon and lynched by the men of the village. The film clearly sees Gómez's capacity for contained fury as a lure, and also wants to capitalize on his telluric associations. Many of the shots in the sequence draw on images of Gómez in *Tierra*: intense facial expressions and white clothing against red landscapes; a man in the throes of psychic conflict; carrying on his shoulders not the dead sheep of the Medem film but a dead man. As it is there, his character is represented as strangely influenced by telluric forces (here emanating from the fiery core rather than heavenly ether); as there too, feuding between males is the catalyst of crisis. There is an explicit element of magic in the film (as also in the novel, where Mararía is unambiguously a beautiful and dangerous witch): Mararía's 'aunt' Herminia (Mirta Ibarra) is a *curandera* (a herbalist white witch) who has tried in vain to join Fermín and Mararía and to keep her from Bertrand. When—after the intervention of war in Spain, then in Europe (all dealt with in less than a minute)—Fermín returns he attempts to double for the long-dead Bertrand in ways so uncanny as to call up the suspicion of spells gone wrong. He returns in the very seaplane that had first brought Bertrand; insists on using the bedroom in which Mararía and Bertrand had made love; forces himself on her (having taken to drink during the war) in a flawed attempt at emulating the passion of the dead man; and stands in as father to the young Jesusito. When the child dies, drowned one day playing in the saltpans, Mararía goes mad, her aunt's use of fire and herbal waters cannot unlock her, and she goes one night to the beach which is superstitiously thought to be that to which all drowned bodies eventually return, and some with life restored. Here Fermín again forces another substitution of himself for the dead Bertrand, trying to make love to her on the same spot—and in the same directed moves—as she and Bertrand had themselves first done. This ghosting further maddens her, and, calling both for her dead son and dead lover, she half deliberately stumbles into the bonfires lit to conjure the dead and allows herself to be burned; like Bertrand she is surrendered to the flames, and like him she is carried by Fermín across a bleak landscape. In this, the last scene of the film, Gómez is memorably (despite the film's limited commercial impact) rendered archetypal: the man from the North, a scientist, distant from the emotional and spiritual meanings of a place where women are pivotal, is sucked into telluric and tragic mayhem, a failed saviour trudging across the desert under whose surface there is real as well as meta-phorical ash, fire, and smoke. A masculinity built on notions of reason and civilization, protected by its own emotional chill and physically signalled uprightness, falls into the melt.

This is, then, in extreme form the deep and turbulent Gómez representing a masculinity conformed by class and professional values, by a dangerous ignorance of the powers of emotion, and by sexual rivalry. The period setting acts as a crucible for the now characteristic transformational reaction as control, reliability, and wholesomeness slip away revealing, apparently, the raw dramatic substance. Unlike the form of heritage film discussed by Monk (1997: part 2), and despite its visual exuberance and tendency to ensemble acting, *Mararía* (like the two Miró films too, for their distinct reasons) identifies the male protagonist strongly and monogamously with the single hero (in Monk's terms) because of this star-contextualized revelation of male trouble beneath the stout exterior. So too, but to different effect, does chronologically the last film I am able to deal with here, *El portero* / *The Goalkeeper* (Gonzalo Suárez, 2000). This positions Gómez as a sturdy presence in the nostalgic national past, drawing to himself potentially violent rivalries but in the end neutralizing them, and helping a Spanish audience, as in *Secretos del corazón*, to convince itself that it has exorcized the ghosts of the Civil War. As a retired goalie making a living out of his one-man travelling exhibition of skills, his character Ramiro Forteza arrives in 1948 in a remote Asturian seaside town which is a representational micro-cosm oddly not dissimilar (coming as it does from an otherwise markedly serious director) to that of the comedy *Belle Époque* (see Ch. 6), complete with doubting priest, civil guards, dazzling exteriors, love interest, and the politics of war sizzling away at the periphery (here the guerrilla warfare of the resistance, the *maquis*). Coverage of the shooting soon incorporated into the anecdotal archive the hard training sessions and broken rib Gómez put himself through for the strenuous aspects of the role:[6] and there is a sense in which this anyway allegorical film also served to keep the reassuringly uncomplicated—and vulnerable—aspects of the Gómez star persona in trim while in other projects it was becoming dense with psychological accretions. As he himself comments in interview, Forteza is an accidental hero, taking up the cause of the disempowered but in a quiet and gentle film in which '[t]rata que el espectador se relaje y se olvide un poco de todo' (the point is for the audience to go and relax and forget everything for a bit) (Fundación

---

[6] For example *Fotogramas*, Nov. 1999 (232–3) and Sept. 2000 (109): http://www.telepolis.com/cgi-bin/t30/!CINECRITICAS?dir=portero (6 Nov. 2001).

Octaedro 2001). However, director Gonzalo Suárez remarks, in relation to the role of Forteza, on 'la intensidad sobria que [Carmelo Gómez] confiere a sus personajes' (the sober intensity he puts into his characters) (*Todocine* 2000*b*); and when Javier Bardem, the subject of the next chapter, played next to him in *Entre las piernas / Between Your Legs* (Manuel Gómez Pereira, 1999) he declared to the press his 'fear' of Gómez's superior abilities, his impressive growth as actor, and the fact that 'él tiene cosas que yo no podré tener nunca' (there are things about him that I will never have) (Martín-Lunas 1998)—again it must have been that 'sober intensity' which struck Bardem, coming through in this particular film in the tightly controlled despair and jealousy of (again) a detective discovering amid the tangle of criminality and male violence his wife's own infidelity (with Bardem as a sexaholic screen-writer, and with an intensity all his own).

TABLE 3. *Filmography*

Year	Title	English title(s) (official titles in italics; literal in roman)	Director	Billing	Audience figures and takings	Other information
1988	*Bajarse al moro*	Going Down to Morocco	Fernando Colomo	Minor	414,737 / €830,828	
1988	*Loco veneno*	Crazy Poison	Miguel Hermoso	Minor	87,995 / €160,612	
1992	*Vacas*	Cows	Julio Medem	Top	152,031 / €370,703	
1992	*Después del sueño*	After the Dream	Mario Camus	Top	64,480 / €148,692	
1993	*La ardilla roja*	The Red Squirrel	Julio Medem	5th	178,139 / €477,855	
1994	*Canción de cuna*	Cradle Song	Jose Luis Garcí	8th	232,147 / €702,052	One of several remakes
1994	*El detective y la muerte*	Death and the Detective	Gonzalo Suárez	2nd	131,113 / €319,645	Minor production interests Holland and Poland
1994	*Días contados*	Numbered Days / Running out of Time	Imanol Uribe	Top	687,783 / €1,947,955	Goya for Best Leading Male
1995	*Entre rojas*	Left-Wing Women	Azucena Rodríguez	5th	49,340 / €146,135	
1996	*Tierra*	Earth (Australia only; elsewhere as original)	Julio Medem	Top	226,174 / €710,246	
1996	*El perro del hortelano*	The Dog in the Manger	Pilar Miró	2nd	975,677 / €3,221,942	Fotogramas de Plata for best actor
1996	*Tu nombre envenena mis sueños*	Your Name Poisons my Dreams	Pilar Miró	Top	136,598 / €429,441	
1997	*Territorio comanche*	Comanche Territory	Gerardo Herrera	2nd	196,528 / €665,770	Co-pro Spain, Germany, France
1997	*Secretos del corazón*	Secrets of the Heart	Montxo Armendáriz	Top	1,199,768 / €4,273,752	
1998	*Mararía*		Antonio José Betancor	Top	132,819 / €455,899	
1998	*Extraños*	Strangers	Imanol Uribe	Top	75,452 / €265,967	
1999	*Entre las piernas*	Between Your Legs	Manuel Gómez Pereira	3rd	923,196 / €3,470,643	
2000	*El portero*	The Goalkeeper	Gonzalo Suárez	Top	145,890 / €609,680	
2000	*La gran vida*	Living It Up	Antonio Cuadri	2nd	351,974 / €1,426,432	
2000	*La Playa de los galgos*	Greyhound Beach	Mario Camus	Top	62,615 / €298,006	
2001	*Nos miran*	They're Watching Us	Norberto López Amado	Top	No figures available	Co-pro Italy, Spain

Television series

La Regenta (dir. Fernando Gómez Leite) 1995

Shorts

Versión simultánea con traducción original (Simultaneous Version with Original Translation) (Santiago Matallana, 1989)
Andeo (Luis Valles, 1998)

4 Javier Bardem (b. 1969)

In and out of *machismo*

Of the actors I am concerned with it is Javier Bardem who most often is discussed explicitly in terms of masculinity, being represented at the popular end of the film publications market within Spain as, in the first part of his career, brutally attractive, full of *morbo* (another variant of that perverse sex appeal attributed to and refuted by Banderas), and as the archetypal and (comically) shameless *macho*. He has been seen from outside in middle- to highbrow commentaries—often with considerable but revealing inaccuracy—as epitomizing not only a general set of Spanish masculinities but a geographically non-defined *machismo*. This is an interpretation due in part to the relative unfamiliarity of non-Spanish audiences with a change of emphasis in the actor's projected self-image and in the roles taken up. There is a marked shift from the heavily ironic and broad-brush mode of José Juan Bigas Luna to more ostentatiously thoughtful roles, as we shall see, which remained little noticed until 2000 and the release abroad of *Segunda piel / Second Skin* (Gerardo Vera, 1999). Like Banderas and Sanz, in their different ways, he is an established sex symbol who to an unusual degree has—at all stages of his career to date, and despite the shift into seriousness just mentioned—attracted commentary on his physical presence and the sensuality of both his everyday demeanour and his acting (Fouz-Hernández 1999: 49–51). Thus (female) interviewers are able to be knowingly and wittily flirtatious, openly referring to his physical attractions, parodically using the clichés against which Bardem rebels, and drawing from their interviewee intelligent complicity (Torres 1993; Rigalt 1997). The opening in France of *Huevos de oro / Golden Balls* (Bigas Luna, 1993) (with the title oversimply translated as *Macho*) was accompanied by a photo spread in the Paris magazine *Glamour* of Bardem half naked in bed; reviews of *Éxtasis* (Ecstasy) (Mariano Barroso, 1995) and *Perdita Durango* (1997) (especially) have frequent recourse to the vocabulary of wildness, conviction, impact, violence, strength.[1] An entry in a popular dictionary begins its

---

[1] For example, in *Fotogramas*, 1829 (March 1996): 16; *Imágenes de actualidad*, 165 (Dec. 1997): 118. See also Merikaetxebarria 1994 (additionally emphasizing the existence of a complementary melancholy and sensitive aspect).

Fig. 8. Javier Bardem, with Stefania Sandrelli and Jordi Mollà in *Jamón, jamón*.

Fig. 9. Javier Bardem in *Los lobos de Washington*.

description of Bardem by characteristically mixing body and mind: 'Actor de aspecto rotundamente carnal, presencia impactante y excelentes dotes interpretativas' (a distinctly sensual-looking actor of impressive physical presence and outstanding talent) (*Cinerama* 1996: 19); and a mainstream website points up the contrast between his popularity with directors, his adaptability, and sensitivity, and yet his 'aspecto rudo, su nariz rota y su corpulencia física [que] le dan cierto aire tosco' (his rough appearance, broken nose, and heavy build [which] give him a certain air of coarseness) (Todocine 2000*a*). Commonplace in early interviews and latterly on fan websites are references to his selection for the Spanish national amateur rugby team, his interest in and (now abandoned) practice of boxing, weight training, and the by all accounts somewhat laddish series of late night bars with which he has been associated, originally in partnership with his brother Carlos.[2] As with Brando (Bardem's nickname, used both by Bigas Luna and Gonzalo Suárez: Torrecillas 1994),[3] an impressive physique speaks of intellectual and imaginative stature and of charisma; and were Bardem French, comments a reviewer of *Éxtasis*, he would be a world-wide star—his head, his profile, is 'portentous', a gift to the camera like a preclassical Greek statue's (Segovia 1996). Like Belmondo he is 'bello tenebroso' (sinisterly handsome) (Ferrando 1994).

He also had early in his career a prominent part in the fantasy social and cultural life of 30-something Madrid, in part, perhaps, because of those bars (and a series of photographs of him dancing shirtless in Pacha: de Laiglesia 1992: 120); and in part because of the high profile and historically embedded meanings of the dynasty from which he comes. His brother Carlos and sister Mónica are both established actors, as is, more famously, his mother, Pilar Bardem, with a distinguished career as a character actress on television and in classic and recent art-house cinema—in Medem's *Vacas* and Agustín Díaz Yañes's *Nadie hablará de nosotras cuando hayamos muerto* (Nobody Will Talk About Us When We're Dead) (1995), winning the Premio Goya for her category, and as Doña Centro in Almodóvar's *Live Flesh*. His uncle, Juan Antonio Bardem, is one of the country's most famous names in film-making (Hopewell 1986: 51–8, 107–10; Stone 2002: 41–57). His cousin, Miguel

[2] See, for example, *Diario 16* (Madrid) 5 April 1994: 43; *La Información de Madrid*, 17 Aug. 1994; *El Mundo (Magazine)*, 10 Sept. 1994: 40; de Laiglesia 1992: 120; http: // alcazaba.unex.es / ~pavirey / pavirey.html (18 Dec. 2000).
[3] Bardem's name was being suggested for a production by José Tamayo of *A Streetcar Named Desire* in 1993; it is interesting to reflect not only on how he would have inflected that role but also whether he might subsequently have been approached by Almodóvar to take it on again in the play within a film that informs the thematics of *Todo sobre mi madre / All About My Mother*.

Bardem, is script writer and co-director (*Más que amor, frenesí / More Than Love, Frenzy*: 1999), and director of the short *La madre* and young actors' showcase (but also with Pilar Bardem), *La mujer más fea del mundo* (The World's Ugliest Woman) (1999). Like Banderas, he became early on in his career a significant element in the social and cultural currency of contemporary Spain, and of Madrid specifically, but unlike Banderas he was already embedded into its cultural life, and unlike him too he stayed. By 1997 he was being named as a key player in the new generation said to be anti-1980s consumerist individualism, los JASP (Jóvenes, aunque sobradamente / suficientemente preparados) (Young but well / exceedingly well prepared).[4]

But while, as a profile in *Cinerama* had it, he may be brutishly passionate and sexual and ready to put 'toda la carne en el asador' (the whole joint of meat on the spit) to put human feeling into his roles (*Cinerama* 1995), this primary image of him is not instinctual or spontaneous but constructed and studied. In his early career it helped him, according to the magazine, to get ahead of the designer set, 'con sangre de horchata' (those with milkshake for blood). Moreover, as José Arroyo has pointed out,[5] the superficial public image of the actor is complicated not only by the (albeit somewhat crude) parodies of *machismo* in Bigas's films and an ironic distance from his characters but by homoeroticism, and indeed, a certain queerness. Bardem's first prominent role, as Arroyo noted, was after all as a gay man paid to perform in a threesome in José Juan Bigas Luna's classily erotic *Las edades de Lulú / The Ages of Lulu* (1990), and his first sex scenes there involved explicit anal penetration (as well as a sadomasochistic structure of instruction and subservience). A later crossover between screen role and star image in this respect comes in the darkly grotesque exploration of sex addiction *Entre las piernas / Between Your Legs* (Manuel Gómez Pereira, 1999) where in an early sequence Bardem's character narrates in detail to a recent pickup, by mobile phone, his first out-of-the-ordinary sexual experience—a homosexually biased threesome involving golden showers—thus writing his body into a perverse and, to the listening woman, stimulating erotic history. His roles as straight actor playing a gay prostitute in the romantic farce and thriller *Boca a boca / Mouth to Mouth* (Gómez Pereira, 1995), as out gay man *Segunda piel / Second Skin*, and as dissident queer writer

---

[4] In *Fotogramas*, 1,839 (Jan. 1997): 28, along with Spanish actors Silke and Coque Malla (and, less convincingly, Leonardo di Caprio and Winona Ryder). The acronym is calqued on the North American WASP but the Spanish grouping is far more liberal—left wing indeed—and, at least theoretically, intended to be racially and ethnically inclusive.

[5] Unpublished paper presented at the day-conference Masculinity and Cultural Change in Europe, at the Centre for Research into Film, University of Newcastle (11 Nov. 1999).

Reinaldo Arenas in *Before Night Falls* (Julian Schnabel, 2000), allow his star persona to signal even more strongly meanings that crucially contradict, or at least intersect critically, with the common early image of Bardem as hunk. In the opening minutes of *El amante bilingüe* (see Ch. 1) Bardem has a cameo role as rough young Andalusian stud having sex with the upper-middle-class Catalan wife of the protagonist-narrator. This is a miniature portrait of typical manliness, inflected by caricature class difference: the Andalusian is her shoe-shine boy as well as her toy boy; she is sexually frustrated by social and marital restraints, he is savage and sexual and liberating. It anticipates the encounter between Bardem's Raúl and the typical bored bourgeois woman Conchita (Stefania Sandrelli) in Bigas Luna's *Jamón, jamón* (1992) where, despite the North-Eastern inland setting of the film (in Aragon) Bardem's character is shot through with Southern Mediterranean 'masculinity ideals' of the sort that Gilmore (1990: 30–55) extrapolates from his socio-anthropological analysis of case studies in Andalusia. There are ostentatious displays of manliness as effective and instrumental (doing, working, go-getting), representations of man as provider and taker of erotic initiatives, of men as out-of-doors, and women as living inside. Much of this is manifested both in *Jamón, jamón* and in Bigas Luna's next Bardem-centred piece *Huevos de oro / Golden Balls* (1993) which gave rise to the inaccurate and persistent connection of Bardem with the *macho ibérico* (Iberian *macho*)[6] and the long process of denial and escape from typecasting (Martín 1993: 6; Merikaetxebarria 1994; see also Fouz-Hernández 1999) as well as in a varied choice of roles.

In *Jamón, jamón*, as is fairly well known, Bardem acts out in the character of Raúl an 'absurdly stereotypical masculinity', which is linked to a critique of consumerism (Jordan and Morgan-Tamosunas 1998: 142) and which turns to murderous violence at the end, when, as Deleyto (1999: 282) argues, the 'two representatives of masculinity are defeated' and the film pivots back into its real dual preoccupation, that with motherhood and prostitution. Food, sex, class differences, and male rivalries underscore the ritual qualities of the relationships between the characters, the play on clichés of masculinity and Spanishness (Morgan and Jordan 1994), and a 'grotesque, dark, [but] humorous portrayal of [the] famous "Mediterranean sensibility"' (63). When the film shifts from 'saturnalian comedy' (Deleyto 1999: 273) to its heavily intertexualized tragic finale,

---

[6] The Spanish term has specifically Spanish (rather than Spanish and Portuguese) connotations of a red-neck world-view, land-locked isolationism, immemorial tradition, and, not least, the indigenous pig—*cerdo ibérico*—known for its superior meat (ham, cured and eaten raw).

Bardem manages a difficult transition, and is able to hold the theatrical moment despite visual interferences of traces of Goya, Buñuel, and Westerns, and despite the biblical overlays (Cain and Abel; the desert landscape; the shepherd with his flock; and the pictorial tradition of the Pietà). The frenzied perversion of virile ideals of doing and competing that is the bludgeoning of his rival José Luis (Jordi Mollà) with one of the cured hams, which it has been his job to guard and advertise, turns, through the murder, into the utter destruction of those same virile ideals. The enacted realization of this is etched on the contorted face of Raúl as he crouches in a mix of physical and psychic pain over the recently dead body of his rival and in a tragically belated outburst against the symbol of his enslavement to material goods, the badge of the Mercedes that Conchita owns and to which he has aspired. What he seems to register in these moments is the shocked acceptance of the punishment for performing excessively and without nuance those masculine ideals that ought to have brought sexual and material success. In *Huevos de oro* there is a similar trajectory towards a punished masculinity. Bardem's character Benito early on makes the gross comic declaration that he lives to put up buildings and have erections, and constantly draws attention to his genitalia (Fouz-Hernández 1999: 48), and his body is spectacularly and competitively displayed (54–5), while all the time the film piles metaphorical emasculation high (58–60) and builds to a crisis of 'psychological castration' (59). The revelation of the redundancy of the performance of masculinity through Benito's 'overcompensating phallic language', and his eventual infantilization (63) point, albeit coarsely, towards psychological meanings of some complexity which in Bardem's subsequent career were to accrue to his persona and which he was intelligently to explore.

The tormented male

In the fantasy thriller *El detective y la muerte / Death and the Detective* (Gonzalo Suárez, 1994) Bardem plays—to simplify a very convoluted plot with no conventional characters—an ex-boxer detective Cornelio who is initially employed or coerced by the dying husband of his lover, La Duquesa (The Duchess). He is to bring her back to the fortified and heavily defended mansion, The Blue House, where her daughter, sexually involved with her father, has made it known that her mother must soon die. The opening five minutes of the film place emphasis on his physicality: he is tracked down by his ex-sparring partner, El Hombre Oscuro

(The Dark Man) (played by Carmelo Gómez) to the shores of a rocky and deserted Northern beach. In a striking surprise shot he emerges, full-frontal, naked, and magnificent, from the waves and is soon temporarily engaging in manly homosocial banter with The Dark Man. Bardem's emergence from the sea stays in the memory as an image of a reverse Venus, some sea-god, or at very least a shipwrecked character in some classic drama, due to engage in symbolic rather than real action. This is retrospectively reinforced by the fact that at another level of diagesis Cornelio, known to all but his ex-sparring partner simply as El Detective, is an allegorical figure—a fallen, damaged, and vulnerable knight on a quest for goodness, love, and resurrection; and his dying employer is an aspect or avatar of Death itself (La Gran Mierda: Dirty Death),[7] who can conjure up ghost images of mother and daughter that are visible and responsive to their living counterparts. There is, though, also a sense, as Stone (2002: 197) puts it, of Bardem 'exploring rather than exploiting his animality' as well as the abundant coding of him as mysterious and unreal. As elements of Hans Christian Andersen's 'The Story of A Mother' (the film's core inspiration) and Bluebeard's Castle interlace, the role connects generically more and more with action thrillers. Distracted from his ostensible task by the peculiar exigencies and probably deliberate discontinuities of the script, The Detective becomes involved, now in the burnt-out ruins of war- or riot-torn Poland, with an ex-prostitute named 'María, like all the others' (as she says). The icily cruel Hombre Oscuro has exercised on María's crying baby a particular skill of his, the suffocation of his victims; she, convinced by him that he has merely taken away the baby's breath and that Death can restore it (as in the Andersen tale), has involved The Detective in taking her to the Blue House. Here, in the final reel, the Duchess herself dies, suffocated at the hands of The Dark Man, The Detective is shot and dies, and, as anticipated in a gnomic utterance about fate, checks, and balances from Dirty Death, María's child has his breath returned to him.

Alongside his mythic trajectory from apparent birth, or rebirth, from the waters to death for the sake of others, there is a ritual passage undertaken by The Detective through certain stages of masculine agency in the world. He negotiates an emotional space between nostalgic comradeship and fearful rivalry with The Dark Man. He has an intensely erotic last scene with the Duchess (to the strains of Marlene Dietrich singing 'I've Been in Love Before') which establishes him, in yet another generic direction, as passionate, reckless, dominant, but enthralled (and in fact drugged) male lover of heroic screen romance

---

[7] The substitution in the Spanish of Mierda (Shit) for Muerte (Death) allows no adequate translation.

tradition, enveloped in the dominant deep reds of the *mise en scène* at this stage. He encounters a kind of innocent woman in the besotted María. Most powerfully and hardest of all, he has to struggle, at his own dying father's hospital bed, to articulate his remorse—as the classic bad, neglectful son—in the context of a common ground formed only of memories of fishing trips during which neither man had ever spoken. Thus on the one hand the allegorical elements of the film require Bardem to attune his presentation of character towards the wide gestures of serious pantomime and move through a narrative of clearly defined, large spaces (from rocky seashore to war zone, ruined complex to vast mansion); while on the other hand, in his encounters with the failure of love and the flaws of paternal-filial relations (as well, to a lesser extent, in his homosocial relationship with The Dark Man), a troubled inwardness is required, a difficult balance where the emotional range to be displayed is informed, precisely, by blocked emotion.

Bardem has commented on the difficulties of performance in this film, the unusually long hours of preparation for the role, and director Suárez's interest in helping him achieve 'algo que no he trabajado hasta ahora, que es la contención de la emoción' (something that I haven't worked on before, and that is the containment of emotion) (Torrecillas 1994). The hospital scene, picking up on notes of frustration and regret associated with the affair with The Duchess, bears out Bardem's comments on the demands of working around the 'prohibition' and 'frustration' associated with 'containment'; this is notably so in the tense, close-up shots of the reactions of The Detective endeavouring but failing to comply with his father's whispered plea to cut off his oxygen supply to put him out of his pain. Speaking again of the difficulties of the role, and alluding to that change of direction in his career, Bardem noted in his performance 'una composición interior, de miradas más que de palabras [. . .] un tono diferente de interpretación al que estaba acostumbrado' (an internalized composition of feeling, made up of looks rather than words [. . .] a different tone of acting from what I had been used to) (Gil 1994).

There is significant overlap in Bardem's role in this peculiar film with Gómez's own style of obscurely tormented detective in *Extraños* and (despite its obvious lack of containment) *Tu nombre envenena mis sueños* (discussed in Ch. 3); like Gómez Bardem exploits the tensions between masculine physicality and interiority, turning the classic severally faceted quest of the film noir detective more towards existential uncertainty than towards narrative or moral resolution—because of a relative lack of intrigue and action—and completing the turn, for himself as actor, towards the recuperation of a more obviously thoughtful, actorly style that always anyway underlay his playing, early on, of the archetypal and parodic Spanish male. It bore out his claims of 1992 to champion individualism—'personalidad y [. . .] singularidad' (personality and [. . .] uniqueness)—in acting, free of formal training, but necessitating hard intellectual effort and the channelling of will and energy (de Laiglesia 1992: 118, 121).

If the route towards this new range and inwardness in *El detective y la muerte* is one that runs through territories of archetype and myth, it is arrived at in *Días contados* (see Ch. 3) by way of the classic technique of the observation of everyday reality, and his playing of Lisardo, the junkie and police informer, is as much a disturbing triumph of self-aware mimesis as is Jordi Mollà's of Daniel in *La Buena estrella* (see Ch. 5). In *Éxtasis* an equally sombre role requires the exploitation of this new, raw interiority. The film is doubly anchored in Spanish cultural history with one line going out to arguably the nation's most famous play of the literary Golden Age, Calderón de la Barca's *La vida es sueño* (*Life is a Dream*)—with a protagonist who discovers himself to be (as spoken by Bardem's character) 'compuesto de hombre y fiera' (made up of elements of man and beast)—a production of which is part of the main narrative. Another line ties up with the metaphorical mode of Spanish art cinema directors of the late 1970s and early 1980s (Jordan and Morgan-Tamosunas 1998: 98–9), not least in its studied use of music for atmosphere and a quotient of image to word favouring the former. Another goes down into the preoccupations and thematics of a belatedly high-profile representation in post-Franco cinema of urban youth cultures (Allinson 2000: 270–2). Disaffected youngsters Ona, Robert (Bardem's character), and Max (Daniel Guzmán) decide to extort or steal money from their families to gain independence. They mount a raid on Ona's father's small store at the start of the film and their ensuing conversation centres on the dysfunctionality of family life. Max has been abandoned early in life by his father, now a rich and successful theatre director, Daniel (Federico Luppi); Robert, armed with this knowledge, makes plans to impersonate Max (while the latter is in jail) and presents himself at a casting session, crucially with one green contact lens in— the proof of his filial status, as Max has one brown and one green eye. Although Daniel marks down the new 'Max' as 'absurd' and 'false' on his casting notes—and Bardem smartly plays the audition just the right side of unconvincing—the 'revelation' from 'Max' that he is his son begins an escalation of deceptions and self-deceptions that lead to Daniel's offering the lead part of the wronged son Prince Segismundo of the famous play to 'Max' (principally on the grounds that he has 'energy and spontaneity'). Daniel slips into the role of father—'me gusta la idea de tener un hijo' (I like the idea of having a son) he confides to 'Max'. In turn, in a carefully calibrated series of reactions to key moments on the way to the final robbery of Daniel's expensive art and watch collection, Bardem has his character alter from a position of hostile indifference (the role-playing is just a job; Daniel unpleasant, and loaded) to conflicted emotional engagement and subtle manifestations of the injured boy who psychically underpins the tough, self-possessed criminal. He registers first mild jealousy, both sexual and material (he twice has sex with Daniel's wife; and Daniel's life and home are more than comfortable), then confusion over his identity and desires, sharpened by the high-profile intervention at key moments of the play. The lines 'qué es la vida? Un frenesí . . .' (what is life? Frenzied confusion) and 'que toda la vida es sueño, y los sueños sueños son' (all life is but a dream, and dreams all dreams) bear in on the character of Robert. In an intense rehearsal scene the power relations between father and son, director and actor fuse as Daniel has 'Max' attempt a physically demanding scene (doubly demanding for Bardem depicting it) which involves climbing a rope while declaiming a key tragic soliloquy ('ay mísero de mí . . .' (ah, wretch that I am . . .)). In the film's climax Daniel stumbles on the trio in the act of robbery, overhears the true Max—out of jail soon after the start of the whole project—giving vent to his own rage and confusion (this, after all, really is his father, whom he needs to hate and yet be loved by) and witnesses a brutal scrap between Max and Robert that leaves Max, beaten to the floor and kicked, temporarily unconscious. In this, another scenario of tension and extreme physicality, the false Max's need really to be Daniel's son is matched by Daniel's own need to have one. As the two men hold each other's shoulders, forehead to forehead in dramatic side-view two-shot—Daniel bleeding—there is a locking into one another of psychological, emotional, social, and dramatic motifs strongly focused on Bardem's performance of the strong but vulnerable Robert, who is himself but another, torn between a false family with a solid future and an alternative family with none. Bardem's face in profile registers the panic of indecision as he hesitates between the route back into the apartment at Daniel's invitation and the route to the street and reunion with his friends.

Bardem is outstandingly good at registering psychological and dramatic fullness through non-verbal representation in establishing moments. Just as *Éxtasis* sets its mood—physical, tense, freighted with emotional issues—by opening on him waiting in the getaway car and looking rivetingly unwholesome, so too it is Bardem who marks with unsettling marginality the start (and duration) of Mariano Barroso's *Los lobos de Washington* (The Washington Wolves) (1999, with Bardem as producer).

Walking unsteadily along a rain-soaked pavement, on which the camera looks down transmitting dejection, and with a realistically shambolic cityscape in the far background, open land strewn with bricks in the middle and foreground, Bardem (as Alberto) hunches up, turning his build into something arrestingly ill-set, muttering to himself about money and trust, trying to rehearse something to himself. Alberto is an alcoholic whose marriage and small-time garage business are in desolation behind him; Bardem plays his linked weaknesses—lack of will, lack of wit, addiction —with a controlled repertoire of downcast glances, avoidances of eye contact, and a particularly memorable and shocking tic of taking drink (in brandy glass or hip-flask) in a grotesque parody of shame, twisting rapidly to one side, drinking away from the line of sight of those around him. Alberto confronts escalating complications around a car-deal scam, is at one point being challenged by his friend Miguel (who is and has long been going out with Alberto's now ex-wife) with a story that does not add up concerning his ex-wife and a car accident, has to care for his semi-autistic young half-brother, and frets about his plans to take his own (he wrongly thinks) 11-year-old son to the circus, which is just driving in to town. Bardem conveys the inability to focus, the haze of alcohol and hangover, and the sense of immense but unrecognizable pain and confusion, by a series of hand movements to forehead, mouth, and temples. There are twitches of the mouth, as if it is seeking the words to restore control (as in the opening sequence); there are looks that give the audience to understand that his character half chooses not to understand himself the full extent of his implication in complexity and possible damage.

The film specializes in desolate, large, enclosed spaces—the practically empty workshop-garage in which Alberto lives, off a bar; an underground car park; a tunnel on the city's road system; the municipal car pound—and Bardem uses his presence to fill these spaces with his character's own desolation and echoing pointlessness. Like the wolves of the title—caged, on their way to the site of the travelling circus (and first seen with soundtrack over of a radio chat show on the theme of guilt)— Alberto and Miguel circle round in a car trying to scheme their way out of their lack of purpose. Miguel's favourite theme is that of dignity —cruelly belied by his guilty affair and his trade in vile knick-knacks for car interiors—and he associates the circus, advertised around town, with all that conspires to remove dignity, as figured in the caged wolves and the star attraction, the Human Bullet. The Human Bullet—distorted images of whom form most of the title sequence and whose act and its aftermath closes the film—is indeed an icon of absurdity, crystallizing a built-in debasement of standard masculinity's obsession with ostentatious self-projection. But it is he, as an incidental character in the right place at the right time, who walks off with the money from the scam—which Alberto has pathetically mislaid—and who closes the loop that ties up this fable of failure and male fecklessness.

Bardem's body and homosocial conflict: *Carne trémula*

By thematic contrast—and in an anticipation of Banderas's entry into adventure as Zorro—the big budget Hispano-Mexican production *Perdita Durango* (Alex de la Iglesia, 1997; after the novel by Barry Gifford) had two years previously removed Bardem both from a problematized Spain as setting and from his quiet and exploratory style of acting. In it he plays a violent, passionate, Romeo (Romeo Dolorosa) living on the edge and on the Mexican–US frontier. An unsettling, unstable, even manic, performance of the role is due in part to the film's generic polyvalence, with threads and snatches of psychological thriller, crossing-the-border movie, bandit film, violence, adventure, and eroticism, and tales of fated lovers driven—and driven mad—by their loner status. It is also due to the aesthetic and technical predilections of the director whose cult success *El día de la bestia* (The Day of the Beast, 1995) is a noisy, shocking, gothic piece whose only half-parodic ultra-violence, excessiveness, and lack of control permeate plot, characterization, structure, and look (Jordan and Morgan-Tamosunas 1998: 194–5; and Allinson 1997: 320–2). But finally it is due, perhaps, to the violent if temporary dislocation of Bardem's removal from that very specifically Spanish machinery of star production which I have talked about in my Introduction, one that builds not primarily on globalized values and expectations (though it does in part, inevitably) but on domestic, national patterns of thought, behaviour, collective memory, and consumption. His performance is as adrift as is the character he plays.

In the same year, however, there is a very emphatic coming home and a locking into the domestic mainstream tradition in the form of work with Pedro Almodóvar, in *Carne trémula / Live Flesh* (1997). Whereas Banderas, taken much earlier in his career into the Almodóvar machine, had complained that the director would not allow him to act, suggesting an excessive malleability or lack of confidence in himself, Bardem comes to the director with an already powerful history. His complex performance of the character of the jealous husband, ex-policeman, and paraplegic sportsman David draws with considerable autonomy on the history of his own performances of masculinity under stress for facets of his character's motivations and behaviour. Through him and the other two male leads, José Sancho and Liberto Rabal, Almodóvar arguably makes a 'surprising [. . .] rediscovery of masculinity' (P. J. Smith 2000: 183) which links to a new concern with character, 'psychological, social, and historical depth' (186).

Almodóvar implicitly twists the Ruth Rendell title even more than he does her plot to make his film one about flesh and the body: in Francesca Neri's sophisticated, 'foreign' look (used seminally in *Jamón, jamón*: Deleyto 1999) and in Ángela Molina's striking, handsome, sensual middle age; in the many sex scenes; in the pain of childbirth in the opening sequence —Penelope Cruz, '[giving] birth to herself as a mature actress' (Stone 2002: 200)—and in the damage of being dependent on drugs and/or love (in Neri); in the humiliations and physical hurts of being in a violent relationship (Molina). José Sancho, playing David's alcoholic, sexually jealous, and wife-beating detective partner, evokes in body shape and language, and in his lined face, the anger and defeat of one who has self-destructively pursued the masculinity ideals of possessiveness, control over life, and professional efficacy, and presents 'an older, more aggressive masculinity' contrasted to David's and even Víctor's (Allinson 2001: 88–9). Liberto Rabal's Víctor is driven by competition (and his name, whose ludicrous obviousness is part of the point) to build his body and sexual expertise in order to win Elena, David's wife; but Rabal's body is meanwhile almost pornographically exploited (see Ch. 7). Bardem's character and Rabal's are embroiled in a contest the premise of which is that bodies matter, that they are deployed in the strenuous performance of being a man. The focus in the film is often on the exertions of the visually very present body to prevail, to prove itself, and to surpass an image of itself; a process that takes place in the enmeshing context of theoretical questions of gender and masculinity and their construction through sport (Parker 1996), social class, and regimes of desire, as well, again, as questions about screen performance and the production of 'cinema'. As P. J. Smith (2000: 182) has observed, 'it was inspired casting against type to have such an uncompromisingly physical actor as Javier Bardem [. . .] play David' (183): in fact the ostensibly absent physicality is acutely enhanced and reinscribed in Bardem's body by the restrictions on it, or half of it, in this film. While *Mouth to Mouth* (discussed in the next section) was a film lightly structured around male sexuality as presentation and dramatic performance, *Live Flesh* approaches with melodramatic intensity the strenuous, the competitive, and the anxious in the hegemonic masculinity ideal (Beneke 1997: 36–43, 138–9). Bardem's multiple disempowerment in relation to Víctor crystallizes such issues: his belief that the young, sexy, and able-bodied Víctor deliberately pulled the trigger in the crime-scene skirmish that initiated his disability constructs one disadvantage; his eventual, certain knowledge that Víctor is after Elena creates a sense of powerlessness; his loss of her, and his departure, are conclusive.

David's first appearance in the film, in a flashback prologue, is as the cool, mobile, active detective in the second of two plot-establishing preludes set in the past. As in most action movies and straightforward film noir, his and his character's masculinities are classically constructed in this section of the film in terms of masterful acting and presence from Bardem; and from David, his character, in terms of control over narrative and of goal-oriented behaviour (patrolling the anarchic streets of Madrid, responding purposefully to the emergency that will none the less and ironically cost him his able-bodiedness, and trying to bring under rational control the violent and self-hating outbursts of his partner). The pleasures for the audience are, initially, those of recognition of the familiar form and physiognomy of the actor, accentuated by a number of conventional cinematographic techniques—in the car medium close-ups and a raw key light with no fill show a handsome, gleamingly close-shaven jawbone in profile, and dwell on the angles and volumes of a nose and forehead unmistakably Bardem's, and frontal shots (old-style through-the-windscreen ones) offer up, coyly and in half shadow, the spectacle of those powerful shoulders; and second (less immediately perceived) the pleasure, in Paul Willemen's (1981: 16) words on Westerns of 'seeing the male "exist" (that is walk, move, ride, fight) in or through cityscapes, landscapes or [. . .] history'.

This crucial movement through space is arrestingly refigured when Bardem first appears on screen in the narrative present, however, in a scene of double paradoxical confinement. The jailed Víctor watches a Barcelona paralympics basketball match whose star player is David—in a sequence, on the TV screen, 'dynamically edited to a pounding track from Afro Celt Sound System' (P. J. Smith 2000: 184); Víctor sees in the crowd Elena, the ex-addict with whom he once had sex and for whom he still has an obsession, and who was the supposed victim at the scene that led to David's disablement by gun-shot. Instead of the full, dark cinematic treatment of the male in the seductive streets of before, the image is now desperately poorly mediated in crackly but gaudy colour and sound by television: we even see that the set is bolted to its casing. The classic pent-up physicality that attaches to Rabal's character in this prison sequence (seen also obsessively and sweatily exercising in his cell —a compact, petite Stallone) and the tension between the constraints of the wheelchair and extreme mobility of body and image in the television sequence build up an expectation of release. The form it takes is a surprising one (or it would be so if it were not for the director's reputation). Víctor's intent gaze on David in action is a quizzical framing of the game's 'assertion of the physical and tactical features of conventional notions of masculinity' (Morgan-Tamosunas forthcoming) which blurs the border between rivalry and homoerotic sadism.

The rock music is replaced with the retro, Mexican-bluesy 'Sufre como yo' (Suffer like I do) (performed by Catalan independent singer-songwriter Albert Plà) now in the diagetic frame of the prison recreation room. This sonic and lyrical context, along with subjective close-up framings of Víctor's eyes and head, linked to POV shots of the continuing television coverage, calls a lot into question. Víctor plots his revenge for his imprisonment and forms his tactics to win Elena to the accompaniment of a violently impassioned song sung—in high, gender-indeterminate register, strangled by intensity—by a jilted, cast-off lover to the object of his desire. The slow, sensual build up of melody, tempo, and instrumentation involves David and Víctor, Bardem and Rabal, in a queer way as themselves exclusively the erotic antagonists, with the woman left aside. It is David at whom Víctor is looking so intensely as the words of the song are superimposed on his visualized thoughts; subsequently it is Víctor by whom David becomes obsessed in exchange. There is a classic man on man, love-hate homosocial pattern to all this,[8] overlaid with something more bodily, more erotic than that: if Víctor envies David Elena's body, David envies Víctor his—it is, perversely, an object of desire and admiration to him as much as it is supposed to be to the audience.

With Víctor out of prison, and spotted by David at his wife's father's funeral, David makes his way to his rival's home to confront him. This is positioned in a slum shockingly revealed as close by Madrid's most famous money-glorifying and 'phallic' folly (ibid.), the leaning double Kio towers at the top of the Castellana boulevard, and the area—the script later reveals—is being cleared to make way for the Prince of Asturias motorway bypass. David's struggle to get across the rubble-strewn terrain —filmed in close detail, including Medem-style ground-level shots of wheels against pebbles—and Víctor's predestined domicile here (the place was his prostitute mother's), map in a number of complex ways onto the losing battles of the urban underclass to retain a place in the thrusting new city. Although Almodóvar seems not to be really interested in this scene as framing a political issue, but more as a melodramatic motif, its highlighting of the destructive effects of years of capitalist enterprise and the thrusting ambitions of Madrid's urban planners cannot be left

---

[8] Also discussed, in the context of an interesting and pertinent expansion of ideas on sport and rivalry, in Fouz-Hernández 2002: ch. 3.

aside. David's trajectory is also one towards an elimination of differences between himself and Víctor and in simple symbolic terms he has come to the same place of devastation and marginality. The two are levelled as the ground is to be levelled.

This happens first in a series of simple narrative checks and balances around the joint issue of empowerment and physical capacity and achievement. Although in this encounter (as well as in a subsequent one at Elena's workplace) David's physical disadvantage *vis-à-vis* Víctor is powerfully, and choreographically, embodied on screen (ibid.), Víctor's strenuous effort at male rivalry and his self-doubt are always made visible: a defiant and cruel display of press-ups is followed by an uncertain, breathless look at the departing David, which has a childish edge of fear of reprisal, and perhaps of fear of castration, as Morgan-Tamosunas convincingly suggests. The disabled body of the successful and driven star athlete confronts the body of the drifter, the social loser, but the boy with the looks and the athletic sex life. It has been argued that the film's treatment of disability is 'impeccable', full of respect (P. J. Smith 2000: 184) and in line with an increase in the availability of positive, Spanish cultural representations of disability (Conway 2000: 256). Certainly this is borne out by combative and self-determining representation, along with very close attention elsewhere in the film to David's victories over obstacles to access both to places and to a fulfilling sex life for himself and Elena; but, rather in line with Almodóvar's earlier treatment of gay issues, questions of class, status, wealth, and the access to time for self-fulfilment, are elided in this representation. David is successful, a star, surrounded by Habitat furnishings, as noticed by Smith (ibid.), with a big car, and big music playing in it, living in airy adaptable spaces in a smart home paid for in part by Elena's family money. Just like Víctor is attempting to do, he has made it, fought against the odds, and as a character has developed very much according to 'the orthodox structuring codes' of classic cinema of masculinity, having moved 'through destruction, to re-emergence and regeneration' (P. Smith 1995: 81) towards a position where his body holds for the audience an erotic, scopophiliac charge. He also, spying on and taking photos of Víctor, is the voyeuristic owner of the gaze and controller of the stories of the images and lives of others.

Secondly, the levelling occurs as part of a homosocial dynamic and in the concomitant double matrix of affective and social influences. The fame, by this stage, of *Jamón, jamón*, and the memory of Bardem within it mean that features of the relationship of rivalry between Bardem's character Raúl and José Luis (Jordi Mollà) in the earlier film are carried over into the relationship between David and Víctor in *Live Flesh*. Moreover, as

J. Arroyo (1998) has pointed out, the audience's memory of Bardem's *Golden Balls* role—in the latter part of that film as a wheelchair user—and of how there 'an excess of testosterone' had led to masculine self-destruction also contributes to the effectiveness of the joint exploration through Bardem and Rabal of apparently instinctual, animalistic, and tribal elements in male behaviour. When David and Víctor are united in cheering at a spectacular goal by Atlético de Madrid's José Luis Pérez Caminero in the televised match playing on-screen in the room, and rue-fully acknowledge their common ground, not just as supporters but as men appearing to themselves to be striving towards a masculine ideal, inhibitions come down in the moment of shared sporting triumph and reflected glory (Beneke 1997: 58). More important still, their 'collusion in the perpetuation of a coded system that has just been debunked' (Morgan-Tamosunas forthcoming) displaces the earlier ritualized violence of the scene. Víctor's previous threatening presence and sexual cocki-ness; his towering above the seated David; David's punch to Víctor's balls in retaliation to the other man's goading and posing: these are elided as the two men find that they are, vociferously, boyishly, and vicariously united in and by competition and success. They are, provisionally, the same. The commercialized and mediatized competition that is football, now not only makes them men but lifts them out of their essentially domestic rivalry to become participants in an imagined community based on allegiances to birthplace, neighbourhood, home town, and nation, and not least to manhood. Both of them glory for a moment in the male body as a driver and controller of actions (Connell 1995: 49); and as Víctor allows, or is unable to prevent, his more youthful enthusiasm for this phenomenon to carry his cheering on after David's, Bardem is able to have the older, more accomplished man he plays cast a paternal, indulgent, amused, and sympathetic look at the younger man as he glances down and across from his chair at Víctor on his futon on the floor.

As Almodóvar has observed of Bardem, 'there's a certain tenderness that is captured by the camera in all his performances, and a kind of mas-culine nobility that appears in all his characters' (*Guardian Unlimited* 2001), and such qualities subtend the homosociality and suppressed viol-ence of these scenes. The wash of sensuality that is part of the film's texture (and of its promotional materials) laps around these two men as around all the other combinations of character; the sexual energy directed by David to Elena in the early part of the narrative, when trun-cated by her switch of erotic allegiance to Víctor, gets transferred only slightly altered—into voyeuristic attention and a fascination with the meanings of the other man's body—onto Víctor; David, in the prison scene, becomes the object of the gaze and the swooning lyrics supposed for a moment to be Víctor's; David's favoured in-car music—bolero—makes of him at key moments not so much tender and noble as wounded and brave, like the archetypal, suffering singer of that genre, as well as subject obliquely to the gender subversive and often homoerotic connotations that Almodóvar famously gives the form (Knights 2001: 11–12). These queer qualities—in the end minor elements of the film itself, despite the inescapable, popular categorization of the director—are now a high-profile part of the Bardem range.

Bardem playing queer

As Llamas and Vidarte (2001: 114) observe it is common enough for heterosexual actors when taking on homosexual roles to be praised for their courage and for the credibility of their performance, the credibility being seen in relation to common perceptions of homosexuality as 'interpretación de atosigantes artificios' (a performance riddled with artificiality) (ibid.) as against the authenticity and essential truthfulness of heterosexuality (115). It is precisely this latter that is so playfully undermined in Manuel Gómez Pereira's 1995 comedy *Boca a boca / Mouth to Mouth*.[9] The film sees Bardem, as in most of his mid-1990s films, still acting his way out of *macho* typecasting, as well as essaying a variety of performance styles and generic positionings—romance, farce, thriller—opposite Aitana Sánchez-Gijón (representing a new generation of Spanish actors) and Josep María Flotats (who brings to the film the codings —and aura—of his distinguished career as stage actor and director). There is an extreme emphasis on performance in the plot and in its execution. Bardem plays an out-of-work actor—with the credibly improbable name of Víctor Ventura—obsessed with Robert de Niro (cross-matching with Bardem's own early interest in Al Pacino) who takes on a job as a telephone sex-line worker (as in Spike Lee's *Girl 6*, 1996, and with similar ramifications). For one job in particular he has to feign homosexuality for the client, a closeted and uptight married professional. Bardem exploits his ambivalence of look and type knowingly in a series of comical shifts between the old, sensual *macho* Bardem (the style needed by Víctor in the roles he is forced into) and the presentation (when his Víctor is in character) of the softly spoken, bespectacled student type

---

[9] Grossing 374.2 million pesetas in 1995.

(recalling, slightly, Banderas as Carlos in *Mujeres* and a whole hinterland of similar cinematic types). In the man-to-man sex-line sequences there is an engagement with aural drag, as Víctor dons the words of a set of desires in a parody of the very sexuality that takes actual shape, for the closeted client, in their initial telephone exchanges. All this leads to a lively revisiting of some old dramatic and philosophical favourites—ideas around appearance and reality—but it also invites a re-evaluation of those long-standing ideas in sociology on identity as performance which are fruitfully applicable to thinking through queer identities (Esterberg 1996), on 'meaning, process, "invented identities" and the cultural constructedness of communities' (Stein and Plummer 1996: 131). Víctor's—and Bardem's—performance of a sexual preference and desire not his own, and the centrality to the farce of the after all extremely serious charade of the married homosexual, keep pointing to the sexual constructedness of identity.

As Jordan and Morgan-Tamosunas (1998: 84) briefly remark, 'surprisingly, despite its subject matter, the film offers little in the way of visual spectacle to titillate the spectator'. Indeed the sensuality of the title, once the film is rolling, converts into or is enmeshed with textuality (words not kisses); and extreme close-ups of the lips of sex-line workers and their clients in intense conversation enact this conversion too. Against this abstraction, however, there are the more immediate and intriguing pleasures of the prominence of the physical body of Bardem on-screen subject to regimes of practice and representation more usually associated with the objectification of women: namely prostitution within the plot, and a fetishistic fragmentation and intensity of attention to the detail of feigned and then real sexual arousal. Scenes in the sex-line office draw attention to Victor's body as highly responsive, subject to impulses, sweats, and flushes as he attempts to control his embarrassment and the erotic responses of his clients, and loses his own uptight cool. He becomes so excited in conversation with the client he eventually falls for, Amanda (Sánchez Gijón), that he becomes tight around the collar and crotch, and needs to avail himself of the privacy of a booth, allowing the camera unrestricted close-ups of the flushed and captive actor surprised by sudden transfers out of pretence into authenticity. To his male client, Ricardo, huddled over his car phone, he coos down the line inciting him to put his fingers to his underarm, touch himself, on his neck, his throat, and he mimics those same actions—followed in close-up—as he urges him to listen and associate those other sensory pleasures with his voice. The audience is also drawn into this, to Bardem's body and voice, and by way of the switching back and forth between the two enclosed spaces of the sex-line booth and the car.

In parallel to Víctor's involvement with Ricardo, his 'real' life sees him struggling to make something of his drama school training by promoting himself as a Latin lover to the casting director of a US production team. A friend, acting as his agent, has set up an interview, and sends him off to prepare himself in the restaurant toilet. By improbable coincidence, Ricardo (whom he has not yet met) stumbles on him doing voice exercises, rehearsing basic lines in English, touching up his slicked-back hair in front of the toilet mirror. Immediately attracted to him, and visibly *au fait* if nervous with toilet pick-up possibilities, a flustered Ricardo bumps into him, and drops a briefcase spilling North American gay porn mags onto the floor, only to deny that they are his. As Ricardo, then, jumps in and out of his sexuality, Víctor too is busy practising an identity of his own, yet not of his own. His transformation into a caricature Spaniard through the pressures of the industry of desire and the need to play up to the casting director, his voice exercises, rocky English, dodgy clothes, olive oil to smooth his hair, and too much aftershave, all make of him a depersonalized, carnivalesquely over-determined token of masculinity. Bardem makes it clear, through his combination of wry detachment from his role (and its roles) and exuberant conscious hamming, that the naïf Víctor's strenuous efforts to work in film (and be worthy of his dad, who worked as an usher) are matched by men's strenuous efforts to be, and remain, real men (a common concern in Gómez Pereira's usually less convoluted comedies).

The embedding in a subplot about the film industry's notions of Spanishness, of issues concerning the constructedness of gender, sexuality, and desire, of performance, textuality, and identity, means that the film moves beyond the scope of an erotic comedy of manners and that subgenre's usual mimetic-parodic purposes. As well as having the conventional appeal of the subfarcical comedy of error and complication (the *comedia de enredo*) the film, largely through Bardem, becomes a mainstream instance of the tying together of conflicting intuitions of subject formation, making curiously visible the star as character undergoing and inciting processes of on- and off-screen formative identifications with national, sexual, and gender stereotypes. In particular, what the film has satirical reference to—and what Bardem is able effectively to distance himself from—is (part of) the US film industry's sensationalism, its bad taste (the loud-mouthed and poorly dressed director demands Coca-Cola in the exquisite French restaurant), and, particularly, the clichéd and outdated North American interest—as with Antonio Banderas—in the Latin Lover. It was perhaps partly because he represented such a stand against Hollywood, made in the context of a complicated, elegant, and accessible performance, that Bardem was voted, by readers of *El País*'s cultural supplement, best Spanish actor of 1995, beating not only veteran Francisco (Paco) Rabal but also—in quite another register—the ascendant cult figure Santiago Segura (for his role in Alex de la Iglesia's *El día de la bestia*).[10]

In a shift away from comedies, though in a logical continuation of *Mouth to Mouth*'s problematizations of sexual desire and gender roles, Gómez Pereira also used Bardem (and Carmelo Gómez, and Victoria Abril) in *Entre las piernas / Between Your Legs* in 1999. Here he plays Javier, a scriptwriter who meets up with fellow sex addict and radio presenter Miranda (Victoria Abril), wife to ironically named police detective Félix (Gómez). Javier's dependence on a telephone sex-line and the association of both him and Miranda with verbal production draws our attention not only to the parallels being drawn between the need for sex and the need to tell stories (noticed by Losilla 1999) but also—as in *Mouth to Mouth*—to the symbolic-linguistic construction of sexuality and to the fascinating proximities of fiction, fantasy, desires, illusions, and lies.

Something of the desperation of Raúl in *Jamón, jamón* carries forward into Bardem's Javier as he discovers mismatch after mismatch between his aspiration as a male, his behaviour as a man, and the exaggerated effects of hegemonic masculinity; and the role anticipates the dramatic exploration of damaging inauthenticity in *Segunda piel / Second Skin*. Here Bardem plays Diego, a more-or-less out wealthy gay professional (who is, however, extraordinarily devoid of gay friends or interests). He falls for Alberto (Jordi Mollà), again a closeted, married man; not only is he strung along by Alberto's fundamental lie—his failure to declare his family life or to verbalize until the end the extent of his psycho-sexual problem—but he is drawn into falling in love by the story that is Alberto's leit-motif (and which provided the working title of the film, 'Donde acaba el mar': Where the Ocean Ends)—his childhood dream to go down to the shore's edge, where he might forget himself, where all is well, and all is quiet. For the second time Bardem finds himself playing a man addicted to another's false narrative; but for the first time he finds himself playing a 'real' gay character, and there are some telling—if perhaps endearing—false notes in the performance which I shall return to shortly.

The high-profile, on-screen performance of a passionate, carnal, homosexual love affair by two of modern Spain's most famous hetero-sexual film personalities (their 'best character actors and sexiest symbols', according to *Variety*: Holland 2000), and of icons of different sorts of masculinity ('new' and thoughtful in Mollà; muscular and forceful in

---

[10] Research published in *El País* (*Tentaciones*), 29 Dec. 1995.

Bardem; or 'pretty-boy' and 'beefy' in Holland's terms) caused considerable excitement (Garrido 2000: 94). So too did its promise to be '[una]
radiografía de la homosexualidad oculta' (an X-Ray of the hidden issue
of homosexuality) (Ponga 2000), sensationally flagged prior to release,
and visually emphasized in the title sequence. The frankness of the
gay sex scenes, with little mainstream precedent in Spain (Alfeo Álvarez
2001; Belatagui 2001), or, indeed, Hollywood (Pretorius 2000), was also
a draw. The two actors had first worked together, memorably, in *Jamón,
jamón*, and there had engaged in a kind of homoerotic courtship based
around male rivalry that ended in the murder by Bardem's character of
Mollà's, the former momentarily cradling the latter in his arms on the
dusty killing ground in arguably the second homoerotic pietà (*Law
of Desire*'s being the first) of Spanish cinema's late twentieth-century
history. They had maintained a close friendship throughout the 1990s,
and Bardem is telling some sort of truth when he emphasizes that the
love scenes were not problematic precisely because of the closeness
(Verchili 2000); he is also, though, telling another rather complicated story:
not simply that he and Jordi, that two straight Spanish males, can bond
tenderly as friends and professionals but rather that Spanish cinema, or
a segment of it, has come to a place where two of its stars can have same-
sex sex with each other, and that this can be represented not only with
visual directness but in relation to some uncomfortable and undecidable
questions to do with performance and depth identity, changeability,
fluidity, and illusion.

A certain anxiety nevertheless accompanies the discussion of their
on-screen liaison: 'Jordi tiene un buen par de glúteos y yo me agarraba
a ellos' (Jordi has a great pair of buttocks and I held on to those) is
Bardem's laddish diversionary tactic; 'fue divertido y nada traumático'
(it was fun and not traumatic at all) (ibid.). In Bardem's case, this picks
up on earlier declarations. Just as his career was taking off Bardem
had given a number of interviews where he volunteered the view that
women were put off by his hard, brutal looks (in *Jamón, jamón* principally), that he had more male than female fans, and only men paid him
compliments (*piropos*) on the streets (gathered in Rivera 1994); furthermore he had openly acknowledged his homoerotic appeal, albeit in
unreconstructed and either oddly misinformed or mischievous terms by
suggesting that gay men do not like other gay men, they prefer real men
('les gustan los hombres'), and that is what his looks ('mi físico') provided (6). Furthermore, and redundantly, 'No me gustan los hombres,
pero si algún día me gustasen, no tendría ningún problema' (I don't go
for men, but if one day I were to then it wouldn't be a problem for me)
(6). Some of this carries over into the role of Diego whom Bardem plays

on the borderlines between massive, assured physicality and emotional fragility, between sensual vitality and frozen calm:[11] it is not just a case of 'his pugilist's features creating interesting tensions with his character's sensitivity' (Holland 2000) but more of a deeper unease.

In the film it is not only Alberto who is emotionally blocked. For all that he keeps slamming shut the closet door from the inside he does at least do it with some considerable show of spirit. Diego, on the other hand, is almost dysfunctionally passive in the face of Alberto's failure to commit,[12] and is straight-acting almost to the extent of complete effacement of his sexuality. While on the one hand a second break—post-*Law of Desire*—with Spanish cinema's tradition of representation of gay men as camp queens or harmless confidants is positive (Retamar 2001), the 'naturalidad y normalidad' (natural, normal manner) of his self-presentation, and of Bardem's representation (Vidal 2000) fits in well with, and may well have been promoted by, the conservative, liberal humanist approach of Vera both to the scripting and direction and to the publicizing of the film. Although Stone's (2002) description of the film as 'lurid soap opera' is as uncalled for as his application of the word 'simpering' to Diego (198), the film is a peculiar mix of the excessive and the highly conventional dramatically, cinematically, and in terms of narrative development and *mise-en-scène*. Vera's insistence in interview on the importance in the film of pain and feelings ('sentimientos') over and above the specifics of character (Vidal 2000) shows through in the intensity of the breakdown of Alberto and his marriage (and a tight, nuanced performance from Ariadna Gil as Elena, his wife) but leaves Bardem with a role ill provided with appropriate emotional material. Diego's undoubted self-confidence and public 'acceptance' of his 'condition' (as one critic puts it—Garrido 2000: 95) is displayed to a very limited circle of colleagues and one close woman friend (although in her case, not least because she is played by Cecilia Roth, there is strength of character more than enough to go around), and Bardem finds himself pulled into a stereotypical role as the gay man adrift taken in hand by the strong woman. Furthermore, as already suggested, Diego has little or no credible gay trace, no contact with a community, no back history, and, improbably—given his wealth and his looks—no one gay around him. While at least one gay critic (Casado 2000) has come out in e-print declaring that he can

---

[11] It is perhaps worth surmising that sheer tiredness may have been the cause of a certain unevenness in expressive control, since this was the third film in six months in which Bardem had been involved.

[12] As observed in an acute reading of this aspect by Shalini Chanda in ch. 2 of 'The Problematization of Masculinity in Post-1990 Spanish Cinema', unpublished M.Phil. thesis, Faculty of Modern and Medieval Languages, University of Cambridge, 2001.

identify with Diego, and can recognize the situation as a common one, the fact is that Diego is too like a film star to allow this: he has an improbably comfortable lifestyle, expensive casual clothes whose swirl and cut are much exploited; a costly apartment; and even the conference he has to attend is lavish and takes place by the sea. He is more than a little aloof. Because Bardem is groomed to a peak of suave handsomeness which is only enhanced by crisis, a Hollywood-style irresistibility accrues to his character visually, making him look like the George Clooney of *One Fine Day* (Michael Hoffman, 1996) more than yet another Spanish gay man being brought down by hysterical, internalized homophobia and the heterosexist imperatives of coupledom, sexual fidelity, and fixity in gender roles.

It was only in Julian Schnabel's *Before Night Falls*, a film whose anti-Castro politics Bardem was at first put off by (Belategui 2001; Cendrós 2001), that he was able, famously now, to get a full creative grasp on a gay character, marking the film with his now brilliantly understated star personality, with his sense of the interplay of emotion and idea, and his physical presence (Preston 2001; Retamar 2001; P. J. Smith 2001*a*). The film, for all its lack of subtlety elsewhere, saw those skills at physical and emotional transformation—for years valued within Spain, and identified in him by Almodóvar (*Guardian Unlimited* 2001)—given its second major 'world' exposure.[13] The first Spanish actor to be nominated for an Oscar, Bardem nevertheless remains carefully sceptical of the value, and the politics, of the award, and of the hyping of his personality (Belategui 2001; *Guardian Unlimited* 2001) and appears to be set on exploring the opportunities to extend his range through a continuing engagement with the more specific cultural material of the new Spanish canon.

[13] With $4.5m. gross takings to December 2001 for *Before Night Falls*, and $8.6m. for *Live Flesh* (figures taken from the unofficial but useful compendium database at worldwideboxoffice.com (4 Dec. 2001)). See, for example, *El Mundo* (*Cultura*), 22 Dec. 2000: http: // www.el-mundo.es / 2000 / 12 / 22 / cultura / 22N0131.html (30 Aug. 2001).

TABLE 4. *Filmography*

Year	Title	English title(s) (official in italics; literal in roman)	Director	Billing	Audience figures and takings	Other information
1990	*Las edades de Lulú*	*The Ages of Lulu*	José Juan Bigas Luna	6th	882,297 €2,099,610	
1991	*Tacones lejanos*	*High Heels*	Pedro Almodóvar	Minor	2,072,847 €5,233,988	
1991	*Amo tu cama rica*	I Love Your Cosy Bed	Emilio Martínez Lázaro	Minor	216,753 €554,876	
1992	*Jamón, jamón*	*Jamón, jamón*	José Juan Bigas Luna	5th	673,467 €1,808,589	Unión de Actores, Best Actor; Fotogramas de Plata, Best Actor; Sant Jordi, Best Actor
1993	*Huidos*	The Escape	Félix Sáncho Gracia	5th	54,461 €105,601	
1993	*El amante bilingüe*	The Bilingual Lover	Vicente Aranda	4th	273,218 €738,397	
1993	*Huevos de oro*	Golden Balls	José Juan Bigas Luna	Top	477,967 €1,382,216	
1994	*El detective y la muerte*	Death and the Detective	Gonzalo Suárez	Top	131,113 €319,645	San Sebastián Festival Concha de Plata for Best Supporting Actor
1994	*Días contados*	*Numbered Days*	Imanol Uribe	Top	687,783 €1,947,955	San Sebastián Concha de Plata Best Actor; Premio Fernando Rey; Goya for Best Supporting Actor

TABLE 4. (*continued*)

Year	Title	English title(s) (official in italics; literal in Roman)	Director	Billing	Audience figures and takings	Other information
1995	*Boca a boca*	*Mouth to Mouth*	Manuel Gómez Pereira	Top	763,548 €2,263,495	Fotogramas de Plata for Best Actor; Goya for Best Leading Male
1996	*Éxtasis*	Ecstasy	Mariano Barroso	Top	290,908 €934,362	
1997	*Carne trémula*	*Live Flesh*	Pedro Almodóvar	2nd	1,433,173 €4,990,272	Fotogramas de Plata for Best Actor; Goya for Best Leading Male
1997	*Perdita Durango*		Alex de la Iglesia	2nd	779,816 €2,573,607	Co-pro Spain, Mexico. Fotogramas de Plata for Best Actor
1997	*El amor perjudica seriamente la salud*	Love Can Seriously Damage Your Health	Manuel Gómez Pereira	Minor	1,057,447 €3,631,183	Co-pro Spain, France
1997	*Torrente, el brazo tonto de la ley*	Torrente, the Stupid Arm of the Law	Santiago Segura	Minor	3,010,664 €10,902,55	
1999	*Entre las piernas*	Between Your Legs	Manuel Gómez Pereira	2nd	923,196 €3,470,643	
1999	*Los lobos de Washington*	The Washington Wolves	Mariano Barroso	Top	110,706 €432,913	Bardem as joint executive producer with Barroso
1999	*Segunda piel*	*Second Skin*	Gonzalo Vera	Top	550,282 €2,194,527	Fotogramas de Plata for Best Actor (beating Carmelo Gómez and Eduardo Noriega)

Shorts

Pronòstic reservat / *Pronóstico reservado* (Judgment Reserved) (Antonio Mollà, 1994)
La madre (The Mother) (Miguel Bardem, 1995)

English language productions

Before Night Falls (Julian Schnabel, 2000)
The Dancer Upstairs (John Malkovich, 2001)

Television series

Segunda enseñanza (Secondary Education) TVE, 1985
Brigada central (Police HQ) TVE, 1988
El día por delante (The Day Ahead) TVE, 1989

Fig. 10. Jordi Mollà (left) with Andrea Ramírez, Antonio Resines, and Maribel Verdú in *La buena Estrella.*

Fig. 11. Jordi Mollà in *Nadie conoce a nadie.*

5 Jordi Mollà (b. 1968)

Performing crisis

Although arguably less glamorous than the other stars considered here, and in at least one authoritative dictionary (Borau 1998: 590) considered a secondary player, Jordi Mollà has a very rapidly rising profile in the 1990s (see Filmography), and his name is aligned with major successes in the national cinema such as *Jamón, jamón* (1992) (with cumulative audience figures of over 670,000) *Segunda piel / Second Skin* (1999) (550,000), and *Nadie conoce a nadie / Nobody Knows Anyone* (1999) (with box office sales across fourteen countries, and significant DVD distribution).[1] Despite his downbeat and studiously serious (and not universally liked) public image, indeed, Mollà is one of only three names, along with Bardem and Cruz, associated in a recent major stock-taking dossier with a putative Spanish star system and cited as one of the industry's principal box-office draws (*Fotogramas* 2000: 220).

Breaking with the more-or-less chronological pattern of previous chapters, my discussion of Mollà starts with *Segunda piel*, in order to develop further the implications there of the close collaboration of the two, by that stage famous stars, and in order to focus from the start on the specifically 'serious' theatrical qualities that are the mark of this actor. These are well displayed in his negotiations of the tensions arising out of his character Alberto's inability in this film to negotiate the impossible threshold between the two lives—the two 'skins'—he tries to inhabit (as a married man and as a man who wants to have sex with men), his refusal to recognize the accumulated damage of past denial and the possibility of any alternative future, and his concomitant inability to shed one phase of life to move on into the other. Alberto is precariously on the edge of being discovered and having to discover 'who he is' partly (though not wholly) in a problematic, essentialist identification of sexuality and identity (Jagose 1996: 58–71). The look he dons, the second skin of conformity, allows him to inhabit the professional and the marital-domestic spheres (though he is made by Mollà to pluck

---

[1] See distributor Sogecable's 2001 Annual Report at http://www.sogecable.es/actividades/Produccion.pdf (28 Aug. 2001).

occasionally at his smart jackets as if they did not belong to him): in the one respectable, responsible, but dynamic; in the other manly, modern, and desirable (in that he, his look, bears traces of the younger, sexier man his wife Elena (Ariadna Gil) once married).

Key encounters and moments requiring (but seldom getting) decisive action in the film are set at physical thresholds: in doorways, with doors at centre screen as background, on a hotel terrace, in and outside the ambiguous, high concrete space of an aircraft engineering hangar (Alberto's place of work). Mollà's character is false or fearful on his returns through the front door and entrance corridor to the family home, always too quickly out of the door of his lover Diego's apartment, reluctant to open his office door to the importunate, hurt, and desperate Diego. As well as marking out the sexual political polarities of in and out, and concentrating attention on the subversive potential in homosexuality's 'precarious position at/as the border' (Fuss 1991: 6), the film's interiors have another, contrasting structural effect. Its smart domestic, night club, hotel, and restaurant settings provide a containing presence of habit, social privilege, and normalization, cocooning the protagonists and blunting the critique while giving the film a pleasing enough aura of high production-value commodity (letting it, at once, rub comparative shoulders with the US subgenre of films about the tribulations of moneyed gays). They also allow the development of director Gerardo Vera's (much praised) talents as theatre set designer further to enhance the piece. There are two foundational domestic interiors, the smart marital home and Diego's soberly luxurious flat (originally both were scenes of interrogation about sexual activity, as one of the non-included sequences available on the DVD version of the film reveals)[2] and in both Mollà has his character display an elusiveness that draws with psychological realism on childish defensive ploys. With Diego, after an early lovemaking scene which he cuts short in response to a mobile phone call from home (though he says it is from work), he meets Diego's pleas that he stay to supper, to eat his favourite dish, with a sudden, strange collapse into childish blurting out of his reluctance, a rocking forwards, and an exaggerated holding of head in hands at the horror of missing this treat, all half-designed to avoid Diego's gaze and the fact that he has engineered his own absence from the feast. This piece of business then finds its more serious counterpart in the brief recounting to Diego of childhood dreams of finding the place where the ocean ends (alluded to in Ch. 4). This is a micro-narrative which, although it opens up part of him to Diego, allows Alberto to take further

---

[2] Manga Films, 2000.

refuge from decision, reasserts his dependence on thin fantasies of escapism, and is deployed as a saving moment outside the two temporal sequences that are overlapping yet must not overlap—an afternoon with Diego, and the return to Elena and home. In this latter domestic interior, seated on the sofa across the room from her, he faces her questioning. Mollà starts with a look of childlike apprehension, moves into blank staring at her, then to closed eyes, head turning away from her, then half-swooping down towards the chest as if to draw breath and courage, eyes screwing up on the verge of tears, mouth quivering not just because of tearfulness but because of the impossibility of the words that it is replacing with excuses.

A similar range of emotion and elusiveness is explored at an attempted reconciliatory restaurant scene later. There is a childish moment of rage when Elena will not play along with plans to move away and make a fresh start; and an adolescent denial in the face of her insistence that they talk frankly. Downcast eyes, a stammering mouth, and near tearfulness are accompanied by shakings of the head that acknowledge the philosophical and moral depths of what needs to be and cannot be explored, a bitter smile at the impossibility of being asked outright how long he has been sleeping with men. Mollà delivers the response cutting short at 'no me . . .' (I've n . . .), and Alberto makes a hurried, choking exit from the restaurant when Elena utters the words 'la verdad' (the truth). This anorexic reflex rejection of the only thing that might nourish him (telling the truth to Elena and himself), and simultaneously of the concomitant unspeakable that he must render abject (sex with men and the possibility of another form of love), marks out Alberto's space.

Consolidating the impressions of him as a cerebral actor (to which I shall be returning), and in consonance with the film's concentration on inner turmoil and moral dilemma, Mollà works consistently with head and face as sites of drama here. Customarily long-haired, he makes much of the shortish hair designated for him for the role, which, combined with grey jackets and grey complexion, mark his indecisiveness, his libidinal liminality and—along with the stubbly beard—his closeness to but safe distance from a 30-something, 1990s, urban gay 'look' (he looks, in fact, much more gay than Bardem's openly gay character). On Alberto's entrances into his family home—which follow on from encounters with Diego—his hand goes up to smooth his hair forwards with the palm of the hand in a gesture that is simultaneously coded as a kind of guilty self-benediction, as the simple, sordid precaution of the adulterer returning home, as an attempt to calm himself, and as quiet despair. This last coding comes in a muted variant on a histrionic standard of heel of hand to forehead, deployed vigorously in the tense and brilliantly studied living-room scene already discussed where Alberto is confronted with the main facts of his 'adultery' and blunders into a false confession (about a liaison with a woman friend from university days) that compounds his guilt.

This anticipates the scene that Vera chooses to mark the end and not the beginning (as it might as easily have been in a more gay-affirmative piece) of the drama of identity; that in which Alberto, now separated from Elena, begins to confront his inability to act authentically, to commit to his homosexuality and to Diego; a scene that precipitates his panicked exit to the street, his reckless mounting of his motorbike (that other token of near gayness), and a fatal accident—the film's punishment of him for being the man who almost knew too much, and for being not only the fallen homosexual but the fallen heterosexual as well. In this scene— with his back up against first one wall in his bleak apartment then the other—he pulls at his chin, beard, and hair, and repeatedly, shockingly, slaps his own face as he breaks through from one side of the membrane of prohibition and repression to confront not an unacceptable answer but a conundrum of identity: if he has lied since childhood, gone along with family expectations, trained for and joined his profession out of patri-lineal custom, if he has married, lied to himself on the issue that even now he will not articulate, then, he asks, 'si no soy . . . si no soy ese Alberto, ¿quién soy?' (if I am not that . . . if I am not that Alberto, then who am I?). The hesitation over even his own name at this extreme moment is a sharp sign of how Mollà's character's dilemma is really, or could be, a postmodern one—that of how to construct, in the ruins of shattered selfhood, a provisional and unprecedented identity in the flux of desire and in the embrace of otherness. But it forms itself around a common, and emphatically theatrical, modernist, and existential concern with the recapture of lost plenitude, with truthful and meaningful interven-tion in the world, and with nothing less than the self (all movingly enough). In this, as in his other screen performances, Mollà advertises the Spanish histrionic tradition's shared fascination for neo- or post-Stanislavskian deep performance—the scene is disturbing and moving in the extreme; but I would suggest that it is partly disturbing because it directs us straight to an important tension in the small crop of 'new' 'gay' films in Spain in the 1990s that, although by definition and through their marketing objectives they intend to represent structures of relationship and identity that are alternative to the normative hetero-sexual, at the same time struggle to transform this other conventional material. Participating in what Alfeo Álvarez (2001) labels a period-specific 'modalidad integrada' (integrated mode), and representing

homosexuality in ways that fail to reveal awareness of its social and
ideological constructedness, they end up, sooner or later and in longer or
shorter durations, getting interested in what is normal, what is human,
what is central, fixed, and susceptible of empathy and identification, being
sometimes of bogus momentousness (145), and at other times of enter-
tainingly forgettable frivolity. Such tensions are to be found between Vera's
suggestion in interview that the film has autobiographical elements and
his declaration that Alberto 'really exists' (*Estrella Digital* 2000), and Mollà's
presentation of his character that pulls away from a rehumanizing, indi-
vidualizing tendency. The strenuous performance of identity crisis and
loss of control is a powerful adaptation both of the old traditional
Method and of techniques of alienation and is as much a representation
of abstractions as it is one of a tragic, human type: Mollà embodies here
instability, the panic of desire, and the bruising imposition of an outsiderdom so raw that it would be difficult—even if we are 'comfortably
entrenched on the inside' (Fuss 1991: 5) of cosy, middle-class, cultural
consumerism—to idealize and romanticize Alberto in the falsely sanitizing way of the 'dominant discourse of sexual difference' (ibid.) which
ignores the possibility that 'sexual identity may be less a function of knowledge than performance [. . .] than perpetual reinvention' (7–8). Alberto
repeatedly says, at moments of crisis, 'I don't know': he does not know
his current position, how to form any sense of his past, what love is,
whether sex between men is what he wants, or what, more to the point,
he is permitted to want. This—embodied in a repertoire of gestures of
high uncertainty from the actor—is one of the things that give the film
its edge. For all that it takes refuge in normalizing discourses and is open
to misleading universalizations in terms such as 'love' and 'sincerity' (all
much promoted by Vera and his interviewers: for example, Reviriego 2000:
58; Vidal 2000),[3] it does nevertheless render wholly visible, albeit in one
limited class stratum, the fragility of heterosexual as well as homosexual identities, the politics of the closet, and the disruptive, perhaps
cleansing force of a small but caustic narrative stream running down the
middle of the streets of western, comfortably married life in Madrid.[4]

---

[3] Interviewed on TVE1, in 'Cartelera' on 15 Jan. 2000, Mollà briefly observed of his character that
'busca un espejo [...] y lo rompe en pedazos [...] creo que le pasa a mucha gente' (he looks
for a mirror [...] and smashes it into pieces [...] I reckon that happens to many of us): he is right
enough, but the sound-bite seems apologetic and robs the film of its specificity.

[4] However, the women interviewed by the mainstream women's magazine *Dunia* (Goicoechea 1987)
more than a decade before the film's conception, and the untroubled contextualization there
of the issue of women having gay male sexual partners (64), perhaps point to a substantial
constituency to whom neither the reminder nor the film can have had much relevance. Neither
poor Elena nor her mother would seem to have been *Dunia* readers; and nor would Vera.

It shocks us with the tragedy of emptiness and destruction that appears to lie behind but is in fact created by social, emotional, and domestic conventions. It crosses over and finds a space—or a space in the process of formation—where not only is a relatively old, modernist concern with the disintegrated and disintegrating self at stake, but where also there is nourishment for more recent critical urges to collapse effectively the binaries of insider/outsider, same/other, heterosexual/homosexual.

This is precisely the sort of tricky intellectual territory that Mollà has steadily been gaining a reputation for. The image of Mollà that emerges from the press and television—to mixed reception—is that he is the most intellectual in his achievements and aspirations of the 1960s-born cohort of actors (though he has said that he sees himself as not widely read: Ponga 1997: 44). Like Gómez, his connections with theatre are strong (though not ongoing); unlike all the other older actors discussed here he underwent three years of formal drama training at the Institut de Teatre in Barcelona, worked with the Teatre Lliure, and undertook short courses in Italy, Bulgaria, and—working briefly at the Actors Studio—New York; he is a film-maker in his own right; and a novelist.[5] Journalist Teresa Gallardo, interviewing Mollà in early 1996 reacted to him in a way typical of coverage of his persona: a coffee and a few minutes with Mollà inspires philosophical thoughts, she wrote, and it is hard to escape 'dissection' by 'those [blue] eyes' (Gallardo 1996: 35). An atypical early career also led to his being labelled as 'raro' (used for example in Navarro 1997: 27). He had success with *Jamón, jamón* but then went a year without work and had nothing substantial until 1995 (see below); he maintains several creative interests all at once; does not live in Madrid; has an interest in outsider figures, evidenced by his own film *Walter Peralta*, and referred to in many interviews; and constantly expresses a lack of preference for any particular genre or style of film in roles taken up. This latter aspect of his 'rareza' (oddness) can be traced in what at first appears to suggest a continuity, a series of appearances in films—including *Segunda piel*—that might be said to contribute to the subtradition of Spanish gay and queer cinema, problematic though that category is (Alfeo Álvarez 2001).

---

[5] The short *Walter Peralta* (1994) won First Prize at the prestigious Alcalá de Henares Festival and Premio Nacional de Cinematografía de la Generalitat de Catalunya; it was followed up with *No me importaría irme contigo. Walter Peralta* was broadcast on 21 Nov. 2000 on TVE2's prestigious *Versión española*: an indication of Mollà's growing general stature (although he has made no further films). His novels are: *Les primeras vegades / Las Primeras Veces* (1999) and *Agua Estancada* (2000), a wry, well-structured first-person narrative about solitude, the death of love, a writer who cannot write, the nature of imagination, and the evils of the commercialization of literature.

Mollà playing queer: antecedents

After the gap following the success of *Jamón, jamón* (discussed below) and Mollà's establishment as a recognizable screen personality, associated from the outset with troubled masculinity, there came two roles in films with substantial gay elements of plot. These small roles gain prominence partly through the decision of yet another successful young Spanish screen actor to take on a gay role. Mollà thus followed Arias (in *La muerte de Mikel*), Banderas (in the several roles discussed in Ch. 2), and Sanz (in *Hotel y domicilio*: see Ch. 6). The first, in the comedy *Alegre ma non troppo*, positioned him as a fleeting object of gay male desire (see Fouz-Hernández and Perriam 2000: 100). More substantial was his involvement in what was to become a key cultural point of reference for a generation and a surprise commercial success (Fouz-Hernández 2000: Stone 2002: 144–5), *Historias del Kronen* (Stories of the Kronen) (Montxo Armendáriz, 1995; after the novel by José Ángel Mañas). Getting second billing after Juan Diego Botto (see Ch. 7), Mollà in fact plays an ensemble role as one of a gang of disaffected middle-class youths, a role that only in the last third of the film becomes concentrated down into a character study and never actually supplants Botto. As Mollà himself has observed (Gallardo 1996: 36), at the time of this film there was a notable opening up of screen opportunities for younger actors and a growing fashion for film representations of Spanish youth, of the damaged and marginalized, and of violence (Mollà is accurate in joining all three topic areas, although less so if he is implying that the first is anything more than a resurgence). Examining repression, circular and sterile sexual exploration, lack of communication across generations, and rebellion against social and family conventions, the film positions Mollà—playing a non-out gay man—at the crux between disaffection, homophobia internalized and externalized, and young heterosexual masculinities in rebellion.

Like Bardem when reflecting on *Segunda piel*, Mollà on *Kronen* was not without a certain liberal, normalizing, and (in style and vocabulary) almost laddish issue-avoidance in interview: 'yo de lo de ser homosexual me olvidé totalmente [. . .] Sólo a mitad de rodaje me dije: ¡Ostia, este tío es homosexual! Pero, bueno, también se trataba de una persona normal y corriente' (me, I completely forgot about the business of being homosexual [. . .] It was only half-way through filming I said to myself: Shit! this guy's homosexual. But, you know, we were also dealing with a normal, run-of-the-mill person here) (ibid. 36). This reveals an interesting take on 'normal' and 'homosexual', given the gently nuanced accumulation of stolen glances, reactions of petty jealousy, and moments of pique that Mollà uses to structure his character Roberto's tense relationship with good-looking, straight boy tearaway Juan Diego Botto as Carlos (who correctly considers Roberto to be repressed and convention-bound, and twice tells him so). More than merely homosocially motiv-ated are: Roberto's failed attempt to help a drunken Carlos back to his bedroom, holding him that bit too tightly; his direct looks at the other's crotch while the two watch pornographic slasher videos together—and, indeed, a sturdy invitation to feel it; his insistence that he wants more than just girls and sex but 'affection, friendship' instead; and the con-stant insistence that 'We're friends, aren't we?'

The film's and Roberto's crisis also involves sex and violence on videotape, but this time home-filmed at a wild party. In a reprise and reversal of the earlier incident, Carlos notes Roberto's sexual excitement at the (heterosexual) gropings and couplings going on around them in the garden (one blond male friend is the particular object of Roberto's attention); he bets him he has an erection, puts the video camera down, and gives him a rapid and brutal hand-job. Mollà sharply represents in the medium close-up that frames his upper body in these seconds a mixture of cocaine- and ecstasy-induced emotional paralysis and grief that this should be the way the longed-for contact has been made. When the numbed Roberto nevertheless goes to kiss Carlos, he is verbally rebuffed and roughly pushed to the ground and away back inside. There, with the video camera repositioned, Carlos forces a diabetic and effeminate member of the group to drink a bottle of whisky, causing a seizure and his death in hospital. This is a conscious punishment of perceived weakness and an assertion of his pre-eminence in this group of males by the fascistically inclined Carlos; it is also a punishment of homosexuality (there is a problematic but clearly intended juxtaposition of illness and effeminacy here: Fouz-Hernández 2000: 94). Similarly, Carlos's subsequent taunting of Roberto by dancing around the scene of the crime with the tape, threatening to give it in to the police, is 'an attempt to punish both Roberto and himself, at an unconscious level, for their [. . .] masturbation and the death [. . .] at the ill-fated party' (95). The tape, of course, holds both the scenes of rape-like masturba-tion and of the forced drinking violation, images of same-sex sex and of death, a loop of homophobic guilt that is meant to entrap Roberto into ceaseless blame and to reassert, in criminal modality, youthful *machismo*. Thus Mollà plays a young man who, though not actually dying, has his life suspended. The film ends on this taunting and we do not know what happens to the tape. His is a masculine subjectivity based on being the victim of male aggression, of a perverse bonding.

Curiously, Mollà's next gay role, in *Perdona bonita pero Lucas me quería a mí / Excuse Me Duckie, But Lucas Loved Me* (Félix Sabroso and Dunia

Ayaso, 1996), also invites associations between gay sexuality and violent death (though here not that of a near-queer character as in *Kronen* but that of the ultra-straight, muscular Lucas of the title). The tone is completely different, though, and Mollà's playing of Alberto—a long-haired, pot-smoking, romantic idealist with a fey manner and a job in a Karaoke bar frequented by Saga-style tourists—is light and engaging. The film's situational premise is that of three flatmates who need a fourth— Lucas—and each flatmate is a (supposed) type of homosexual man: one neurotic, overweight, and mother-fixated, another gym- and fashion-obsessed, vain, and bitchy, and Mollà's character sensitive. Mollà seems to have used this caricature aspect of the role, in fact, to construct a Banderas-style disavowal: 'acepté el papel porque está tratado en clave de comedia' (I took the role because it's dealt with in comic mode) (Navarro 1997: 26). None the less, *Perdona* . . . was the first Spanish film to target itself explicitly in its marketing on a gay and gay-sympathetic audience, and it is precisely its comic modality—and Mollà's co-mingling in performance of caricature and depth impersonation—that problematizes and opens up the issue of representation of homosexuality on the Spanish screen, inevitably implicating the actor's growing star persona in a discourse of otherness both industrial (the formation of an alternative, independent, but popular cinema) and identificatory (the performance and reception of more-or-less believable modern Spanish gay men—or their exaggerated tokens at least—on screen).

On the front of Sogepac's 1996 video-box cover Mollà features in a line-up of the cast, all with limbs comically akimbo, the men in caricature poses meant to designate their primary characteristics. Mollà looks ditsy and mystified, the other two look queeny and hysterical. In the fore-ground lies the knife and blood-encrusted semi-naked body of Lucas, winking sexily out at the viewer-buyer. So far so safe (if zany). However, the imagery on the back cover points towards a more troubled reading of sexuality. The three men appear each in a still, displaying caricatured shock and horror (at the moment of discovery of Lucas's murdered body) with captions punning on the word 'loca'—mad, as referring to the film's blackish farcical comedy, and 'queen', printed three times, once for each face—all of which points up the film's collusion with hetero-sexist strategies of holding off gayness as other and holding up its supposed picturesque excesses as ridiculous but safe (all these are points made by Fouz-Hernández in Fouz-Hernández and Perriam 2000: 103–5). However, the moment of discovery that is depicted here ushers in a confessional (if still satirically comical) second half of the film, based on the interrogation of the three men by two women police detectives (the senior of whom turns out to have been Lucas's ex, the junior of whom is, in Almodovaresque manner, both an incompetent officer and a travesty of femininity). This is a confessional scenario that not only suggests, belittlingly, that the men's—gay men's—sex lives 'exist only in conversation [. . .] as wishful fantasies' (105) (each lies about a supposed relationship with the dead man) but that there is so much psychological dysfunction between them, so much that is hidden, and so much deception, that obliquely they are to blame for the death. They sit side by side on the sofa as on a bench for the accused; Lucas's ex most certainly holds them to blame for what has happened; and they blame each other. Even though the murder is actually committed by a husband jealous of his wife's dalliance with Lucas, their interrogation and terrorizing is a combination of classic film come-uppance for the transgressive 'feminine' (Williams 1983; Modleski 1988)—translated here to effeminacy —and a comic variant on the poltergeist film: the eight knives stuck into poor Lucas have a parodic, referential look to them; they might easily have been propelled by some invisible force fuelled by the evil in the flat's atmosphere, and this evil might easily have been outed by the hysteria of these men. The comedy notwithstanding, this film involves Mollà again in a story of punishment for gayness. Although it is true, as Jordan and Morgan-Tamosunas (1998: 152) have implied, that the film appears progressive and vaguely postmodern in that it 'avoids turning homosexuality into an issue, representing gay identity as just another option in the contemporary social collage'—a point also made, with more comparative and contextualizing detail in Alfeo Álvarez (2000: 145)—that 'issue' does arise to problematize itself again.

From mother's boy to rough diamond

However, it is heterosexuality, and specifically Spanish variants of it, that is at issue in Mollà's entry into prominence as a screen personality— if not yet, by some years, a star. As already discussed in Ch. 4, Bigas Luna's *Jamón, jamón* has become something of a rough and ready prism through which to observe an ambiguous, parodic representation of aspects of *machismo*. If Bardem's Raúl and Juan Diego's sinister, frozen-hearted Manuel construct between them there the physical and mental brutalities of patriarchal masculinity exaggeratedly epitomized, Mollà's role as José Luis serves the slightly more subtle purpose of being at once that masculinity's other and its familiar. The year after the film's opening, Bardem himself drew attention to Mollà's largely unrecognized pre-eminence among his generation of actors, affirming that the role of José Luis was the film's most difficult (Martín 1993: 7).

The double relationship of sexual rivalry with Raúl and filial conflict with Manuel which supplies key tensions to the dynamic of the film and its representations of masculinity is one whose interlocking clichés it must have been difficult to prevent setting hard into the heaviest of dramatic cement. José Luis is disadvantaged in relation to Raúl by his weedy looks, implied lack of lustre in sex (we assume he is as passive with Silvia as he is with her part-prostitute mother Carmen), his clumsiness in making Silvia pregnant, and by his class (part of Bigas Luna's crude schema is a century-old representation of the working class as sexual and the upper middle as repressed). In relation to Manuel, he is classically bound into a system whereby he is disdained and discounted by his father precisely for roles imposed and expected by him, that of the obedient son and interested heir to the family business. His sexual relationship with Carmen is a shadow of his father's earlier affair with her. He is controlled by his possessive, destructive, monstrous-feminine mother (Deleyto 1999: 279–80), and pseudo-Oedipally struggling with his father for her love. When he and his friends line up to urinate outside the sex club in an early scene, psychosocially speaking size matters: they taunt him about his subservience, he blusters, and one of them remarks of the underwear and the penis visible to them at his open fly, 'Sansón: ¡polla de maricón!' (Samson, hard as rock: José Luis, fairy's cock!) (Samson being the trade name of underwear made at the factory). Deleyto has suggested that 'the excessive potency of Raúl and the excessive emasculation of José Luis' are part of a 'packaged product' purveyed by the film, 'male sexuality' (278), and the young Mollà's role is certainly often reduced in terms of imaginative range in performance by both the polarity and the packaging. On the other hand, his subsequent career gains density by its early concentrated association with typical emasculation (and its violent obverse) and it is in the reactions to Bardem as Raúl, and in a series of parallelisms between the two characters, that Mollà is able to find some finer modulations of the masculine dilemmas and discontents of José Luis.

Silvia—whose focalizing role and shift from virtuous to voracious are subtly expounded by Deleyto (276–8)—is the territory where the defining similarities and differences are honed by rivalry and the supposed instincts of rebellion (in José Luis), conquest (in Raúl), and possession (in both). They become the boring, wheedling boyfriend who sees her as a satisfying mother, and the exciting, new, no-nonsense man who sees her as a powerfully sexual woman. When, under the Osborne bull hoarding on the top of the hill and in melodramatic pre-thunder storm circumstances, José Luis tries to force himself on her, he comes to the simply enough arrived at realization that she wants not him but Raúl. He leaps up in rage and knocks off the hoarding's rickety testicle, verbalizing the obvious connotation as regards the stud Raúl (but with the script necessarily leaving it to Silvia to observe to his retreating form that it is he who lacks the balls). Down at the roadside café Africa (named parodically to signify wilderness adventure and old film romance) he sees the two in an intensely physical embrace and is the jilted outsider in the rain looking on. Yet out of this stock sequence and these high-profile codes Mollà begins to find variation and shading. Within the barely contained violence of the hilltop scene, through facial gesture, body language, and a voice modulating from quietly threatening, through desperate, to enraged, he invests the scene with an anger directed not so much at Silvia and Raúl as at himself and his weakness—thus activating a more interesting micro-investigation of the family dynamics of motherhood, masculinity, consumerism, and control. Looking in on the café scene he turns the blankness of expression that previously had seemed to signify passivity to what it now seems it has all along really been, a muted violent inner struggle where self-blame, consciousness of powerlessness, and explosive despair are the agents. This, as his acting makes clear, is the pivotal moment for Mollà as José Luis, the trigger for the physical destruction to come, and the first strong sign of the psychological harm that dominates the spaces of the film inhabited by his character. The look returns in later films, notably *Second Skin* which, as we have seen, also ends in the character's melodramatic death in the wake of an emotional débâcle.

The parallels that elide the *macho* and the emasculated operate at varying degrees of intricacy. José Luis's father has had sex with Silvia's mother, so does José Luis; Raúl has had sex with his mother and now will do so with Silvia; both men in different ways are inarticulate; both have a lack where there might be a family; both are needy and greedy; both think they taste basic foods, tortilla and ham, on Silvia's breasts; both are enslaved to consumer capitalism, and in particular the underwear factory; while José Luis is infantilized, Raúl is trapped in adolescence. More than characters they are ciphers in a problem— the problem of a somewhat generalized socially and psychically con-structed masculinity. At key moments in the film they bond within the same rough-hewn mindset, share a plot, a micro-ideology. They are merely the men in the movie: as Deleyto (1999) shows so well, it is the women that the film can more interestingly be thought to be about.

Mollà's performance of fury in the final scenes—shocking, but emer-ging logically out of the plot's build-up of affronts to his aspirations of manhood—is a dramatically effective representation of masculinity as enchained mimicry, of a kind of compacted, perverse tutelage in which his frenzied character becomes the inevitable masochistic buddy to

Bardem's. In the strangely exalted ending—with its strong cultural codings of Spanish violence and fatalism (Kinder 1993: 157; Morgan and Jordan 1994: 63)—the two cudgel each other grotesquely with ham bones. The coarsely symbolic injury done by José Luis to Raúl—a disabling blow to the testicles—is matched by a fatal blow to his head as brawn violently wins out over brain; but, as all who have ever seen the film will recall, the brawny aggressor is immediately gripped by the dual realization, coming from the heart, that he has ruined his life by taking a life, and that he has killed the thing he narcissistically loved: the (im)possibility of adding to the potency of his spontaneous, instantly attractive animal maleness the longer-term benefits of being a nice, well-heeled, and well-controlled young man. As Raúl bends over the dead man's head—in the same way as he has recently been doubled up over his balls—and weeps, Mollà's character suddenly crystallizes into this configuration, a memorial to masculine aspiration as causative of its own symbolic castration, an image of repression through family dynamics, patriarchal abdication, and the imperatives of consumer society. The dead José Luis and the living—prone and masturbating as he watches his father's ex-lover mimic with grotesque eroticism her own pet parrot— come together as a powerful emblem of psychosexual entrapment and the deadening confinements of traditional gender roles.

By contrast, borrowing a little from Bardem's Raúl's rougher edges, and attempting a kind of distillation of Spanish rough youth movies, Mollà also places himself at the crux of social and family dysfunction in *La buena Estrella / Lucky Star* (Ricardo Franco, 1997) (perhaps better translated as A Gift from Heaven, Estrella being the name of the baby becoming toddler at the core of the plot). Something too of the drugs-and-crime subtheme of *Historias del Kronen* carries over into the film, and Mollà won the Fotogramas de Plata for Best Actor for his role here as the brutish, dope-stunned, but vulnerable petty criminal Daniel. The role is executed unevenly, to some tastes: the gravelly voice and unstable laugh he gives the character in order to point up the contradiction of bravado and insecurity seem at odds with the more refined and extensive register of posture, look, and gesture deployed in the film (and which has much in common with Bardem as Alberto in *Los lobos de Washington*). But the role keys into his own skills at vivid impersonation and into his interests in the marginal, moves him radically away from the narrative context of dysfunctional middle-class families, and, in the new social-realist counter-tradition that we keep returning to with these stars, constructs a personality out of chaos, abandonment, drug use, criminality. The role is a turning point, even though Mollà was outshone by Antonio Resines, twelve years his senior, and winner of the Goya for Best Male Lead for the film.[6] According to Mollà's own testimony (Ponga 1997), preparation for the role included three days spent on downtown streets passing (successfully) for a dope-head and occasional peddler of hash (42), and effected a 'transformation' (41) and a departure from the tonalities of voice and the thoughtfulness of the usual persona of the actor Mollà. The character of Daniel was intensively researched and Mollà declared an identification with his character's fears (Casanova 1998: 120) which seems to be borne out both in the frequent moments of authentic representation of mood and motivation and in the equally frequent moments of misjudgement of tone arising from overstrenuous seeking after authenticity.

Daniel is the true father of Estrella whose mother Marina (played by Maribel Verdú) has left him for the caring, paternal, but clinically impotent butcher Rafael (Resines, unusually here in a non-comic role) who rescues her one night from a fight with Daniel. The reason for Rafael's impotence is simple, and brutal, and leads directly to one crux of the matter of masculinity: he has lost his testicles in an accident, whereas Daniel is all too fired up by what we might loosely think of as testosterone. When Daniel tracks Marina down after a spell in jail and in the immediate aftermath of a violent mugging in which he has been victim, Rafael agrees to allow him to stay in the house to recover from his beating, recognizing too that Maribel still has strong emotional bonds with Daniel. As the agreed three or four days stretches into weeks, a number of classic scenarios of masculinity are played out with the Mollà character as main agency. As Marina continues to be protected by the gentle but sturdy Rafael so too does a continuity establish itself with her earlier rough life with sexually aggressive Daniel who, in a typical moment, ogles, makes crude references to how he wants to have sex with her 'like you like it', then begins to caress and kiss her from behind as she stands ironing, earning the traditional slap to the face that signifies—we see on Verdú's face—as much shamed acknowledgement of the accuracy of the male diagnosis of her need as it does anger at his. Subsequently, when Rafael goes away for a night at his sister's in the country outside Madrid, but returns unexpectedly, Marina and Daniel are indeed having sex upstairs. On going back upstairs after fetching water from the fridge, Daniel realizes that Rafael is sitting silently in a chair; he reveals that he has been there all night; and Daniel's reaction is not one of shame or

---

[6] Resines is extremely well known for his long career in comedy roles (including that in *Todos los hombres sois iguales*, All Men Are the Same: discussed in Ch. 1), for his part in Alex de la Iglesia's angry sci-fi spoof *Acción mutante / Mutant Action* (1991), and, especially, in the television series *A las once en casa* (Home By Eleven); beginning in the same year as the film's release.

fear, rather of rebuke: 'esto no se hace' (you don't do that sort of thing). As with the ironing scene, the sexual politics marginalizes and reduces Marina to a supposition of masculinity's own. She is coded as predictably enmeshed in a micro-narrative of male sexual fulfilment and a surrounding plot of collusion between men to ensure the continuation and reiteration of a hegemonic set of social and sexual circumstances. But so too is masculinity belittled, of course, if this is all it is about, its petty self-perpetuation. This is embodied strongly in Mollà's performance of the Daniel of the first half of the film as pitiable in his repertoire of gross remarks, jokes, and gestures; a bizarre harsh laugh too frequently deployed (both by character and actor). His inability to respond to Rafael's gentle goodness speaks of weakness too.

On the other hand, though, there is a crude forcefulness to Daniel. Mollà has him signify post-coital self-confidence and relaxation in his easy, muscular striding down and back up the stairs in the episode described above; his long hair is well mussed, and he is dressed in bad-taste briefs: he is— as Bardem was in *Jamón, jamón*—apparently pure young *macho*. His lean, tanned body, again in briefs (this time bright red) had occupied the screen and the domestic space on the occasion of Daniel's bloodied first appearance at the house and had signified both the character's physical potency (contrasted to Rafael's already established relative lack of it) and the perversity of attraction to the damaged or tortured masculine body that animates the identifications available to audiences of action (and crime-and-prison) movies (Tasker 1993; Holmlund 1993: 220–4; Fuchs 1993: 197). As Martina tends Daniel in this early scene Mollà keeps switching codes between the anti-heroic and heroic, the display and disposition of Mollà's body making Daniel both magnificent and pathetic, both dominant and on offer. Marina, partly because of this indeterminacy in him, is able to resist being positioned by the needs of either man. She makes her first stand by refusing Daniel's attempt to use the battered beauty of his body to seduce her back into the good/bad old days; and her second by challenging Rafael's emerging shy jealousy and insisting that he can stay in the bathroom and watch the bathing and bandaging if he wishes. Both nostalgic, recidivistic fidelity and domestic monogamy are refused, as is also the usual trajectory of male rivalry. Her subsequent insistence to Rafael that she can love both men, and the danger of losing Estrella, persuades him to allow a complex alternative triangular family structure to form in the house.

Its complexity resides not so much in the unusual juxtaposition of powerful female and good, rather than bad, male (in Rafael), nor in the child-with-two-dads motif, as in the shifting patterns of male role-playing and identification within Daniel and between him and Rafael. While Daniel is helping out in the butcher's shop, Mollà draws on a stock street repertoire of old-fashioned cockiness as Daniel—to Rafael's dismay—flirts and speaks familiarly with the somewhat starchy clientele; similarly, in showing his disdain for what (for him) is represented by Rafael's friend the local priest, he aligns himself with a rebel, underdog class as well as recalling harm done to him in his past at orphanages and special schools. Both are forms of bravado, and it registers bodily as well as verbally. A coarse, vehement rejection of the wiles and cruelties of priests (in their role as teachers and imposers of discipline) is backed in gesture by the signalling of them as abject, other, discountable (a handshake with eyes averted; an arm waved dismissively) and by the implicit inclusion of Rafael in the registering of disgust (emphatic banging of the shop counter and a bitter, smiling look to Rafael inviting his agreement). This young man angry on behalf of his even younger self coincides in the domestic set-up with a return to the surface of expression and emotion of the memories and desires of that damaged child (Rafael's own physical accident of mutilation is a straightforward correlative here). Near Christmas, the whole family group sits around the television; Estrella is taken off to bed, kisses both men; they turn and look tenderly at each other, Resines having Rafael exhibit a quiet and contented acceptance of the strangeness but rightness of their version of family, Mollà allowing a more superficial tenderness to show. As Rafael shifts out of that mood of tolerance, however, and determines to go out for a Christmas drink, the lack of depth in Daniel's reaction becomes more clearly understood as a lack of self-confidence, as fear of solitude, and need of male companionship. He follows Rafael out, invokes communality of resistance to womanly nagging, goes with him to the bar, and—intensely leaning across the table—engages Rafael in close and coarse discussion of the causes and effects of the latter's accident. Both blokey and sympathetic, inappropriate and attentive, in this scene he is not only establishing with Rafael a classic bond but also a discourse in common on loss and physical damage, one which might shield him from his own psychological hurt. Mollà holds back the revelation of the latter, though he suggests it (or it is anyway suggested) in the always intelligent look emerging from the unshaven face and from under his unkempt hair.

It manifests itself in the last third of the film, in fact, not simply as that past damage reasserting itself but—with Daniel again in jail—as terminal, AIDS-related, illness and a new, sharpened consciousness of futility and ending. In the prison interview room, with a glass panel separating the two men, Daniel and Rafael talk, Daniel drawn and, at the end, seized by a coughing fit. Alternating shots at 180° show first one head and next to it, same size, the reflection of the other, then the reverse; instead of the traditional confrontation of rivals (which, for example, we had had in a scene in the country when Rafael had trained his shooting rifle on a stunned, almost accepting, Daniel and toyed with eliminating him in a minor echo of Carlos Saura's *La caza / The Hunt* of 1965), we find ourselves, as Heredero (1997: 28) has suggested, witnessing their careful, and watchful, search for each other's motivations. We see a transference of vulnerabilities and qualities of strength and self-knowledge. In a cleverly paced crescendo of expressivity Mollà moves from quiet concern for the family; to jealousy at the news of another child on its way (his, perhaps?); to rueful recognition that he is in too poor a state for Marina and Estrella to see him; through a low-key and more sincere version of the man-to-man talk of bar scene at Christmas (saying outright now 'eres el único tío legal que he conocido' (you're the only really decent bloke I've met)); to defeat, despair, and the bitter mimicry and repetition of the words of the guard: 'ha pasado el tiempo' (time's up). It has been observed that the whole premise of the story (the eunuch with a heart of gold, the borderline prostitute, the child, the good-for-nothing father) might have led to sensationalist melodrama in the hands of a less able director and script-writing team (ibid. 26), and the melodramatic cliché of coincidence of this prison scene is accordingly transformed by the quiet style of the lighting, shifts of frame, and angle —by a renowned director's know-how—but also by acting technique and well thought through modulations, more on Mollà's part, in fact, than Resines's (whose remit here is to remain a stolid and sensitive foil for the intensity on the other side of the glass). The scene becomes an emotional and dramatic pivot of great force, pitching the acting style and the story into a new phase for the last twenty minutes of the film. Daniel returns, on Estrella's birthday, in an ambulance, near death; in bed—the marital bed—in terror and great pain (tautly played, with minimal facial and bodily movement and none of the vocal excesses of earlier) he pleads unsuccessfully (and out of our earshot) with the good Catholic Rafael, to kill him; finally it is Marina who fetches the hunting rifle and (in consolidation and closure of that earlier near-shooting scene in the country) ends his suffering out of our sight, with a fade to black cueing the gunshot.

More new directions

The conviction and impact of Mollà's performance as Daniel led for a while, according to Mollà, to a spate of scripts in which 'Daniels' were earmarked for him but which he preferred to avoid in favour of completely different roles (Casanova 1998: 120): as Tomás, the daring, handsome, wholesome, bourgeois anti-Franco rebel in *Los años bárbaros / The Stolen Years / Barbaric Years* (Fernando Colomo, 1998) and as the pianist Luis Doria in the literary adaptation *El Pianista* (The Pianist: Mario Gas, 1999). He is commonly reported as being the most versatile of the generation—while implicitly being set apart from Bardem, whose range is of another order—from the point of view of imitations of character type, look, and gestural signature. In Bigas Luna's shamelessly eroticized costume drama thriller *Volavérunt* (1999; adapted from Antonio Larreta's novel of the same name (1980))—the more expensive of two Goya biopics that centenary year (Saura's *Goya en Burdeos / Goya in Bordeaux* being the other)—he plays Prime Minister Manuel de Godoy handsomely. Both in and frequently half out of colourful and pompous clothing Mollà is smoothly lascivious with the Duchess of Alba (Aitana Sánchez-Gijón, outshining Penelope Cruz who plays the smouldering, simple, and sexually exploited model for the famous double picture of the Maja Desnuda). He is demeaningly naughty-boyish with Queen María Luisa of Parma (Stefania Sandrelli—the film's third actor in common with *Jamón, jamón*, reaffirming the sense of a generation's development in which Mollà is enwrapped). He makes an excellent schemer and wielder of political and patriarchal power, judging the balance between collusion with the audience through self-aware parody and obedience to the requirements of the commingled genres here, bio-pic, thriller, and literary adaptation historical drama (after Antonio Larreta's Planeta Prize-winning novel of the same name). Like Carmelo Gómez, then, Mollà has as part of his star persona a clear image in that part of the national cultural imaginary which is constructed of and entertained by pastness.

The on-screen performances of intimacy and crisis in *Second Skin* are productively disrupted and overlapped by the sense of a shared career path for the two actors—predicted early on by Bardem (Martín 1993: 9)—and by their well-known closeness as friends (Ponga 1997: 42). When that film came out in January 2000 another notable, and saleable, partnership was being made in *Nadie conoce a nadie / Nobody Knows Anybody* (Mateo Gil, 1999), overlapping with it for several weeks in Spanish cinemas. This convoluted thriller cast Mollà in antagonistic pairing with Eduardo Noriega (on whose heart-throb status see Ch. 7). In the promotional spots the two names—announced verbally and in textual credit (Noriega's first)—are a key hook; and the paradoxical bonds of rivalry and domination–subordination between them are strong. Noriega's character, Simón, is a composer of crossword puzzles, while Mollà's, Sapo (Toad), carries out a bizarre series of terrorist attacks on Seville in Holy

Week around a video-game scenario, in which he lures Simón into involvement by way of cryptic clues. Both are disaffected: Simón with his career and his love-life, and with being 30-something and directionless (a strong theme in Juan Bonilla's novel on which the film is loosely based); Sapo psychopathically, pitted as he is against all that Holy Week in Seville implies for him—a country incapable of abandoning the trappings of tradition, empty belief, and oppression, and mindlessly still given over to the ritual round of bread and circuses. On his own admission (Belategui 1999) Mollà gives in too much to his desire to take risks with voice (menacing and quiet) and looks (bespectacled, red-headed, manic). He goes much further even than with Daniel in *La buena Estrella*, and the remark that the film is notable for 'un pasadísimo Jordi Mollà, pero al fin y al cabo un actor' (a very over the top Mollà, but still an actor, none the less) (Bellido 1999) is probably fair (even if the rest of the judgement, on Noriega's irredeemable blandness, is questionable).

Sapo's sentiments are keyed to a significant sector of the young and liberal, as well as to an older generation who once admired anti-Francoist references. An alter ego constructed by him in a manuscript autobiography recalls damage at the hands of a sexually perverted, religiously devoted father; his co-players in the game include one who has suffered at the hands of priests at Catholic school, another whose anarchist grandfather was lynched by a rightist mob in the Civil War. In his wildest moment, when he has killed all the players except Simón ('The Chosen One') by blowing up their headquarters under the abandoned Vatican City pavilion on the site of the famous Expo 92, his justification—though extreme—is familiar. Holding Simón at gunpoint in the elevated viewing platform on the Expo site he explains to him (having observed that the city spread before them is like the huge model he has worked with in elaborating the game) that in a life infused with tedium and pointlessness salvation lies in the detailed construction of a new character for oneself (in his case, the Devil) and an alternative story (Seville controlled by the game). In a city where thousands of people shuffle along behind a 'tree-trunk' in procession, what is so odd in belief in the Devil? Who can deny the thrill of living on the edge? he asks. Mollà draws effectively on the whole film repertoire of cool, cruel killers in the delivery of these uncomfortably true, transgressive half-clichés; and his connection to the popular global subgenre (dangerous fantasist holds city to ransom) is enhanced by a repertoire of studied ordinariness, blank dissimulation, tight-lipped smiles, tense movements of the jaw, and sudden violent or vehement looks fired out from behind innocent plain spectacles. The film brings to the fore the business of performance, the connections between narrating and game-playing, the issues of film actors throughout the tradition of box-office movie-making finding themselves in roles where 'an actor's [. . .] unconscious self-image, hidden even from himself, can be brought to the surface and developed' (Griffith 1970: 25). For Mollà—across his range—reads as having just such an extreme fascination with fictionality, one that borders on disturbing just as it contributes to the fascination of his person and personae.

In print, his trademark 'serious', odd, and 'different' image has not prevented his presentation in the glossy press as something of a sex symbol: for example presented provocatively unkempt on the front cover of *Cinemanía* (September 1998) captioned with the adjective 'bárbaro' (wild) (from *Los años bárbaros*, covered in the issue); or in the fashion photo shots in Ponga (1997), in a full-page image, bare-chested in open denim top and unbuttoned jeans with the caption quote drawing attention to his sharp, natural intelligence in a strategy similar to that used to present Bardem and his own perceived contrasting characteristics. In *Son de mar / The Sound of the Sea* (Bigas Luna, 2001)—another adaptation (of Manuel Vicent's novel of the same name)—these contrasts are returned to again in a replaying of another potent (if somewhat clichéd) myth, that of the sexual and emotional awakening of a cerebral man (the teacher played by Mollà) when he discovers the sensuality of the south, specifically the Mediterranean, and sex (with Leonor Watling, with whom he is naked and entwined on the main publicity image). Even here, though, there is scope for the more sombre side of Mollà, as his character goes missing, presumed drowned, but returns years later, when his lover has married into money, to haunt her and imprison them both in a bruising re-enactment of sexual passion with a sinister edge of nihilism.

TABLE 5. *Filmography*

Year	Title	English title (s) (official in italics; literal in roman)	Director	Billing	Audience figures and takings	Other information
1992	*Jamón, jamón*		José Juan Bigas Luna	6th	673,467 €1,808,589	
1993	*Mi hermano del alma*	*My Darling Brother*	Mariano Barroso	Minor	80,751 €207,318	
1993	*Historias de la puta mili*	Stories of Military Service	Manuel Esteban	2nd	570,117 €1,602,746	
1994	*Alegre ma non troppo*	With Gaiety, ma non troppo	Fernando Colomo	7th	210,891 €624,661	
1994	*Todo es mentira*	*It's All Lies / Life's A Bitch*	Álvaro Fernández Armero	3rd	366,794 €1,085,571	
1995	*Historias del Kronen*	Stories of the Kronen	Montxo Armendáriz	2nd	771,950 €2,344,136	
1995	*Los hombres siempre mienten*	Men Always Lie	Antonio del Real	4th	456,889 €1,363,028	
1995	*La flor de mi secreto*	*The Flower of My Secret*	Pedro Almodóvar	Minor	981,688 €3,196,909	
1996	*Celestina, La*	Celestina	Gerardo Vera	6th	443,979 €1,393,595	
1996	*Perdona bonita pero Lucas me quería a mí*	*Excuse Me Duckie, But Lucas Loved Me*	Félix Sabroso and Dunia Ayaso	Top	283,436 €920,246	

TABLE 5. *(continued)*

Year	Title	English title(s) (official in italics; literal in Roman)	Director	Billing	Audience figures and takings	Other information
1997	*La Cible / Romance peligroso*	*The Target to Kill*	Pierre Courrège	6th	21,011 €70,544	Co-pro France, Spain; original in French; dubbed and subtitled into Spanish
1997	*La buena Estrella*	*Lucky Star*	Ricardo Franco	3rd	684,152 €2,398,799	Fotogramas de Plata, Best Actor
1998	*Los años bárbaros*	*The Stolen Years / Barbaric Years*	Fernando Colomo	Top	492,506 €1,826,994	Co-pro Spain, France
1999	*El Pianista*	The Pianist	Mario Gas	Top	43,537 €183,388	Original in Catalán; dubbed and subtitled into Spanish
1999	*Un dólar por los muertos*	*A Dollar for the Dead*	Gene Quintano	3rd	98,903 €378,031	Co-pro USA, Spain; original in English; Dubbed into Spanish
1999	*Volavérunt*	[the subtitle to Goya's famous 'Maja desnuda']	José Juan Bigas Luna	3rd	394,795 €1,532,650	
1999	*Nadie conoce a nadie*	*Nobody Knows Anyone*	Mateo Gil	2nd	1,409,621 €5,526,483	
2000	*Segunda piel*	*Second Skin*	Gerardo Vera	2nd	550,282 €2,194,527	
2001	*Son de mar*	*The Sound of the Sea*	José Juan Bigas Luna	Top	239,663 €998,517	

Shorts

Quizás no sea demasiado tarde / Potser no sigui massa tard (Perhaps It's Not Too Late)
   (Txerra Cirbián, 1988)
Pronòstic reservat / Pronóstico reservado (Judgment Reserved) (Antonio Mollà, 1994)

Television series

La granja (On the Farm) TV3, 1989

Films for television

El joven Picasso (Young Picasso) (Juan Antonio Bardem, 1991)

Fig. 12. Jorge Sanz and Victoria Abril in *Amantes*.

Fig. 13. Jorge Sanz in *Fotogramas* pin-up calendar for 1988.

6 Jorge Sanz (b. 1969)

Cine en las venas (Cinema in the Blood)[1]

Jorge Sanz, though born only in 1969, has the longest career of the actors discussed in this book, with two key directors underpinning his career in the 1980s and 1990s, Vicente Aranda and Fernando Trueba. He had already begun to be dubbed *galán* by his early twenties (Gracia 1992) in the wake of roles played opposite Victoria Abril in *Si te dicen que caí* / *If They Tell You I Fell* (Aranda, 1989) (winning the Goya for Best Actor) and Aranda's television serial *Jinetes del alba* (Riders of the Dawn) (1990: adapted from Jesús Fernández Santos' novel of the same name). Starting his career at the age of 9, by 15 he had played in ten features within and beyond the Spanish film industry. His roles as Paco in Pedro Masó's *La miel* (Honey) (1979) alongside Jane Birkin and as rascally Pepe in the serialized TV film drama *Valentina* (Antonio José Betancor, 1982) were both still remembered in the early 1990s (*Deia Igandea* 1994: 9); and non-Spanish audiences watching his later appearances in US productions *The Break* (Robert Dornhelm, 1996) and *The Garden of Redemption* (Thomas Michael Donnelly, 1997) might have recalled him as the young Conan in *Conan the Barbarian* (John Milius, 1982). His image soon moved on from that of the sweet, the feisty, and the lively—while echoes of these qualities persist well into the 1990s—into being one of strong and unambiguous youthful sex appeal. This appeal was consolidated definitively in Fernando Trueba's *El año de las luces* / *The Year of Enlightenment* (1986), the first of an intermittent series of young adult and adult roles that were to associate Sanz not only with sexuality as an issue, a plot device, and a useful selling point,[2] but also with key historical moments and nationally characteristic social roles. In *Jinetes del alba* he is enmeshed, as a young anarchist soldier, in a storyline sympathetic to the cause of the 1934 Asturias Revolution. In *Si te dicen que*

---

[1] The title of a prominent mid-career interview and photo-shoot (Ponga 1994).

[2] Thus he is 'the Spanish Tom Cruise' (*Tiempo*, 19 Nov. 1990; Ponga 1994); 'object of desire' *Semana*, 5 Aug. 1992; and, retrospectively (and not that kindly), 'teenage heart-throb' ('ídolo de jovencitas') for Europa Press as relayed in *Teletipo (Sociedad)*, 16 Feb. 2000. A characteristically sexy photo shoot is that in Ponga 1994 where the paraphernalia of low-cut vests, wet clothes, hot looks, and tousled hair are used with appropriate abandon.

caí—another adaptation, this time of Juan Marsé's well-known novel (1973/6)—his character Java, a young rag-and-bone merchant in the old quarter of a 1940s Barcelona under tight vigilance from the right, is (obliquely) associated with the resistance and represents the under-class, exploited economically and sexually. In a completely different, and indifferently executed, perspective on the history of the Catalan ter-ritories, *Tramontana* (From Across the Mountains) (Carlos Pérez Ferré, 1991) Sanz plays the focalizing character Arnau, a strapping orphan living rough (and in revealing rags) in the thirteenth-century Pyrenees who tags on to a group of migrant social entrepreneurs headed for Valencian territories due to be liberated by King Jaume I. In this simple tale his image becomes (forgettably) associated with unfocused adven-ture, the landscapes of Eastern Spain, and a key (if here almost totally unresearched) moment in the national histories of Valencia and Spain. In *Morirás en Chafarinas* (You'll Die in Xafarinas) (Pedro Olea, 1995) the association is with the politics of military service and, implicitly, of Spain's presence in its North African provinces; in *Cuba* (Pedro Carvajal, 1999) he is a young colonial officer in 1898; while in *Libertarias / Freedom-fighters* (Aranda, 1996) he has high billing but only brief exposure again as an anarchist soldier, this time in the Civil War.

His roles in historical films do not, then, range widely but there is none the less sufficient variation in type to allow us to think of Sanz in terms of a plurality of views on men's agency in the Spanish past; on the other hand he also succumbs to the homogenizing and distorting effects of 'heritage'-style visualizations of the past (Wright 1985: 78).[3] As with the UK and France (Powrie 1997: 15), the majority of historical films in Spain are literary adaptations and the actor seeking to break new ground fights first against the firm consistency of nostalgia—not just nostalgia for more exciting and defining times, but, as Powrie (14) suggests, for the pleasures of that other form, reading. Such films also, of course, offer what seems the opposite pleasure, that deriving from the convenient sub-stitution for the work of reading which is offered by such adaptations when taken at narrative surface value. The actor, then, becomes the star who is simply the past; the sign of the glamour of action, resistance, or, in Fernando Trueba's *Belle Époque* (1992), a blurred Golden Age in fact more protected from than intersected by historical circumstance. This is not to say that Sanz's is a dated or fusty image (although he never has

[3] There are numerous Spanish products that fit the category better, mostly in the 'rustic' mode (Corner and Harvey 1991: 52–3) and/or with child protagonists (see my discussion of *Secretos del corazón* in Ch. 3); however, the only film with one of this book's actor subjects in a main role that I would consider to be fully a 'heritage' movie—although Jordan supports powerfully *Belle Époque*'s credentials (1999)—is *Volavérunt*, discussed briefly in Ch. 5.

the youth credibility and relative cool of the young Banderas in his better roles): over an unusually long time span (only in 2000 did reports begin to comment on his loss of sex appeal) he has been able to maintain the look and the behavioural style of the fresh-faced hero and rogue; innocent, and precociously perverse; both the comic and the tragic handsome lead. Despite the variations in role, then, and his dual career as film and television actor—with consistently light, comic roles in the latter but with generic variation in the former—and in particular despite the interestingly perverse twist given to his desirability in Vicente Aranda's *Amantes / Lovers* (1991), by the mid-1990s Sanz was beginning to feel the traditional need to react in interview to restrictive typecasting and audience definitions of his roles. Though the reputation as *galán* might be what originates most offers of work in film, Sanz declares that he tries to function 'no [. . .] como galán sino como un actor que cambia sus personajes en cada película' (not as romantic lead but actor, changing character from film to film) (*Deia Igandea* 1994: 10).

In *El año de las luces* the urgent sexuality of Sanz's character, 15-year-old Manolo (the kind of ordinary lad's name typically attaching to his roles), stands at the centre of a schematic portrait of the social and moral climate of the years immediately following the Civil War. He and his much younger brother are taken from the city to a boarding school run by the stereotypical comic duo of sexually aware and available young matron and moralizing, religious fanatic headmistress, Doña Tránsito, who is a dedicated, paranoid voyeur and member of the Sección Femenina (a kind of Francoist Christian Mothers' Union-cum-Girl Guides organization). They are aided by a small crew of younger women, variously feisty, and innocently but provocatively pretty (Maribel Verdú). This set-up, and above all this cast, serve as a clear anticipatory marker of Sanz's predominant screen identity both in that his masculine prowess is triangulated against, defined by, and brought low by narratively prominent women, and in that the two older women are played by Veronica Forqué and Chus Lampreave, backed up by Rafaela Aparicio (as the no-nonsense school cook), all mainstays of post-1980 Spanish comedies, who thus enfold him in a powerful generic tradition. There are numerous points of emphasis on the scandalous presence of his cheeky good looks and his adolescent body in this female and pre-pubescent male domain. He lies in bed quietly masturbating as he nightly watches the silhouette of the young female dormitory monitor as she prepares for bed behind a screen; he meticulously keeps a diary of his ejaculations; one night in an erotically charged scene he allows the comely monitor (in her pseudo-nurse's uniform) to tie his hands to the bedposts, deliciously persuaded of the sinfulness of his acts—but he cannot but break free. Inevitably, when she moves on, he seduces her successor, María José (Maribel Verdú), charmingly, handsomely, and with talk of 'what they do in films'. Doña Tránsito on one of her vigilant perambulations catches him hiding in a toilet with his trousers down and next day, over lunch, notes with hypocritical horror that he has 'una cosa tremenda' (a monstrous thing) between his legs. Matron, to whom this remark is addressed, has noted this and more from the start: she has managed to lean across him and touch him with her cheek within five minutes of his arrival, has had him strip to the waist with the other younger boys for measuring and weighing, and in the end—stereotypically combining sympathetic mother-figure and seducer, unwilling victim and hungry lover—she gives in to him and has him give in to her. Monitored, measured, self-recorded, sized up, and eventually expelled, Manolo's body is processed by the caricature microsystem of Francoism; its masculinity and sexuality is as dangerous as the foreign books that Doña Tránsito insists are removed from the school library and burned, and as the languid foxtrot that at a summer picnic she has replaced by proper, lumpy, earthy, Castilian *jotas*.

For all the levity of this film, the enlightenments suggested in its title are various and paradoxical. Manolo is released temporarily from the world of his soldier-brother, and memories of conflict between men, into an environment where that other masculine world is emptied of meaning as he discovers what it really is to be male, to be subject to desire, in close engagement with women; and yet this environment is also that of prohibition. He bonds with the cook's handyman husband (Manuel Alexandre), an internal exile of sorts because of his apparently shameful former life in Paris and his (incongruously) wide knowledge of French thought (the arch-enemy of traditionalist Spanishness); but this man also is in thrall, silenced, discounted, restricted to his workshop, and as worried about Manolo's debilitating masturbatory incontinence as the women are (though while they fear for his soul, he fears for the youth's manliness). Manolo, then, is caught up in an ideological and somatic rite of passage which has no clear linear trajectory. The patriarchal space of older brother, military, and priestly authority is seen to make no sense, either when he returns to it or as it intervenes through Doña Tránsito; the full realization of his masculine sexuality depends both on its rejection by some of the women all of the time and its variously conflicted acceptance by some of them some of the time. Above all, the women are represented (in irritatingly time-honoured fashion) as holding the key to the change, enabling the transition to enlightenment. Sanz frequently occupies just such a comfortably fuzzy space of dubious or unfinished articulation of gender identity, and usually does so in light comic mode and in relation to what women make of his charms, and his body.

The fallen man

A significant proportion of the films Sanz has chosen to work in—particularly comedies of the 1990s—seek to maintain the 'male norm, perspective and look' discussed many years back by Neale (1993: 19); however, there are others that also, in the figure of their problematically disempowered male protagonist, represent masculinity in tones and situations that blur the norm. In these his body is on display in such a way as to make Sanz singularly framed as a problematic and yet safely iconic sex object, ostensibly typifying conventional, empowered masculinities of various sorts and yet perverse, scandalous, available. The male body, in Sanz on screen, is subjected to systems of representation that conventionally speaking are not appropriate to the object in question: systems, that is, that make a forbidden linkage between the masculine, the passive, the desirable, the disempowered, the weak, and the absurd.

Scenes in *Si te dicen que caí* have Sanz, as Java, stripped and performing sex for money with war-wounded ex-Falangist Don Conrado looking on from his wheelchair behind a curtain. In the first instance he finds himself opposite Victoria Abril, brutally fucking and physically abusing her wretched, pregnant, prostitute character; in the second (though Aranda wipes the images of sex) he is ordered to bed by an effeminate and very young homosexual man. His (flaccid) penis in full-frontal medium-long shot and his thrusting buttocks in medium close-up are made much of in the first case (more than is Abril's body, mostly face down or kneeling on the floor); his shame and fragile manliness ('I'll do the fucking') are painfully revealed in the second. In ironic parody of his hard-man persona and underworld existence, he appears in a morality play directed by Don Conrado as Lucifer, in red cape and tights which pornographically display his cock and balls (towards which the camera tracks mimicking Conrado's gaze). Conrado's sadism—carried over from the war years, which are summarized in flashbacks—is projected onto the stage martyrdom of a saintly young virgin; but backstage, as an extension both of the play and of the fantasy stories that Java and his gang construct, Java in his red gear torments and abuses the same girl tied to a cross, drawing a sharp blade between his and her lips as he forcibly kisses her, then recoiling from the blood-lust ashamed. He is equated in perversity with the character who politically speaking is the enemy, just as he is levelled earlier by prostitution in a violent and shocking inversion of patriarchal power relations (Jordan and Morgan-Tamosunas 1998: 145). As the abused turned abuser—and in a chilling echo of the many treacherous turns of the Civil War—Java is the fallen man, a role that is reprised and extended by Aranda in *Lovers*.

Lovers is an erotic true-story crime thriller with specifically national historical resonances and appealing to a peculiar, multiple form of nostalgia and desire for vicarious adventure. Aranda, Pedro Costa (producer), and Álvaro del Amo (scriptwriter) had already worked on a feature-length episode for a television series based on famous Spanish crimes of the twentieth century,[4] and *Amantes* takes another well-known story, that of the 'Crime at Tetuán de las Victorias', as its basis. Onto this is laid a simpler triple nostalgia, for film noir, for an apparently more black-and-white world in the recallable past, and for the brave days of struggle to emerge from the aftermath of civil conflict. In the opening post-title sequence Sanz is once again coded with soldierly charms. Not only, though, in a uniform, but framed by two key institutions of Francoism—the Catholic Church and the military—and by a symbolic time in the Franco era, the 1950s, with the austere and isolated 1940s over and money coming in from abroad, people on the make, Madrid coming to life again. As the title sequence ends, place and period—'Madrid, Años 50'—are textually indicated on screen; there are horses, the scene appears to be a stable, but the sound-track reveals that there is a simple but formal mass being celebrated in this building, a site caught between the spiritual (as chapel) and the pragmatic secular (as stable) in a way that prefigures one of the film's key and archetypal tensions (between purity and lust-driven crime). The camera travels horizontally along the back row of the congregation, from behind, at shoulder height, revealing uniforms and establishing the altar end of the makeshift chapel as the centre of attention. Halfway through the camera's trajectory the priest is glimpsed centre-screen in medium-long shot; the camera travels on and ends on a horse tethered to one side of the congregation (a metaphorical punctuation mark for the transition not only into the social space but into the mire of the film's main plot). There is a cut to two young boys—'Trini piensa en Paco' says one to the other—then a cut to Trini (Maribel Verdú), demure but sparkly-eyed, in blue coat and dark headscarf. She gazes towards the back of the congregation; representing her coy look, the camera dollies unsteadily up a shallow angle to Paco, first along the notional line of sight, then situating itself and the spectator directly in front of him, moving in for a medium close-up. Paco at the back of the church has usurped the priest at the front. Love interest has overridden other plot-establishing detail. Trini's gaze and the spectator's have become fixed on one prime object of desire. A cut back to Trini shows her stealing another glance back: Paco continues to

---

[4] 'La huella del crimen' (The Traces of Crime): a series of films for television made in the first half of the 1980s, under the general direction of Pedro Costa; with a second series in the early 1990s.

look steadfastly forward, his masculine charms accentuated by this discipline; but as the congregation rises for the elevation of the Host and she has to turn back to the front his eyes do flicker in her direction. He is masculine, but mischievous; and vulnerable too. Having been aligned with Trini's gaze and her thoughts, the spectator—though thinking probably not so much of Paco as of Jorge Sanz in similar roles—is properly seduced into recognizing his status as centre of attraction as the camera lingers in the intimacy of a medium close-up. That little gesture of acknowledgement of the admiring gaze is as much from Sanz for the spectator as it is from Paco for Trini.

Paco's moral and emotional positioning between the pure and innocent Trini, and Luisa (Victoria Abril), his sexy and sexually manipulative young widow landlady has been investigated by Marsha Kinder in relation to the iconographies of Freudian psychoanalysis and of Catholicism. The two women, set up as 'the opposing stereotypes of virgin and whore' (Jacobs 1987: 100–2) provide a schematic melodrama for Paco to operate in as he is caught in a tangle of lust and ingenuousness between evil and good, adventure and duty. Kinder (1995) draws our attention to Trini's association with the Madonna through her blue costume (also perversely associated with Luisa) and the picture of the Immaculate Conception (Kinder 207) which she takes with her on her last journey. Trini is coded as the pure, family-oriented woman, the 'patriarchal woman' (206) to whom Paco eventually gravitates on Christmas Eve having been seduced in the preceding days by Luisa who is, Kinder suggests, a 'profane alternative to the Madonna' (206). His profound ambivalence in relation to Trini, and his fatal attraction to Luisa, is due in large part to his freedom—gained through the attritional effects of Luisa on traditionally ideologized masculinity—to refuse to submit to the patriarchal law (P. Evans 1999c: 94–5, 98). If Paco is in this way empowered, so too Kinder emphasizes the subversive ways in which the sex scenes of the early parts of the film empower Luisa, and represent her sexuality as an amalgam of aggression, 'phallic power', tenderness, and vulnerability. 'Not only [. . .] is she the sexual subject who actively pursues her own desire and who first seduces Paco but she continues to control the lovemaking' (210). It is possible, moreover, to recover from this—and other love scenes in the film—an inversion of that norm whereby in cinema the woman is (in the often quoted phrases) 'image [. . .] spectacle, object to be looked at, vision of beauty' and the female body is represented as '*locus* of sexuality, site of visual pleasure, or lure of the gaze' (de Lauretis 1984: 37). But these representations of the body of Paco and of 'Jorge Sanz'—the young male star forming his image and career classically in relation to the more established female star (here Victoria

Abril on a plateau of achievement)—construct a space full of equivocal meanings. The male body finds itself here passive and looked at, fixed in the *locus* of sexuality. When Luisa comes into the bedroom on the first night of sex she leaves retouching the decorations on a Christmas tree and goes over to Paco lying on his side, his soft-lit back to her, on the bed. From dressing the tree she moves to denuding him—removing the sheet that covers him—and with the careful touch that titivated the tree, she prepares his body for her pleasure. The camera follows her hand in close-up as it traces a line down his flank to his buttock: he seems controlled. However, a further caressing close-up shot of him back up from hip to neck, following Luisa's lips now, ends with a 180° switch of camera position to his front, and a close-up of his glamorously lust-flushed face occluding her features and challenging the power of what she is trying to insist on with the words whispered in his ear—'te ha traido la Providencia a esta casa' (Providence had brought you to this house). Now it is apparent that it is his body that inspires the action and the mobility of the camera; it attracts Luisa and animates her, but empowers him. His body, even as it is positioned as object to be gazed at, gives the gaze back to him by way of an idolization of his own desirability. When he turns and mounts her, he first kisses the lips that had been in control, silencing them, then throws a garment over Luisa's face obliterating it and with it her sight. The male norm seems restored.

Nevertheless there are two moments where his masculinity is more forcefully shifted from the conventional paradigms; in the second of these he is required to dress up respectably (in the dead husband's suit) to help Luisa out in one of her deals. In the first, on another day in the early love-making, Luisa—dressed fetishistically in a black basque—commands the prone Paco, in a famous scene, to insert into his anus a pink satin cloth (apparently Sanz's own idea—*Academia* 1996: 49), taking over when he is too inept—'qué torpe eres' (how clumsy you are)—or too coy to carry the manœuvre through. The consequent copulation is done with Luisa on top, the cloth removed by her at the moment of his climax. The scene is one where Sanz is made to masquerade as the ultimately passive male in a striking challenge to taboo. The emblematically pink cloth, how it is used, and other visual breachings of cinematic codes of masculinity—the preponderance of soft-lit close-ups of parts of the male body, for instance, or simply Sanz being looked at so much—all shift the power of the gaze from its accustomed position, that 'male norm, perspective and look' (Neale 1993: 19). Indeed, this is an 'assault on traditional forms of masculinity [while] at other levels, the whole idea of Castilian hegemony is undermined through the attack on the Church and army and their Madrid/Burgos ambience' (P. Evans 1999c: 97).

The second instance of Paco's being required by Luisa to take fabric to his flesh to further her own purposes is that of his being dressed up in the respectable garb of the dead husband's suit (a scene separated from the one just discussed by one depicting a miserable and neglected Trini in thrall to dull domestic drudgery). He is to act as signatory to the agreement of sale (to an unsuspecting provincial) of false deeds to the tobacconist's where Luisa works and whose owner is ill in hospital. Here, with the donning of the suit and Luisa's proffering to him of his share in the cash earned, Paco starts on a downward moral path through dependency on Luisa, complicity with her, shame at taking dirty money after the deal is struck, and demeaning association—for an upright young lad—with a grimy older world of crime, low-hung lights, smoke, and dark suits. Luisa's widowhood combined with the effects of the *años de hambre* have made of her a version of the fallen woman whose characteristics are summarized from various sources by Lea Jacobs (1987): she, like that classic figure of melodrama, is cast out both economically and in terms of class. Lacking a man with money by whom she might be kept she turns to both crime and a form of commonplace prostitution in her initial seduction of Paco, done as it is with half an eye on his charms and half on his potential for changing her situation for the better. Yet he too is fallen, and trammelled by similar plot lines. By attracting Luisa, his body makes him the lure rather than the alluring, an agent of desire not its protagonist; he is in his way a prostitute, a fallen man following what would be, by convention, the woman's path. Luisa's preparations of his body, unclothed and clothed, and her inclusion of him in her small world of relatively rich colour and decor represent a variant of the classic sequence of the fallen woman narrative, one 'in which the heroine is visually transformed, dressed up and surrounded by objects' (ibid. 102).

When Paco and Luisa return from the deal, and when she has given him his money, his initial indignant refusal of it is soon mitigated by Luisa's control of his body and his feelings. She insists he tell her he loves her, but infantilizes him by suggesting that his penis also talk to her; she leads him to bed, straddles him, and casts him in the double role of little boy and tantalized lover, as she sings 'La infanta Doña Eulalia | se perfuma el coño con una dalia | La Infanta Doña Isabel | se lo perfuma con un clavel . . .' (The Princess Dona Eulalia | perfumes her cunt with a dahlia | Princess Dona Annunciation | perfumes hers with a carnation). Having forced him to masturbate himself—she perches astride him at first; then, when he is undressed, makes him take hold of the penis she has already manipulated herself and bring himself to climax while her lips—as before —trace their way up his flank. Nibbling his ear she tells him in sensual detail of the physical effects he has on her and puts the third question of this session: where and how does he intend to spend Christmas Eve? When he replies, erasing the name of Trini, that he'll spend it 'como todos los años', Luisa gives him a spiteful love-bite which he will be forced to hide. His body is thus marked by a soft-core interrogation whose violence is only postponed to the film's climax. Sex—the love-bite, the scarf—marks his entrapment; the suit marks his descent into criminality; the gently enforced self-masturbation not only takes away his power in the ways that Kinder suggests, but implies an unwilling apprenticeship in a career of erotic self-exploitation. All these make his body the sign of the betrayal of the manly values of independent proactivity (his new start in life), decency (his duty to Trini and to the institution of marriage), discipline (his soldierly past), and sexual assertiveness. In his fallen role and in the role as sex object both Paco's and Sanz's performances disrupt the scopic regime, unsettle the pattern of gender power relations.

Again, however, these are performances of masculinity that allow it to reassert its normal ideological structures. Assuming his to-be-looked-at-ness gives the Sanz/Paco amalgam a certain, albeit equivocal, power not least in the amount of attention it seems to need and get from the women, the camera, and the audience. The direction of the sex scenes too presents problems for the assumption by the viewer of a gaze that is not male. Luisa's domination of Paco's body and its responses, her effective removal of the cocksureness that attaches itself to Sanz in his other cinematic roles, are by no means free of association with pornographic male fantasies. Shots of her partly dressed and him either fully dressed or completely naked draw attention away from the male to the fetishized female. Her flower song in the third of the bedroom scenes partly serves to infantilize him, but it also verges on Perfumed-Garden cliché which devalues female sexuality. Her intimate confession about the effects he has on her has strong value as a statement of female desire and self-knowledge, but it is connected, by another loving shot of his body, with the whispered question that repositions her as scheming female and allows him to snap back into assertiveness and veer back to his duty to Trini. His face hardens with this resolve, and although both their faces are in close-up two-shot, Luisa's is very slightly in the background; and when she loses the last word to him this positioning, the psychological effect, and lighting (it is Sanz's glowing complexion and sparkling eyes that gain prominence) confirm her relegation. Richard Dyer draws attention to how 'many male pin-ups counteract the passive, objectifying tendency [of their to-be-looked-at-ness] by having the model tauten his body, glare at us, or away from the viewer, and look as if he is caught in action or movement' (Dyer 1986: 117), and Paco's determination serves a similar purpose here.

A later matching scene between Paco and Trini accentuates the power of the male body to occlude female desires. In bed in her mother's home, Trini tries but fails to excite Paco who, just as he had done with Luisa, looks purposefully out of screen and out of the room's window, upper torso coolly but attractively lit. Trini is in the shadows, shut in, unable to assert her desire either with her body or through verbal seduction. These, however, she will deploy in a completely different, tragic, mode when, having followed Paco north in the half-belief that they might flee the memory and influence of Luisa, she resolves to die. The scene is well known: in the grim, wet-snow-filled square in front of the great patriarchal mass of stone and carvings that is the cathedral at Burgos, in the knowledge of Paco's continuing and exacerbated betrayal of her, she delivers a soliloquy on love, the thwarted ambitions of motherhood, and sacrifice. Handing Paco the knife on which she has been fixated for hours, rigid with cold, fear, and rebuke, she talks him into stabbing her, thus showing herself to be, as Kinder (1993: 207) observes, just as 'passionate and strong-willed' as Luisa.

Sex and death, with the looming shape of religion in the background, give Trini the power of words and make Paco a silent agent in a tragedy that is beyond his control and that belongs not to him and his story, but to the traditions of Hollywood melodrama and to Spanish dramatic traditions. Half-resonances make Trini akin to the distraught Yerma of Lorca's great play: not only does the famous Act II Scene 2 soliloquy ('¡Ay, qué prado de pena!') (García Lorca 1986: 846) (Ah, such a meadowland of pain!) suggest itself as a dramatic intertext here but so too does a reverse image of the paradoxically empowered Yerma who finds a bitter resolution to her pain in the murder of her husband, and therefore of her potential offspring (880). The terrible scene outside the cathedral is, with a certain obviousness, a version of a blood wedding, and the memorable connections made in *Bodas de sangre / Blood Wedding* (like Aranda's film, itself a reworking of a real-life drama) between knives, cold whiteness, death, and (by implication) the phallus, resound even more strongly here (798–9).

Furthermore, Kinder (1993) draws attention to the pull of another tradition in her remarks on the importance to Spanish reworkings of the Oedipal narrative of 'conventions of the Counter-Reformation [. . .] as remolded by the Fascist aesthetic' (138), a 'pictorial language of violent sensuality, spectacle, theatricality, and excess' within which 'Catholic spectators were encouraged to identify emotionally with the eroticized martyrs whom they were trained to admire and adore' (141). In this scene 'the murder retains the aura of Christian ritual, especially since the minimalist representation of violence is limited to a fetishized close-up of the victim's bare feet and a few drops of bright red blood [. . .] on the pure white snow' (208). Kinder sees Trini's plea for death as masochistic (207), as it surely is; but masochism is not passive victimhood, and the dramatic and cinematic privileging of her, the compulsion in her words, and the authority in her martyrdom, empower her. She has in effect not only taken from Luisa the power to provoke her death, but also definitively wrested from Paco his control over his own life. For all that, as P. Evans (1999*c*) argues, the disruptive treatment of and gazing on the idealized male body here, and the submission to Luisa, themselves all give Paco power—power to reject patriarchal norms, to refuse the Oedipal trajectory; he is now the mere agent of a sadistic dynamic that is partly generic (the compulsion of the thriller), partly ideological (guilt, retribution, sacrifice: the Christian edifice), and paradoxically Trini's as well as Luisa's victim. When he races off to the railway station—through the serendipitously symbolic grey slush—and shows Luisa the blood on his hands, it is as if he himself had been the victim of violence. Now it is he who must make a desperate plea to be saved, the plea that Luisa should take him back, relieve him of his guilt, and of the weight of his desire.

Trini has in common with Luisa the ability to direct and control Paco. As the overcautious virgin she at first frustrates his approaches; as the good *novia* (fiancée) she maps out his career, creating a tension between this straight path and the adventure with Luisa that has gained prime importance for him. As the pure 'mother' she shames him into acquiescence (in particular by having him participate in the pretence to her own mother that the two are married) and seems, like the women in *noir* thrillers discussed by Frank Krutnik (1991: 76–85) in relation to masculine identity, desire, and the law, to be the object of a Freudian 'pacting' and over-idealization, a process that involves the risk, here for Paco, of 'some degree of destabilization of his post-Oedipal identity as a man' (84). As Evans's arguments suggest, the strong intertext of the crime-thriller in this film is subjected to some revealing recodings as regards power relations and conventional roles. While Luisa, as a (flawed) kind of *femme fatale*, is able through the intensity of her desire and desirability to disrupt what in relation to investigative thrillers Krutnik describes as 'the linear trajectory of the hero's quest [. . .] his self-defining, male-oriented mission' (97) (in Paco's rather different case, the mission is to make good but honestly), surprisingly Trini too is empowered to shift into the strong role against which the male loses his way and plays out his masochism, his 'disavowal of his masculine identity' (102). For in turning to her, and trying to escape his already emasculating thraldom to Luisa and to crime, Paco disavows the tough and adventurous role of the real man that Luisa needs him to be and that would have been his only salvation once implicated: he disobeys the rule that there is no going back. Moreover this is a going back not just to an innocent past of *noviazgo* and conventional happy future but a going back to mother.

Sanz's role as 'Bruno', a rent-boy unwittingly involved in a murder, then murdered himself, in the contemporary urban thriller *Hotel y domicilio* (In Calls and Out) (Ernesto del Río, 1995) once again constructs him as the passive male caught up in an economy of need. In contrast to the festive explorations of the issues surrounding men paid to perform sex roles for other men in *Boca a boca / Mouth to Mouth* (see Ch. 4) this is a sombre film whose slow pace leaves room for the desperation and lone-liness of the main characters to grow. There is more scope here than in *Lovers*—with its presuppositions about the power of the *femme fatale* over the younger man—for Sanz to seek ways of playing out motivation. In his relations with lonely, middle-aged police forensic pathologist Ángel, Bruno's transition from the self-assurance and shiny body-hugging clothes of the high-class prostitute to emotional dependency and slop-ping around his flat are predicated on a past abusive relationship with corrupt ex-policeman pimp Guillermo. Bruno is, furthermore, in psy-chotherapy with a friend of Ángel's and the film is interspersed with sessions and their taped content in voice-over or, at the end, diagetically. The psychosexual situation between these men is a relatively complex and perverse one.

When Guillermo reappears from jail to claim Bruno and threaten Ángel—whom he refers to as 'mamá', while he is 'papá' to the 'muñeco' (doll) Bruno—Sanz convincingly and subtly plays the signs of abject sex slave, acceding with quietly repressed horror to Guillermo's insistence, on their re-encounter in the warehouse where Guillermo is night secur-ity man, that he slowly eat from the end of a thick baguette—Guillermo's supper—and recognize the inevitability of his return, again explicitly, to 'papá'. Sanz nicely underplays the disgust and reluctance of the forced eating scene while exaggerating to considerable dramatic effect Bruno's trance-like subsequent approach to Guillermo and his falling to his knees in front of his crotch. It is this intolerable scene that precipitates the crisis anticipated by the film's early insistence on images of bodies laid out in the morgue. Ángel, who has been watching, like us, from out-side the warehouse, breaks in, confronts Guillermo, and, in the scuffle throws him to a lower floor, killing him. The disposal of his body and the need for secrecy is then the cause of a further crisis: Bruno's already manifest dependency on Ángel and his bored, lonely hours in his flat become enforced curfew; he decides to flout this, putting them both at risk of discovery, and in an argument Ángel once again commits unpremeditated murder, sending Bruno's head flying against the corner of a table then taking the decision to asphyxiate him while he is unconscious. This death reads not so much as the conventional narrative punishment of the homosexual as the (equally conventional) violent disposal, in film noir and violence movies, of the kept woman who has grown inconvenient. Bruno's pre-killing frustration at periods of abandonment by Ángel ('you could have rung me') turns first to desperate need for company ('don't leave me; I can't stay cooped up here') then spunky revenge ('now you can't get away from me') and defiance ('go on, hit me'). An image of him preparing to break free of the home further aligns him with the conventions of the drama of heterosexual couple dysfunction and with the woman's role: he irons his best flashy shirt at the window, after an American Gigolo-esque bout of home exercise that equates not only to getting made up to go out but also to the reassignment of his body as available to other men as spectacle and commodity. He is out to get laid, perhaps to get paid, and to put false monogamy behind him. He is asking for trouble. And like Juan in *Law of Desire*, he ends up first on the rocks at the foot of the cliffs, and then on the slab.

Comic effects

'Men will always be men, no matter how they are represented, no matter who is looking at them.' This is how Naomi Salaman (1994: 21) summarizes what she calls the 'rigid classical position' taken up by art historians Griselda Pollock and Rozika Parker in their study *Old Mistresses*, a position from which 'men cannot be imagined without their power'. My own arguments about Jorge Sanz's body as spectacle could be led towards a similarly rigid position, of course. The extreme eroticization of Sanz in Aranda's movie, and his narcissistic, troubled victim status and sexual availability in *Hotel y domicilio* are underpinned and safeguarded by the contexts of Aranda's gruffly unreconstructed-male œuvre, the 'masculine' generic context of del Río's film, and by other performances by Sanz that are emphatically heterosexist in their assumptions, especially in the comedies *¿Por qué lo llaman amor cuando quieren decir sexo?* (Why Do They Call it Love when They Mean Sex?) (Manuel Gómez Pereira, 1992), *Tocando fondo* (Rock Bottom) (José Luis Cuerda, 1993), *Los peores años de nuestra vida* / *The Worst Years of Our Lives* (Emilio Martínez-Lázaro, 1994), and *Cha cha chá* (Antonio del Real, 1998), where his character Pablo cruises nonchalantly, with minimal emotional labour, through romantic complication and infidelity only to end up with the same girlfriend as he started out with since, in his erstwhile suitor Lucía's phrase, 'en el fondo es un blando', (deep down he's just too wishy-washy). Like Arias, but to a greater degree, Sanz is involved in the high comic deflation yet reaffirmation of masculine stereotypes and fantasies, and of patriarchal prohibitions. While he takes a full role in the marked tendency in Spanish cinema of the period (and in Hollywood—Lehman 1993: 105–29, 107) to undermine through comedy traditional masculine values, attributes, and behaviours, taking on ostentatiously vulnerable roles (Jordan and Morgan-Tamosunas 1998: 140–1), the balance of his career is none the less towards a nostalgic reclamation of laddishness or towards the representation of a pitiably damaged masculinity which—leavened by comedy and absurdity—sidesteps the uneasy ambiguities of sado-masochistic, spectatorial engagement with the loss (and therefore the presence) of heroic masculinities (Willemen 1981; Neale 1993: 10–15; Tasker 1993: 236–8). If there is disempowerment it is soon brushed off, laughed off, and spruced up; the eroticism is unmanned.

On television too, conveniently temporary disempowerment is explored in low-key mode in Telemadrid's *Colegio Mayor* (Living on Campus) (1993; into a second series in 1994–5)[5] which is built on the earlier *Segunda enseñanza* (Secondary School). Here Sanz plays Ángel, living in mixed-sex Halls of Residence (with Antonio Resines as a wry, bewildered, incompetent Warden), wearing cut-off bomber jackets over T-shirts, sporting pointed sideburns, being hit on by the women, and staying one step ahead of most of the men through the exercise of charm and cunning. This, following comic convention, is seen through and exploited repeatedly by the women, however. In Episode 10, 'Hombres, sólo hombres' (Men, and Men Only), they enlist his help in coaxing all the men in the Hall to pose nude for an exhibition of photography in a 'cultural event' they are planning, on the understanding that he himself will not have to take part. In the end they trick him (he is their real object of interest) into the same position by a blindfolded seduction, giving the lie to his trademark mantra in the episode: 'confía en mi experiencia' (trust me, I know what I'm doing). In Episode 12, 'Nadie es perfecto' (Nobody's Perfect) his *macho* charm faces a (temporary) challenge as he finds himself the not entirely uncooperative object of the insistent attentions of a tall American who has been brought in to boost the basket-ball team's performance. He soon discovers that this tall 'man' is in fact a woman, but the rest of the Hall know only at the end; and

[5] Bought back by TVE with ETB and a consortium of private stations, notably Canal Sur.

for the duration of the episode they have a queer view of Ángel. The self-assured but relieved 'yo sólo gusto a mujeres: es una cuestión de química' (I'm only attractive to women, it's a chemistry thing) scripted for him in the closing scene of the episode is a nice tease that reasserts but lightly disturbs his straightness (and an interesting out-take from rehearsals is tagged on showing him fluffing the lines, clearly anxious).

In this sense virility as represented in Sanz's performances resurfaces unscathed from that earlier melodrama of extreme passion and objectification. The comic roles which dominate Sanz's early- to mid-1990s career domesticate but do not disturb masculinity. The only extremity here is that of farce; by ridiculing *machista* assumptions and pretensions within the safe bounds of convention, in these roles all the failings and insensitivities of types of men are gently accepted and the usual false set of bipolar gender characteristics are redeployed. In *Tocando fondo* Sanz plays Fulgencio, a lower-middle class Madrid youth in his early twenties who drifts into his weak-willed and commercially incompetent uncle's warehousing firm, run on old-fashioned patriarchal lines (and employing a bumbling foreman played by Manuel Alexandre, providing a continuity of association back to *El año de las luces*). The film's flimsily sustained social context is that of the economic downturn of the early 1990s and spiralling unemployment in Spain. The descent to rock bottom of Fulgencio's uncle Andrés (Antonio Resines: Sanz's usual comic sparring partner) is metonymic of the same downward development in matters of certain conventionally 'masculine' competencies (maintaining a family, a marriage, a business). Andrés himself starts off quite far down, and stays at the level of goofy, pretty, and useless young male. He admires his put-upon girlfriend's ability to cook, but with subconsciously learned helplessness cannot even manage an omelette himself; in one sex scene he has drunk too much to get an erection and has to plead to see and clumsily massage her breasts by way of (ineffective) stimulant; in another, overcome by lust in the veterinary surgery where she quietly carries on a competent career, he has to be told what to do (slow down and calm down) and in what position (with her on top). Obviously enough, on the one occasion he witnesses her professional skills she is engaged in a routine castration of a tomcat with which he queasily identifies as she snips. He is, then, vulnerable, more creature than person; propelled but not refined by his manly desires; weak, over-eager, chirpy, yet slow: indeed, '*torpe*'—slow, clumsy, unsophisticated—is, we recall, an epithet thrown at Sanz's character by Victoria Abril's in *Lovers* in a key sex scene, and it blossoms out to surround many of his roles (and, some opine, his performances too).

Much of the pleasure offered by *Belle Époque*—winning the Oscar for best Foreign Language Film 1993—is derived from the represented clumsiness of youthful masculine desire and self-delusion, and the simple, well-tried formula of quick-witted woman versus dim-witted male is given multiple perspective as the lucky innocent Fernando (Sanz) finds himself in hog heaven as the lad who gets laid by four sisters of differing temperament. In this film, Sanz is once more required to develop a character who has just left the institution of military service and there are mild subversions of laws military, political, religious, and moral, underlying the ludic sexuality that is the key note. He sheds his uniform and all it signifies from the moment at the start of the film when he is caught at the roadside by two passing Civil Guards with his trousers archetypically down; later he finds himself dressed up as a maid and seduced by a woman cross-dressed as a soldier; the performativity of masculinity and the interchangeability of some of its classic roles and accoutrements are to the fore. The controlling generic contexts of the film are carnival, musical and romantic comedy, comedies of errors, and the cinema of nostalgia. As Jordan and Morgan-Tamosunas (1998: 58) have observed 'despite the sobering note of the deaths which open and close the film, *Belle Epoque* remains as somewhat uncritical, indulgent celebration of a mythic libertarian Republican Spain', anachronistically tinged by alternative political ideas—or, rather, ideals—of the 1960s to the 1990s (Jordan 1999: 148–51; also Pagés 1993); and Fernando's association with the worldly-wise, anise-pickled, pinko-anarchist painter Manolo (Fernando Fernán Gómez) and his four daughters is equally easy on its sexual politics.

It is, however, precisely this entertaining yet irritating ease that blurs the edges of virility and allows sceptical filmgoers to adjust their gaze without forfeiting the possible initial pleasures of spectacle and fun. The first encounter with Manolo (Fernán Gómez, a living compendium of bluff manliness on the Spanish screen) is rich in this sort of potential. Invited to share a bed with Manolo (the house is chilly) Fernando, ridiculously enough, needs assurance that he is not a *maricón* (queer). Against the camp aural backdrop of Manolo's wife Amalia's singing *zarzuela* (light opera) on the phonograph, Fernando is assured that Manolo is not, and is furthermore incapable of being, unfaithful to Amalia (a reprise of an earlier gag on the mismatch of anarchist, atheist credentials and bourgeois sexual mores). With Amalia's voice replaced by the non-diagetic accompaniment of some of the lighter passages of Antoine Duhamel's theme music (in comic contrast to solemn patriarchal words from Ecclesiastes on death and the destiny of the soul, read out by Fernando to help Manolo to sleep), Fernando moves across the room to a mirror to which the photos of the four daughters are stuck, and with a pulling into soft focus of his low-lit face against a dark ground in the style of classic portraiture, he appears reflected alongside these images, then displaces them as there is a fade to black (and a decrescendo and cessation of the music) during which his image is the last to disappear. Even though his masculinity is safeguarded in the exchange over the bed-sharing, the wash of music and the equation of his with other pretty features make his cocky image fragile in a way that the rest of the film will exploit (through multiple seductions, deceptions and misunderstandings, and his being dressed up for carnival, petted, and teased).

When the voice of the absent Amalia (Mari-Carmen Ramírez) is heard again later on, this time as internally diagetic, another visual and auditory framing becomes apparent: Fernando, the four sisters, and Manolo too, are equal spectators and protagonists in a musical Arcadian interlude of their own. Amalia mounts the steps in the early morning sunshine, to announce her return from her tour of performances, and, with charmingly obvious pertinence, breaks into the alluring *zarzuela* number 'En un país de fábula' (In a Fabled Land).[6] The camera moves out from her and cranes up, and the shot switches back 180° to take in the whole façade of the house. All the onlookers are framed, enchanted, humming along, in the windows, which are both boxes in a theatre and platforms for them as a chorus of performers. That Fernando is the last to be dwelt on in the sequence, and the last to dwell on the scene, implicates him especially in the sentimentality, the melody, and the heavily coded femininity of it all. In such an excessive world, problems of sexual politics and desire become problematically unproblematic (as the gag about Manolo's fidelity at once suggests, there are close limits to the radical).

Sanz is able to participate in some overt gender bending which troubles a whole series of status quos only for the system to wobble back into place at the end, with little irregularities pardoned if wistfully left behind. Fernando falls for all the girls, but especially for Violeta, who is lesbian (or, as Manolo puts it, 'un hombre'), a fact never named as such but accepted festively and nonchalantly by all save Fernando. In sequences set on the day before *domingo de carnaval* (Carnival Sunday) and on the evening of the day itself we see Sanz's body once more in submission. Over the 36-hour period Fernando is twice flung down and made to lie on his back; and between these instances of comic and perhaps touching vulnerability, he is subjected to a very thorough festive

---

[6] From *La tabernera del puerto* by Pablo Sorozabel, Guillermo Fernández Shaw, and Federico Romero.

inversion. Fernando, fondly watched by women's eyes, is mocked as well as appreciated for his sudden prettiness and subordination. Dressed up as a maid and urged to dance with Violeta, he declares 'me da mucha vergüenza'. Sanz's own sense of awkwardness comes through nicely too in his adoption of a waddling gait to disavow effeminateness in the manner of the Tony Curtis of *Some Like It Hot* (pictorially illustrated and briefly elaborated on in *Fotogramas* 1993).

But it is the awkwardness—the queerness—that wins out in the end. Violeta's own cross-dressing and the at least double-edged humour of the seduction and domination scenes (her straddling him in the barn after the dancing, bugle to her lips, just one step ahead of his hurried climax— one of a series of poor sexual performances from him), point up the performativity of gender. For a while the male body and its desires and suppositions are inverted; but the main joke depends on the normalization of heterosexuality, on the charming (and beautifully lit) flightiness of women, on the feminine sex-appeal of the stars, on the worldliness of the older male star, Fernán Gómez, and the magnetism and power to trouble that the younger man possesses. In the end the unsurprising message is that a man may not marry a 'man' (Violeta, that is) and Fernando marries one of the other sisters and leaves the village utopia. Over and above this too, as Butler (1993: 231) observes, 'heterosexuality can augment its hegemony through its denaturalization, as when we see denaturalizing parodies that reidealize heterosexual norms without calling them into question'. The after-image of Jorge on his back, in high heels, made a handsome fool of, is seductive and amusing but its subversive image fights in vain for supremacy with the normalizing jokiness that sustains much of the film and with heterosexuality's own hegemonic safety net.

The performer

Sanz's body is the site and focus of *Belle Époque*'s festive inversions and potential subversions of systems of desire, control, power, authority. In *Lovers* it is the site of melodramatic conflicts and stagings of erotic desire that negate—or for P. Evans (1999*c*) redirect—the conventionally masculine. In both films, however, Sanz's success in the portrayal of lost virility gains him more desirability as a star. Spectacle, masochism, passivity, and masquerade (Cohan and Rae Hark 1993*b*: 3), when located in this particular star's body and performance in these two quite different generic contexts are seen only just at the moment when they are retreating timidly back into the shell of laddish wholesomeness. What is interesting about Sanz in this regard, however, is the insistence with which he is asked to or chooses to return to this liminal place. In common with Banderas, Bardem, and—as we shall see when I return briefly to *Cha cha chá* in the next chapter—Noriega, Sanz is drawn to performing the role of performer, in his case three times: in *Orquesta Club Virginia* (The Virginia Club Band: Manuel Iborra, 1991), *¿Por qué lo llaman amor . . . ?* (1992), and *La niña de tus ojos / The Girl of Your Dreams* (Trueba, 1998);[7] and as with those other actors this double performance highlights aspects of masculinity's trouble with differentiating itself from its other. All three films—characteristically for Sanz roles, *Hotel y domicilio* excepted —make deceptively festive capital out of a homophobia that rises to the surface when Sanz's character finds himself in some extreme situation that is demanded of him as performer.

In *Orquesta Club Virginia* he plays the acoustic guitarist but all-rounder son of the eponymous band's manager (Resines) on tour with the musicians in the Near East, and in lust with Emma Suárez—like Carmelo Gómez's Ángel four years later—who plays a laid-back ur-hippy, with her own band too. Though she openly admires his 'buen culito' (nice little bum), in its period crushed-velvet trousers, and tries to seduce him into her open view of sex, he is too uptight. But one night he ends up dancing in the arms of a queer club-owner who will not take no for an answer, and this provokes a homophobic outburst ('what are we: musicians or sluts?') generating anger directed at his fellow band members (who have sat back and let it happen) and motivated by another set of masculine insecurities altogether. This is compounded of his inability—despite his own long hair and devotion to the Beatles—to swing María's way; his emotional and sexual disadvantage in relation to his father's contemporary, the fast-living and self-destructive El Negro who gets María; and his failure to live up to a vaguely defined half-reactionary macho, half-liberatory progressive code of musicianship (as relayed to him by El Negro himself) that is also vaguely (as the script avows) linked to Spanishness.

---

[7] It seems, from reports and reviews, that Xavier Villaverde's *Continental* (1989)—where Sanz plays a drug dealer—also has at its centre a performance venue (here doubling as a brothel); but this is one of the handful of earlier films in my range, copies of which I was not able to track down in time. Similarly, though for different reasons (the gap between cinema and video release), I failed to see *Almejas y mejillones* (Clams and Mussels) (Marcos Carnevale, 2000). Here Sanz's cross-dressing, inspired by the spirit of the carnival on Tenerife, in order to win the affections of a woman who has recently decided she is lesbian, as well as a gay sub-plot, may well have been pertinent to the interests of this book (although the film was not at all well received, despite the always arresting presence of the actress Silke). There is a semi-official website at http://www.epu21.com/2000/pattagonik/htm/almejas.htm and images of Sanz in drag at http://members.es.tripod.de/silke/himagen/imagfi07.htm (21 Dec. 2001).

In *¿Por qué lo llaman amor . . . ?* Sanz's character, Manu, finds himself persuaded to fill in as part of a double act at the Sex Shop
Hollywood (with Veronica Forqué), advertised by the billboard man
outside as 'typically Espanish porno show [. . .] bellisima ragazza y
macho hispánico'. This involves Manu dressing up in rubberwear;
being catcalled by the other women performers; being gently mocked
for being short; dancing and having sex while watched through portals
by masturbating men; and, in rehearsal, ejaculating prematurely—
'¡piensa que son cuatro pases por noche, chaval!' (Careful sweetheart!
It's four shows a night you know!) is his partner's rebuke, delivered with
Forqué's customary (indeed, automatic pilot) mix of deadpan and outrage. The man he is standing in for is gay, and Manu feels the need to
explain that he himself is not, but is instead 'buena gente' (a decent bloke),
a claim contradicted by the requirements of classically masculine cinematic predicament that he is in (he is involved with a gang of (male) crooks,
owes them thousands, and has to gamble away the wedding money—
inevitably he and Forqué fall in love—to try to repay them). Two slaps
to the face then contribute to his emasculation: one which he gives her
in response to her angry accusation that 'te falta un cojón' (you're only
half a man (lit. you've only got one ball)) and for which he receives the
further rebuke 'y eso que has hecho te hace menos hombre todavía' (and
what you've just done makes you even less of a man still); the other
he gets from his father, which is to say, from the patriarchal family
(played for laughs here: the father is a professor of sexual psychology
at Salamanca; the mother a caricature schemer and interferer). So,
the sex show becomes an arena for the shaming of cocky behaviour;
Manu has little sexual prowess and—until the bitter-sweet ending—less
emotional integrity; and the typically 'macho hispánico', as advertised,
is enjoyably punished in a set of scenarios which associate Sanz with a
somewhat equivocal urge to use his eroticized body on the one hand and
his gift for looking and speaking laddish on the other to make coarse
but constant little incursions into the fragility of the categorizations of
masculinity.

When in *La niña de tus ojos*—in which a troupe of actors are invited
in 1938 by Goebbels to film a typically Spanish musical as an aid to
cordial Francoist–Nazi relations—Sanz's character, Julián Torralba, is
mistakenly taken off to a prison camp and severely beaten up, his
transgressions again have both an intra- and an extra-diagetic dimension. Having translated his on-set Don Juanism into action with the ambas-
sador's wife he is surprised in the act; in fleeing he is confused with an
escaped Jewish prisoner of war; and thus gets a beating not designed
for him but almost deserved by him. Beyond the plot, though, again

the punishment is for an excess of masculine idealization: Torralba is repugnantly insensitive to the women around him; he is panicked when the Aryan hunk assigned to play next to him takes a shine to him and, as in so many Sanz roles, has to make much of distancing himself from the possibility of homosexuality. In the end, despite (and because of) the panache of bandana and moustache (sported, for example, on the main publicity poster), the performance of masculinity is a sham, and a damaging one. Here we are far distant from the carefree, unproblematic 'niño mimado del cine español'[8] (spoiled child of Spanish cinema) which until recently was Sanz's dominant image. Indeed, although behind each spoiled man-child there is a complex set of gender power relations and usually trouble in store.

---

[8] The characteristic title of an interview in a popular TV and cinema listings magazine *Antena Semanal* (30 April 1995).

TABLE 6. *Filmography*

Year	Title	English title(s) (official in italics; literal in roman)	Director	Billing	Audience figures and takings	Other information
1979	*La miel*	Honey	Pedro Masó	6th	902,598 €740,304	Child role
1980	*El canto de la cigarra*	The Song of the Cricket	José María Forqué	Minor	203,138 €187,854	Child role
1980	*Dos y dos, cinco*	Two and Two Makes Five	Lluís Josep Comerón	9th	185,146 €156,122	Co-pro Spain, Mexico
1980	*Los locos vecinos del 2°*	Those Crazy Neighbours on the Second Floor	Juan Bosch	10th	427,737 €362,925	Child role
1981	*Dos pillos y pico*	Two and a Bit Kids	Ignacio Iquino	6th	105,174 €84,932	
1981	*Leyenda del tambor*	The Legend of the Drum	Jordi Grau	Minor	106,628 €113,206	Co-pro Spain, Mexico; Child role
1981	*La rebelión de los pájaros*	The Birds' Rebellion	Lluís Josep Comerón	2nd	297,983 €405,290	Child role
1982	*Mar brava*	Rough Seas	Angelino Fons	2nd	13,558 €14,430	Co-pro Spain, Mexico
1982	*Valentina*		Antonio Betancor	Top	752,917 €1,026,945	Child role

TABLE 6. (*continued*)

Year	Title	English title(s) (official in italics; literal in Roman)	Director	Billing	Audience figures and takings	Other information
1983	*Vivir mañana*	Living for Tomorrow	Nino Quevedo	10th	36,000 €46,416	Child role
1984	*Dos mejor que uno*	Two is Better than One	Ángel Llorente	Minor	52,586 €81,894	Child role
1985	*Mambrú se fue a la guerra*	Mambrú [Marlborough] Went to War	Fernando Fernán Gómez	6th	80,014 €153,974	
1986	*El año de las luces*	*The Year of Enlightenment / The Year of Awakening*	Fernando Trueba	Top	754,011 €1,334,769	
1987	*Gallego*	The Spanish Immigrant	Manuel Octavio Gómez	2nd	66,236 €124,856	Co-pro Spain, Cuba
1988	*El Lute II: Mañana seré libre*	El Lute II: Tomorrow I'll Be Free	Vicente Aranda	3rd	382,764 €681,131	
1989	*Si te dicen que caí*	*If They Tell You I Fell*	Vicente Aranda	2nd	340,702 €700,184	Goya and Fotogramas de Plata, Best Actor
1990	*Continental*		Xavier Villaverde	2nd	103,994 €163,629	
1990	*Monte bajo*	The Foothills	Julián Esteban	2nd	13,567 €26,608	

Year	Title (Spanish)	Title (English)	Director	Ranking	Box office	Notes
1990	Tramontana/Tramuntana	From Across the Mountains	Carlos Pérez Ferré	Top	6,749 €16,171	
1991	Amantes	Lovers / Lovers, A True Story	Vicente Aranda	2nd	697,368 €1,723,766	Fotogramas de Plata, Best Actor
1991	Orquesta Club Virginia	The Virginia Club Band	Manuel Iborra	Top	261,606 €648,695	
1992	Belle Époque		Fernando Trueba	10th	1,817,999 €5,108,652	
1993	¿Por qué lo llaman amor cuando quieren decir sexo?	Why Do They Say Love When They Mean Sex?	Manuel Gómez Pereira	2nd	721,947 €2,004,968	
1993	Tocando fondo	Touching Rock Bottom	José Luis Cuerda	2nd	173,802 €415,529	
1994	Los peores años de nuestra vida	The Worst Years of Our Lives	Emilo Martínez Lázaro	3rd	723,677 €2,157,329	
1995	Morirás en Chafarinas	You'll Die in Xafarinas	Pedro Olea	Top	111,522 €319,058	
1995	Hotel y domicilio	In Calls and Out	Ernesto del Río	Top	77,071 €218,380	
1996	Libertarias	Freedomfighters	Vicente Aranda	4th	594,978 €1,907,592	Co-pro Spain, Italy, Belgium
1996	¿De qué se ríen las mujeres?	What Makes Women Laugh?	Joaquín Oristrel	9th	333,079 €1,075,489	
1997	Torrente, el brazo tonto de la ley	Torrente, the Stupid Arm of the Law	Santiago Segura	Minor	3,010,664 €10,902,560	
1998	Manos de seda	Hands of Silk	César Martínez Herrada	Top	48,927 €181,067	

TABLE 6. (*continued*)

Year	Title	English title(s) (official in italics; literal in Roman)	Director	Billing	Audience figures and takings	Other information
1998	*Cha cha chá*		Antonio Real	4th	855,715 €3,036,142	
1998	*La niña de tus ojos*	*The Girl of Your Dreams*	Fernando Trueba	8th	2,497,759 €9,473,747	
1999	*Cuba*		Pedro Carvajal	7th	No figures available	Co-pro Spain-Cuba
1999	*Paris–Tomboctú*	*Paris–Timbuktu*	Luis García Berlanga	Minor	407,408 €1,580,734	
1999	*Pepe Guindo*		Manuel Iborra	Minor	45,586 €181,028	
2000	*Almejas y mejillones*	*Clams and Mussels*	Marcos Carnevale	1st	332,032 €1,332,694	Co-pro Spain, Argentina
2001	*Sin vergüenza*	*Shameless*	Joaquín Oristrell	7th	233,182 €1,046,156	
2001	*Tuno negro*	*Band of Killers*	Pedro Luis Barbero and Vicente J. Martín	2nd	571,976 €2,273,073	
2001	*I Love You Baby*		Alfonso Albacete and David Menke	Top	114,033 €491,134	
2001	*Clara y Elena*	*Clara and Elena*	Manuel Iborra	2nd	147,140 €632,347	

Television series

Segunda enseñanza (Secondary School) 1986, TVE
Colegio Mayor (Living on Campus) 1993 Telemadrid; 1995, TVE
A las once en casa (Home by Eleven) 1998, TVE

Serialized films for television

La forja de un rebelde (The Forging of a Rebel) (Mario Camus, 1990)
Los jinetes de Alba (Riders of the Dawn) (Vicente Aranda, 1990)

Shorts

Sé que estas ahí (I Know You're There) (Miguel Angel Fernández, 1989)
Chihuahua (Oscar Aibar, 1991)
Evilio (Santiago Segura, 1992)
Hora final (Last Hour) (Julio del Álamo, 1992)
El nacimiento de un imperio (The Birth of an Empire) (Josep M. Borrell, 1997)

English-language productions

Conan the Barbarian (John Milius, 1982)
A Further Gesture, aka *The Break* (Robert Dornhelm, 1996)
The Garden of Redemption (Thomas Michael Donnelly, 1997) (made for television)

Fig. 14. Eduardo Noriega in *Abre los ojos*.

Fig. 15. Fele Martínez and Ana Risueño in *Lágrimas negras*.

7 A Newer Generation

Preamble

The late 1990s saw a considerable promotion of new film acting and a sudden growth of interest in potential stars as the prime producers of meanings for audiences of contemporary Spanish films (*Fotogramas* 1994*b*; Castellano and Costa 1995). This came in the wake of the Almodóvar phenomenon, and in a context of rising numbers of multi-plexes and ticket sales, and big multimedia distribution and exhibition deals (Jordan and Morgan-Tamosunas 1998: 206). In annual upbeat reviews of the state of Spanish cinema in the glossy press, the names of the new wave of directors (as partly represented below) are linked to the fame and faces of their actors in a widespread fashion, and the industry is increasingly dependent on key producers (*Fotogramas* 2000). The public interest, however, is more in groups and generations (that concept so beloved of the Romance languages) of actors than in individuals, at least where film magazines and publicity are concerned (the more general celebrity glossies, leisure, youth, and lesbian and gay magazines continue to idolize the actors one by one).[1] There was already, in the 1990s, a growing sense that the new wave of young actors (and directors), considered collectively, was becoming established as a necessary challenge to a commercially successful Spanish cinema that had become too restricted to films repeatedly casting just a handful of actors in varying combinations: Victoria Abril and Imanol Arias in *A solas contigo*, Abril and Jorge Sanz in *Lovers*, Penélope Cruz and Sanz in *Belle Époque*, Cruz and Bardem in *Jamón, jamón* (1992), Abril and Arias in *Intruso* (1993), and so on. However, certain key names have already started to emerge—partly owing to the introduction to the Spanish industry of

---

[1] It is characteristic that one of the many photo-essays on the subject, in *Fotogramas*, 1,845 (July 1997): 82–8, features three of the actors in prominent position top right opposite the title, arms around one another, and allowing a group dynamic to sweep diagonally down across the whole montage (82). The dynamic is enhanced by the fact that all those featured are in swimwear— Eduardo Noriega barely so (85)—as if all on holiday together. In *Fotogramas*, 1,880 (Aug. 2000) a review of the past year's features shows this to be a consistent strategy (in this particular issue all are dressed in white on the feature's main page). Similarly, half the actors featured as a new Generation Y in Asúa (1998) are posed in pairs.

Fig. 16. Juan Diego Botto and Penelope Cruz in *La Celestina*.

the widespread use of the casting director from the mid-1990s (Castilla 1996). What is more, these have emerged in the same sorts of combinations of twos and threes as had been so successful before: Fele Martínez with Najwa Nimri and Nancho Novo in *Los amantes del círculo polar*; Juan Diego Botto with Cruz in *La Celestina* (all discussed below); Eduardo Noriega with Mollà (also see below). Alternatively they have played moderately prominent roles alongside the bigger stars; Javier Albalà alongside Mollà, Bardem, and Ariadna Gil in *Second Skin*; Liberto Rabal with Bardem in *Live Flesh*. Some of these actors are still caught up in the business of being 'heroes for the under-thirties: life-style stars' (Walker 1970: 333), but others have already shared top billing in major films with a wider target audience. One in particular, Eduardo Noriega, has rapidly overtaken Mollà since this book was started and has become a bankable star with an increasingly international, mainstream reputation.

Eduardo Noriega (b. 1973)

Noriega was born in green and wealthy Santander in the North of Spain—where he began a short career at drama school—and brought to a much publicized new wave of film acting talent in Spain in the 1990s a number of rather posh qualities that went against a significant trend towards gritty youth, drugs, and violence movies (Allinson 1997), against the ever-rising and amazingly lucrative tide of sex comedies, and against the slightly prior subtradition of films parodying *machismo* (notably those by Bigas Luna). In his early roles he brings to the screen and glossy pages a preppy, safe-looking sexiness, a rich-kid aura, and a crystalline received pronunciation (instrumental in Almodóvar's turning him down for the role of Víctor in *Live Flesh*). Madrid-based Alejandro Amenábar— now famous beyond Spain for *The Others* (2001)—is generally credited with launching Noriega (then briefly at drama school in Madrid) as a key new iconic, handsome lead[2] in first feature *Tesis / Thesis* (1995)—a stark, campus-set psychological thriller with snuff-movies its subject matter—which soon gained cult status, especially among 20-something cinema-goers. His second feature film, *Abre los ojos / Open Your Eyes* (1997) draws on a wide range of film intertexts centred on the wounded male hero (from the disfigured to those trapped in apocalyptic, science-fictional time-shifts).

Noriega plays this film's initially handsome, womanizing protagonist, César, a man who is apparently disfigured in a car crash that propels him into a waking nightmare of narrative Chinese boxes in which he never knows which reality he has awakened to. A social services psychiatrist, assigned to César in the prison where he is (again, apparently) being held on a charge of murder, tries to coax out of him a meaningful therapeutic and justificatory account of what has happened. The story involves the callously *machista* stealing of the virginal and lovely Sofía (Penélope Cruz: another of the film's powerful popular attractions) from his normal-laddish best friend Pelayo (Fele Martínez, to whom I shall be returning) and the bewildering interchangeability, subsequently, of Sofía and a vampish and destructive Nuria (Najwa Nimri). It also involves César's quest for a return to him of his lost good looks by advanced surgery and the use of a prosthetic face, much focused upon as an ironically overdetermined sign of the unreliability of appearances (and by extension of looks and images). What appears to resolve the plot is a version of reality in which César is in fact 'living' in an unstable dream in the mid-twenty-first century, in thrall to the ultimate in consumer products: an extended, virtual life. By representing the destruction of César's looks in the context of a shining hypermodern Madrid it constructs a critique of cinema's marketing of good looks and society's consumption of this dream, much as *Tesis* had offered a critique of the film industry before (Allinson 1997: 327); and by presenting a newly scarified image of Noriega it heightens by contrast the usual pleasure in his looks.

[2] See Ponga 1999; *El País (Semanal)*, 23 Nov. 1997: 86; *Acción*, 92 (June 2000): 33.

In amongst the wreckage of César's identity, and pivoted about the destruction of his sex appeal, lies his shattered sense of self-worth as an unreconstructed, if modern, newish male. He takes pride in his appearance, wealth, car, and pulling power; he has a cocksure competitive streak; an embedded set of problems around his dead parents (orphanhood providing a biographical cross-match to Noriega himself) is revealed in therapy sessions where the psychiatrist (Chete Lera) soon begins to stand in for that father; and there is an extended intertextual linkage to Hitchcock's *Vertigo* around the Nuria/Sofía exchange, and that film's own deconstructions of masculine integrity (Perriam forthcoming). All these features link Noriega to the new tradition of 'framed' men and to critiques of modes of masculinity such as those explored by Jordan and Morgan-Tamosunas (1998: 140–54); in particular they link him with suggestions of a return of the threat of woman as other (146–7). Here, however, this older style of representation is interestingly combined with the parallel presentation of a male identity thwarted in its attempt to coalesce around its own attraction to and recoil from the monstrous feminine and informed by a new sensitivity to the futility of goal-oriented and competitive behaviours, as well as attuned to the values of community, emotional commitment, and deep self-knowledge.

In the commercially very successful *Nadie conoce a nadie* (1999) (discussed in relation to Mollà in Ch. 5) Noriega is also placed in an extreme position where radical re-evaluations have to be undertaken. More explicitly than in *Open Your Eyes*, he plays the classic cinema figure of the (relatively) innocent individual caught up in the revelation and playing-out of horrors that break the frame of reality and force the hitherto self-absorbed male protagonist to identify and engage with others' suffering, and with issues of social import. The film's setting in Seville in Holy Week—'bolt[ing] an ultra-Spanish body onto a Hollywood-inspired chassis' (Holland 1999)—gives it, as previously suggested, a range of nation- and region-specific reference. It is of obvious significance that the crucial moments of violence in Sapo's game of terror should be directed against time-honoured traditions and beliefs (the processions of Seville's Holy Week and their inescapable connections with the right wing, its past, and its money). Spanish audiences will also have been quick to see a critique of the more recent idolatries that were the Expo 92 celebrations and constructions at Seville (with their connections to the new 'socialists'; the 'New Spain'; and, eventually, corruption and the end of an era). But in particular it is targeted at a youth audience through its premise of the electronically facilitated role-play game that turns 'real', and its use of Noriega. While there is scope for horrified identification with Mollà's rebel character, Noriega invites stronger and more various identifications: socially with the young man in crisis; sympathetically and erotically with the beautiful body threatened by imprisonment, coercion, and exhaustion; intellectually and dramatically with the man who becomes the unwilling witness to violence and the confessor to the psychopathic perpetrator of it. Noriega here plays the man who stands in for us, taking the blows, focalizing our own fearful gaze.

In the co-production *Plata quemada* / *Burning Money* directed by Argentinian Marcelo Piñeyro (2000) (based on the main crime story that underpins Ricardo Piglia's complex novel of the same name), it is Noriega who plays the disturbed and criminal young man confronting a world opposed. Whereas in *Nadie conoce a nadie* institutionalized superstition, through Sapo's eyes, acts as a stupefacient, here (as his name rather obviously suggests) Ángel is inspired by an extreme interpretation of Catholic personal morality, and paradoxically driven to sin. The film is an old-fashioned romanticization of violence and crime in one aspect— Ángel and his lover-cum-brother substitute El Nene (Leonardo Sbaraglia) are bank robbers whose actions map onto hazy political opposition to authority (and particularly the political regimes of the River Plate region in the 1970s)—but it is also what Alfeo Álvarez (2001: 146) characterizes as 'un abierto canto homoerótico al glorioso cuerpo despojado, castigado por el deseo, el dolor y la culpa' (an openly homoerotic paean to the denuded body, lashed by desire, pain, and guilt). It is acutely interested in the bodies of its two protagonists. Ángel tortures himself, the disturbingly erotic El Nene, and the audience by persisting in the belief that to spill semen is to lose one's purity, and Noriega becomes an image charged with a sense of thrilling prohibition. The final shoot-out, where the two are left taking on the Uruguayan military and taking off their shirts (ostensibly to use them as bonfires to make the tear gas rise to the ceiling of the room in which they are at bay), is as much a ritualistic release of sexual tension as a conventional piece of action. Genet, Burroughs, or Greg Araki might all subscribe to the sly reclaiming of the extreme heterosexual virility of the conventional action film (as also the generic promiscuity of the film: at once crime, road, gangland, and forbidden love movie). It places Noriega squarely (perhaps, given his default demeanour, in both senses) within a queer field of representation and reception,[3] as well as giving him, like Arias, a perverse edge.

In the ghost-story thriller *El espinazo del diablo* / *The Devil's Backbone* (Guillermo del Toro, 2001), set in an orphanage at the end of the Civil War, Noriega is 'now hardened into a convincingly repellent

---

[3] As witness the film's distribution in the USA by Strand Releasing (for whose product range see http://www.strandrel.com), its circuit of the Lesbian and Gay Film Festivals (e.g. Miami and London), and its winning of the up-and-coming Spanish gay magazine *Shangay Express*'s prize for best cinematic representation of homosexuality in 2001.

macho' (P. J. Smith 2001*b*: 39), greedy for sex and for money, emotionally dysfunctional, and revealed to be a child-murderer. The orphanage (with an unexploded bomb in its patio, and a ghost in its cellar) serves as a microcosm of the Spain of the times, much as the village and the house in Erice's *The Spirit of the Beehive* (1973), with which there are other elements in common (P. J. Smith 2001*b*: 38); but it is also an exploration of violence, and the ghosts of violence (Altares 2001: 10). In terms of Noriega's career the film builds on the productive tension between extreme good looks and extreme bad conduct that marked *Tesis* and of which Noriega was well aware (Serrano 2001: 20, 22). His first appearance, preceded by establishing shots of a fearsomely barren central Spain and framed by the fortress-like gate and walls of the orphanage, make him seem a Western-style tough, squinting into a merciless sun, whose cruelty is, in classic manner, etched onto him. His character Jacinto is the frustrated action hero—both jailor and escapee—as he plots to steal the gold that the orphanage's widowed owner Carmen (Marisa Paredes) is keeping safe for the republican cause her husband had supported; he is the cause of a devastating explosion (half designed to blow the safe, half to wipe out the past) that enriches the final reel with spectacular war and crime motifs and recontextualizes Noriega. Although he is the dominant male to the surrounding boys in his role as caretaker and enforcer of rough discipline, he is also the archetype of their condition, the saddest and the loneliest of the inmates (as Carmen reminds him) but damaged by this and his terrible secret—the brutal but accidental killing of one of the boys. For this film and for Daniel Calparsoro's *Guerreros* (Warriors) (still awaiting release in early 2002) Noriega took to the gym to build his chest and biceps (Ponga 2001: 96), working up a body image already exploited in the many shirtless moments of *Burnt Money*, as well as in the much-circulated fashion and publicity photo of him in jeans, vest, and tattooed biceps leaning back provocatively on the open bonnet of a car, with a virgin white but ragged cloth sticking out of his pocket coding him as rough but ready, hard but clean (Ponga 1999: 118). The quality of its other stars—Paredes (of *All About My Mother*) and Federico Luppi (of the key Latin American male stars probably the one with the highest profile in Spain)—also make the film a sign of the firming up of Noriega's status. The role was originally written with Bardem in mind (Ponga 2001: 96) and the interchangeability of body type and perceived ability moves him up a weight (though he modestly says the opposite in the interview I am citing (96)). Del Toro's insistence on a combination of method acting and improvisation for all the roles (98) seems to have helped Noriega find a way to overcome the caricature potential in his role, and he essays some effectively terrifying looks and actions. Jacinto's violent end—stuck in armpits and sides with sharpened sticks by the enraged boys, and toppled into the cistern where the dead boy's body and its ghost reside—again remits to the Western, to violent crime and horror genres (as well as to *Lord of the Flies*) in its spectacularization of the tortured male body, and of evil turned upon itself. Any sense of Noriega's remaining a *galán* in the sense of pretty but talentless has gone. It was anyway already denied by his strenuous repertory circuit of crime, action, fantasy thriller, comedy—a point made to him in the interview by Ponga (102).

In this same interview Noriega reveals his intense awareness of the importance to him of being the object of the gaze, in this case in the context of the relationship—erotically homosocial to judge from Noriega's words—of actor and director: 'necesito que haya una mirada cómplice, saber que hay un tío que me está guiñando, [los directores] son tu primer espectador' (I need the knowing look, to know that there's a guy out there winking at you, encouraging you, [directors] are your first audience) (100). In the lightest possible way this fact of star psychology is dramatized in *Cha cha chá* (Antonio del Real, 1997) where Noriega plays an unconvincingly lower middle class student, aspiring to be a male model, who is enlisted by Lucía (Ana Álvarez) to seduce María (Ana Adánez) away from Pablo (Jorge Sanz), with whom Lucía is in love. Noriega plays his character Antonio's satisfaction at learning all the right things to say to María—a social class above him—amusingly and self-reflexively, acknowledging in little gestural asides not only his own harmless narcissism but also sending up some classic inadequacies of young manhood. Antonio learns to say how important communication is to a relationship, and Noriega plays it with transparent slickness; Lucía trains Antonio to pose, and Noriega does so with nicely judged overenthusiasm and competitiveness; above all, when it transpires that Antonio and Pablo are long-lost friends, both actors overplay the joyous homosociality of the reunion—aided by the director's interpretation of the requirements of the genre—talking incessantly, and to the exclusion of the women, embracing, slapping each other on the back, jumping into a fountain, and effectively resolving the plot by the exchange of the true commitment at issue, as expressed by Antonio: 'yo quiero a Pablo' (Pablo's a friend, I love him), which blows the continuing execution of Lucía's plans out of the water.

In yet another generic area, like Arias, Gómez, and Mollà, Noriega now has a profile as a fantasy part of Spanish history. As well as *The Devil's Backbone*, there are three films that posit Noriega as the more-or-less heroic embodiment of national, historical meanings. The romantic historical drama *El invierno de las Anjanas* (The Winter We Prayed to the

Angels) (Pedro Telechea, 2000) is set in 1898—the year of the loss of Spain's colonies abroad—and casts Noriega, here a north-coast fisherman, as part of the common national tragedy of thousands sent off to war to die in futility. As with Mollà's character in *Son de mar* in the following year, the man supposed dead returns to the woman he loves (but who has been consigned, by her right-wing brother-in-law, to an asylum); the return from the dead in this film marks Noriega with heroic, romantic value (the reunited lovers confront the forces of social and political oppression) in contrast to the stain of evil revealed by the ghostly return of the dead child in *The Devil's Backbone*. Manuel Gutiérrez Aragón's *Visionarios* (Visionaries) (2001) is a historical reconstruction of a case of miraculous appearances—those of the Virgin of Ezkioga prophesying the victory of Catholicism over Republicanism—and is set in rural Guipúzcoa in the pre-Civil War 1930s. It explores the relationships between popular religion, war, national destiny, and love (between Noriega and Rubio, playing a young woman who has visions of the Virgin). As well as giving him generic breadth, the film also supplies a crucial star match for Noriega, in a series of links to Carmelo Gómez: the setting echoes *Vacas*, his co-star Ingrid Rubio recalls *Extraños*, and Emma Suárez and Karra Elejalde, *Tierra*. Finally, the war-associated role in Calparsoro's *Guerreros* (Warriors: 2001)—about a platoon of Spanish soldiers on a peace mission in Kosovo in 2000—again has a link to Gómez, and to Arias, in its similarity (to judge by pre-release synopses and interviews) to *Territorio Comanche* (discussed in Ch. 1) as well as having Noriega represent in low key a form of national and European hero. (There is also an interesting connection with a younger generation of actors in that Noriega is working alongside Eloy Azorín—best known as Esteban, the teenage son whose death is the plot detonator in Almodóvar's *All About My Mother*—who also gained a high profile in 2001 in Vicente Aranda's bio-pic, *Juana la loca / Mad Love*.)[4]

Fele Martínez (b. 1975)

Fele Martínez's image as the intense, slightly geeky loner and horror-film buff, Chema, in *Tesis* (see above, under Noriega) is one that has maintained its potency in young Spanish cinema-goers' memories (with a recent boost through a re-release on DVD). The role built on an

---

[4] This was the only Spanish product to make the top 25 in Spain at the end of 2001, grossing $6m (Reuters/Variety 2001).

already fairly substantial young stage-acting career in Alicante and subsequently (though, like Noriega, briefly) in Madrid, and it won him the Young Actor of the Year award in the 1996 Goyas. His theatre career is marked by a propensity for experimental performance (still pursued in stage appearances, for example with the company Teatro Acción Futura, and his own theatre group Sex Peare), and Martínez was invited subsequently to take some memorable risks with difficult, troubled, withdrawn, and emotionally insightful characters, particularly in Ricardo Franco's *Lágrimas negras* (Dark Tears) and Julio Medem's *Los amantes del círculo polar / Lovers of the Arctic Circle* (both 1998). By contrast, *Tesis*—the cinematic start of Martínez's moody, anti-heroic, and slightly chill constructions of character—had already had the effect in extra-filmic discourse of associating him with Amenábar, Noriega, and Ana Torrent (famous for her role as the child witness of other horrors in *The Spirit of the Beehive* (1973)), and with the self-conscious revitalization of the Spanish pantheon of film actors. Spooky inwardness is transformed into arrogant sexiness as he poses with (a somewhat eclipsed) Noriega in black leather under the headline 'Los hombres de Amenábar' (the Amenábar men);[5] the film has become a commonplace for reporters and academics identifying pivotal moments in Spanish cinema of the late twentieth century, both for its combination of young actors and for its albeit parodic opening up to North American popular themes; the Goya, as he has acknowledged in interview, put pressure on him to fulfil the promise, and made '[el] chico tímido de Alicante' (the timid boy from Alicante) a famous personality right at the start of his film career (Martialay 2000: 92–6, 96).

As Pelayo, César's plain but presentable, normal-laddish best friend from whom César steals Sofía in *Open Your Eyes*, Martínez plays a popularly familiar type of young male: anxious about his looks, his pulling power, his general prowess in the world, and semi-comically focused on, yet made ineffectual by, the sheer energy of his sexual neediness. The character draws on the potential for eliciting audience sympathy that lies in its model—Hollywood teen and college movies or TV series—as well as gathering to itself a specific connection to the Woody Allen/Alvy Singer character in a brief but important allusion to *Annie Hall* (1977) early in the film. Pelayo also represents decency and integrity set against the self-serving exploitation of looks and women by his sexier friend (in the pre-accident phases of the film). But this floppy-haired niceness is cross-cut with steelier, more sinister strands; and this is a marker of the Martínez persona. In César's nightmare it is Pelayo who is coolly

---

[5] In *El País* (*Semanal*), 23 Nov. 1997: 86.

responsible for the psychological tortures undergone, and both from within and outside César's POV Pelayo, finely tuned by Martínez, can be seen to be, or be suspected of, quietly registering satisfaction at the superiority afforded to him by the destruction of his friend's good looks, lifestyle, and even sanity.

It is in Medem's *Los amantes del círculo polar* and its psychological representation of loss and love that Martínez has the scope to develop a full profile. The complex visualization of emotion that characterizes the film, and the consistently tight framing of the lovers (Hernández Ruiz 1998: 31) puts heavy demands on the actors, and shooting was preceded by a month of rehearsals with Medem, according to Martínez, encouraging minute scrutiny of character, emotion, and motivation (Isasi 1999: 54). On the other hand, this is not a film that favours the animation through performance of immediately re-felt passion and distress by actors, but rather one that treats acting somewhat statically as part of its look, and part of its field of sentiment. Medem's decision to film the sequences from end to beginning and to place unusual emphasis on the editing process (seven months, against nine weeks of filming) give it a complex structure (Stone 2002: 178)—or, on a less enthusiastic view, make it 'an alienating jigsaw puzzle' (Romney 2000: 49)—and mean that acting, the contiguous presence of the stars in real time, and narrative continuity are all radically set aside. This, along with a dependence on voice-over to provide meaning—or 'questionable profundities' (48)—and motivation, means that Martínez and Najwa Nimri (as Ana) need frequently to provide blank faces and stock reactions to facilitate the subsequent, editorial alterations as much as they need to register intense emotion. It is partly by way of directorial manipulations of sequence and image rather than by way of performance that Otto's point of view becomes linked to the real and the contingent (in his decisive break with his family and decision to become a night-shift courier pilot, in a resigned quest for oblivion), that Ana's comes to depend on the imaginary and aspirational (Hernández Ruiz 1998: 31, 32), and that the look of the two young stars has persistence in the memory of their audiences.

Martínez does, however, also achieve a memorable look and style through old-fashioned acting. A traumatic reaction to the death of his mother, and the full realization of the impossibility of his love for his half-sister give rise to the dynamic extremes of his throwing himself against the corridor walls at the crematorium and the garishly wallpapered walls of the tiny rented room he has fled home to, as well as to a soberly attempted suicide off snowy mountain cliffs. These only accentuate the surrounding, outwardly impassive, intensity of the performance. Martínez is able to use his long hair to accentuate the melancholy set of an oval face—as when Otto looks in through the windows on his abandoned father, ship-wrecked in front of the television—and also, in half profile, to accentuate the cheekbones and soulful eyes to which much of his attractiveness to his fan base is owing. Reflected in the eyes of the apparently dead Ana, sprawled in the road where she has been knocked down, the face becomes a tragic mask. In this final sequence his eyes, slowly closed in upon, mesmerize the audience and act as the visual bridge to the film's brief epilogue—a shot of the crashed plane (from which he has ejected—unless this is a dream of Ana's) lying in the snow, and the dedication to the director's father, who had died just after the completion of *Tierra*.

This dedication has resonance back into the film's internal concerns: blood lines, destinies, a dead mother, an emotionally disabled father (Nancho Novo), a disjuncture between Otto and Ana (true lovers) and their parents' generation (unfaithful and inconstant lovers)—features that Stone (2002) suggests are typical of a generation of film-makers 'that has little memory of the dictatorship but which certainly shared in the emotional fallout of their parents' suffering' (179). Another, similarly oblique, attachment is made between what is acted out and the story of Spain in that not only does Nimri's Ana have a look in her eyes that recalls her dreamy namesake from Erice's *The Spirit of the Beehive*—that key exploration of national and psychological trauma (and redemption)—but Otto's name and occupation are also time-lines dropped back into a crucial moment in the national history. The name is that of a German bomber pilot, involved in the raid on Guernika, found by Otto's grandfather caught up in his parachute in the trees (as Otto himself ends up being); German reparations for the action feature in snatches of television coverage within the plot: in an unresolved but none the less haunting way the losses, separations, and brutalities of war, and specifically the Spanish Civil War, and the attrition of the Basques, are echoed in the domestic and romantic tragedies of abandonment, death, and missed encounters of the present.

Lágrimas negras (Dark Tears) (Ricardo Franco, completed by Fernando Bauluz, 1999) again casts Martínez as the younger man scarred by family history: when a toddler, told by his father that his mother, who has gone off with another man, has died; and later, left traumatized and mystified by his father's real suicide. A soft-lit, classic sex scene with his steady girlfriend Alicia early in the first reel establishes him as erotically desirable—smooth-skinned, lean, now with mid-length dark hair—but also troubled (post-coital conversation is about his visit to his therapist). His mugging by two desperate drug-users, Isabel (Ariadna Gil) and Cinta (Ana Risueño), leads to his overnight kidnapping, sexual humiliation, and rape—hands and feet tied, in an industrial wasteland—by Isabel; it also leads to the start of a strong perverse fixation by Andrés on his aggressor, fed by his predisposition to a fascination—as a nice, middle-class professional photographer of nature scenes—for scenes of social deprivation and mental extremity. Added to this is the discovery that he already has video footage and stills of Isabel, taken at a mental institution, which is featured in the film's opening moments. She has a double life and is, when dried out, glamorous, idle, rich, and calling herself Ana. In this persona Andrés dates her, having tracked her down, still unsure that she is the real Isabel. In the Retiro park he tells her his family history in a classic, long park-bench scene shot statically and frontally and played with sobriety and poignancy. Martínez's fear and emotional daring are projected by his facing forward, with simple nervous fingering of the camera that is always with him, by movements of the jawbone, and sudden sideways looks nicely balanced between provocatively coltish and vulnerably childish. 'Ana''s revelation that her mother had committed suicide, shortly after the family's last visit to this park, prompts a change of tableau as Martínez now half turns towards her and centimetre by centimetre moves closer, visibly facing his as well as her grief. When she shifts suddenly into a tearful prophecy of the brevity of their incipient romance Andrés starts back, appalled, and showing, as she strokes his hair, the physical memory of the earlier rape—his eyes move downwards and sideways, away from her and her hand; gulping he is immobilized by horror and desire.

This fine-grained type of performance from Martínez pervades the film, and is offset by his character's double sexual life—the conventional, clean relationship with Alicia, and the desperate, fearful, ambiguous, and much more sexy couplings with Isabel, in the first of which she tells him her real name and during which his suspicions about his attraction to her have to be confronted. When Isabel, in a long, dramatic scene on an austerely lovely Atlantic beach persuades him that her madness and addiction are unbearable and that he must, if he loves her, kill her, it is Martínez's ability to register facially the transition from paralysed horror to desperate and impassioned determination to do her will that, along with Ariadna Gil's convincing passive, deep despair (reworked for *Second Skin* a year later), saves the film's apotheosis from cliché.

In another modality, in the same year, his role in *El arte de morir* (The Art of Dying) (Álvaro Fernández Almero, 1999) returned Martínez to the thriller genre in which he started. Here he is disturbing, pale, and emotionally paralysed as the guilt-wracked Iván,[6] one of a group of

---

[6] In characteristic pose on the publicity poster and video cover: see http://cinemania.simplenet.com/carteles/video/El_Arte_De_Morir.htm (17 Jan. 2002).

20-somethings who are to different degrees involved in the death of a friend—an avant-garde painter obsessed with the theme of death—and who one by one themselves die off. The film once more associates him, as had *Tesis*, with the horror genre and with popular Hollywood; again, as with the Amenábar films, he is part of a key team of young actors, here with Gustavo Salmerón (as the dead painter), Adrià Collado, Lucía Jiménez, María Esteve (Clara), and Sergio Peris-Mencheta.[7]

He gains a European dimension, and a place in the historical genre, in the Portuguese director María de Medeiros's account of the April Revolution of 1974, *Capitanes de abril* (Captains of April) (2001). A love affair opposite Silke (who played the sensual Mari in *Tierra*, see Ch. 3) set in contemporary underclass Madrid, in *¿Tú qué harías por amor?* (Carlos Suarte Medrano, 2001), gives him both sexual and social credibility with his fan base. This, mixed with the range and subtlety of expression of the roles under the more art-house direction of Medem and Franco, make him one of the more substantially coded and widely recognized rising stars.

Liberto Rabal (b. 1975)

The final stages of writing of this book have corresponded with an unexpectedly fallow period in the film career of Liberto Rabal, hailed as the latest of the *chicos Almodóvar* (Almodóvar boys) at the time of *Carne trémula / Live Flesh* (Aznar, 1997).[8] Rabal, like Bardem, comes from a family of names illustrious in the world of Spanish arts and culture (he is the grandson of the famed novelist of the mid-twentieth century Carmen Laforet, and the veteran actor Francisco Rabal, who was still alive as Liberto's career took off). He comes to the screen coded with glamour and social meaning by these connections,[9] but no less importantly with a clear complexion, sex-symbol potential, and a well-designed, chunky physique which Aznar (1997) somewhat, but not entirely fancifully likens to the early Brando's. In *El tiempo de la felicidad* (Happy Years) (Manuel Iborra, 1997) one of the group of late teenagers summering on Ibiza—among them an aspiring film director, León, played by Rabal—

---

7 A useful link to some of their other roles is at http://www.zinema.com/2000/pelicula/elartede.htm. (4 Jan. 2002).

8 Also *Mundo*, 1997; *Tiempo*, 14 April 1997, as 'el sucesor de Banderas' (Banderas's successor).

9 Aznar (1997: 86) talks of 'el apellido de oro' (the golden surname); *Ya*, 6 April 1997: 35, of the Rabal blood running through his veins; *Elle*, 1 Aug. 1997: 53, of 'los genes bien puestos' (a nice set of genes).

says to the other, Juan (Carlos Fuentes) that he should become an actor, he is so good-looking. 'Ser actor es para maricones o vanidosos' (acting's for queers or narcissists) is Juan's response. Part of Rabal's career seems to have been concerned to address just this anxiety and to circumvent the givens of a particular look. What gives an edge to his performance in *Live Flesh* is, as well as his association on screen with two bigger stars, a determined straightening out and masculinizing of a role embedded in the double context of the 'Almodóvar boys' and of a typically Almodovarian penchant for strong mothers and fatal attractions.

His first major role came in the nostalgic, pseudo-historical, and commercially successful literary adaptation *Tranvía a la Malvarrosa / The Tram to Malvarrosa Beach* (José Luis García Sánchez, 1996) (whose title gave journalists another, more spurious, chance to make the Brando connection). Playing opposite Ariadna Gil, Rabal is exploited, in his innocence and sex appeal, by the script and camera as a latterday Jorge Sanz, and like so many of that actor's roles Rabal's here puts youthful masculinity through some straightforward trials (love in wartime; conflicts of loyalty) to allow it lightly to settle back ostensibly proven at the end. Although Rabal's character, Manuel, goes through the mill of sexual and political awakening, he is implicated in the film's dénouement in applause—literally, at a sun-kissed beachside wedding party—for the institutions of heterosexuality and the conventions of the happy ending. Similarly, in his television appearances since *Live Flesh*, particularly in the hugely popular, light comedy series on TVE-1, *A las once en casa* (Home by Eleven) from October 1998, Rabal has continued to play the straight, sensitive, and romantically uncomplicated newish man in the guise of a discreetly tattooed and bleached blond artist rebel.

In 1996 when *Tranvía a la Malvarrosa* came out so did what is perhaps Spain's first postmodern queer film, *Más que amor, frenesí / Not Love, Just Frenzy* (Alfonso Albacete, Miguel Bardem, and David Menkes) in which Rabal's character (a straight male model) is enmeshed in a plot involving all manner of alternative relationships and desires and is clearly there for his appeal to a gay audience. Appealing also to a young heterosexual female public in the next few years, magazine and television appearances have made abundant use of open shirts, attractive stubble, rolled-up sleeves, and the image of a man who is straight but persuadable; innocent and knowing; gentle but muscular; perhaps, in clichéd and falsely contrasted terms, feminine and masculine; ambiguous, after all.[10]

---

[10] For example, *La Revista de El Mundo*, 1997; *ABC* (*Ocio*), 27 March 1997, where he is dubbed 'El galán del siglo XXI' (A Leading Man for the 21st Century)—a prophecy yet to be fulfilled.

In *Live Flesh* the role of Víctor (in which Sanz was originally cast) allowed Rabal to bring an intellectually and emotionally full performance to the screen very much against the grain of the public reception of him as above all a sex symbol—of 'the full-lipped Antonio Banderas school of feverishly beautiful leading men' (*Advocate* 1999)—against readings and media representations of him as ambiguous, and against Almodóvar's clear exploitation of his body and looks. Almodóvar had in his previous films paid unusual attention, of course, to the eroticized male body, particularly in *Law of Desire* where Antonio Banderas's star career took off in the context of a number of naked men, and later in the (brief but memorable) use of the already internationally famous erotic form of the dancer Joaquín Cortés in *The Flower of My Secret*. On the one hand the blatant imitation forced upon Rabal of the close-cropped, manic, sensual look of Banderas's Ricki in *Átame*, and a now famous scene of him 'emerg[ing] naked and gleaming from the smoke of a flaming frying pan' (*Advocate* 1999) might be seen as restrictive and exploitative; on the other, Rabal has (perhaps dutifully, and in contradistinction to other actors' impressions of the director) paid tribute to Almodóvar's encouragement inventively to build the character of Víctor for himself (Casanova 1999).

If in *Tranvía a la Malvarrosa* Ariadna Gil's presence and back-history as a young star eclipsed Rabal, in *Live Flesh* Ángela Molina brings him on in a reversal of the classic dynamic (Clark Gable and Vivien Leigh; Humphrey Bogart and Ingrid Bergman; Burt Lancaster and Deborah Kerr; or Richard Gere and Julia Roberts). Just as crucial, though, is the relationship between him and Bardem. The end of the film returns Rabal, through Víctor, to a certain straight normality: he is saved from the excessive world of passion and jealousy, and has overcome the intense bonding and rivalry with David; he is redeemed *vis-à-vis* his mother; he is involved in a pleasing cyclical pattern whereby his own emergency birth in the Christmas-time streets is matched by that of his own son; and he is empowered by the script to speak on behalf of the nation, no less, as he declares, patriarchally, that all is well and all are free, that now, in Spain, no one has had to be afraid for many years. The moment, for all its proximity to corniness and its undeniable inaccuracy as sociological comment (which nation? which racial and economic groups are included in this utopian vision?), is part of a perceived new social and political accentuation in Almodóvar's œuvre to that date, placing the actors in a context where 'recent Spanish history is finally acknowledged' (J. Arroyo 1998) and within a 'national narrative' and a 'political framing of [. . .] personal melodrama' (P. J. Smith 2000: 184, 185). However, it is also true that this is a film where 'lo icónico domina a lo ideológico de manera rotunda' (the iconic decisively outweighs the ideological), and the sociopolitical elements of the narrative of Víctor's life are displaced by a focus on passionate emotions, on the one hand, and the grander, general themes of human weakness, guilt, love, and redemptive or cathartic death (Alcover 1997). More coherent too as a source of individualized dramatic motivations for Rabal's character than the socio-historical prologue and epilogue are the instances of a micro-politics of masculine rivalry, bonding, and disavowal, as discussed in relation to Bardem in Ch. 4. Playing next to Bardem, Rabal is able to develop a dynamic and emotionally nuanced model of young heterosexual masculinity which, though it is less convincing with regard to class (the actor's family connections do not rub off so easily and he makes an unconvincing working-class lad), allows full audience recognition of *machista* patterns of jealousy, competition, and fear of failure, as well as—in more caricatural vein, and as much due to Molina as Bardem—of the inferiority in erotic expertise of the younger man. The film, then, firmed him up as an icon of social change in Spain but also as a heightened representative of male heterosexual desires and drives.

Juan Diego Botto (b. 1976)

A familiar early photograph (*Fotogramas* 1994b) shows Juan Diego Botto with incipient moustache but boyish, wide-eyed look, shirt wide open to a smooth and lightly muscled chest. This type of image, his intensely studied acting style, his playing of problem men, and his deep brown eyes, all give him a strong following among female audiences and magazine buyers, and, as we shall see, a potential gay following too. Botto's paradigmatic role for the early to mid-1990s was that of the younger man—the romantic ingénue with sex appeal and a nice complexion but with intriguing, underlying problems—in *En brazos de la mujer madura* (In the Arms of Older Women) (Manuel Lombardero, 1997: an adaptation of Stephen Vizinczy's novel *In Praise of Older Women* (1965)). There his division of erotic loyalties is, without subtlety but not without dramatic effect, mapped onto the brutal social divisions of the immediate post-Civil War days in Barcelona. Living with his right-wing mother and her Falangist lover, Andrés (Botto) has an affair with the liberal intellectual neighbour's wife and, at the same time, is haunted by reminders of his sexual and sentimental education in the war behind Republican lines. The film, complete with clumsy references to *Le Rouge et le noir*, builds him as the classic heterosexual, flawed romantic hero caught up in character in the flux of history and destiny, and, as an actor, implicated in some unambiguously exploitative displays of his flawless, youthful body and look of ready, innocent availability. It highlights what was to become a trademark: the easy manner and soft if lean body that denotes a straight-living and straightforward persona and character, but a character none the less with a conflicted emotional life that is metaphorically and causally related to social and psychosexual problematics. This duality also underlies Botto's low-key performance as 'Hache' ('H' for *hijo*, son, as his father only ever calls him) in Adolfo Aristarain's *Martín (Hache)* / *Martin (H)* (1997) and sensitively explores the dynamics of a middle-class father–son relationship whose gaps and silences are exacerbated by an exiled father's bitter disenchantment with Argentina (Botto's own birthplace) and a son's construction of late-adolescent masculinity as a site of serene passivity but also as a damaging place from which to observe the emotional dysfunctionality and sexual disappointments of male heterosexual adult middle age. The film made him the choice as Spanish representative at the MEDIA-sponsored Young European Actors showcase in the 1998 Berlin Film Festival, building on a reputation already paradigmatically established in *Historias del Kronen* (1995: discussed in Ch. 5), which had won him the Goya for Best New Actor.

His character Carlos in that film is a complex (if classic), dangerous combination of teenage rebellion, homophobia, and anxiously self-affirming violent masculinity. The brutal series of glaring silences, dares, and initiation rites that punctuate the film, and its sheer pace, link it and Carlos to a critique of young, wealthy, urban youth, the alienation of younger males by upper middle-class family life, and the social pressures and ethical omissions of the consumerist city (Jordan and Morgan-Tamosunas 1998: 99; Fouz Hernández 2000; Stone 2002: 144–5). Botto is set in a similar context in Daniel Calparsoro's *Asfalto* (Asphalt) (1999), an exploration and extreme aestheticization of urban violence, alienation, and dark fantasies, as well as of heroic virility, homoeroticism, rebellion, and pan-sexuality (Palacios 2000); and in the mass-murderer thriller *Plenilunio* (Full Moon) (Imanol Uribe, 2000), as a psychotically misogynistic child-killer, he plays out an extreme masculine dysfunction set in parallel to a plot-line investigating—as is habitual with Uribe—the violent clash of the State and the separatist terrorism of ETA. The oblique connections between the two forms of violence—part of the pseudo-sociological, pseudo-religious stock-in-trade of this genre and its cross-tracings of the origins of evil—are pivoted about the investigating detective (Miguel Ángel Solá) who has had to flee his post in the Basque country because of the wave of threats against professionals and public figures in the late 1990s. His wife has herself been tipped into madness by the threats; and his tracking down of the killer coincides with his own murder by a marksman. Early in the hunt the local priest advises him to look into the eyes of his suspects, for surely they must bear the evidence of evil; and in the prison, just before his death, he, along with the camera, does just this. These eyes—the main motif of the publicity campaign for the film—are seen horribly, and melodramatically in the moonlight by the witnessing audience at the moments of kill, and are the traumatic, repressed memory secreted in the mind of the one surviving victim. They are the same eyes that in Botto habitually signal innocence, openness, vulnerability, and safe sexiness and their melodramatic conversion sends a satisfying thrill through the audience for this film.

Sobreviviré / I Will Survive (Alfonso Albacete and David Menkes, 1999) had explored a different type of duality, but again added substantially to the fascination and saleability of this young star. Here, like Antonio Banderas and Carmelo Gómez before him, he plays opposite Emma Suárez whose customary sex appeal and strong acting are meant to convince the audience that her character Marga—the would-be survivor of the title—can straighten out a mixed-up gay man, such as that played by Botto (who manfully picks his way through a script fraught with didactic set pieces about respecting everyone's 'difference'). Although his character, the gentle Iñaki, seems to Marga to be fun and sensitive and, when he comes out to her, Just Gay Enough not to leave her for another life, he is somewhat problematically attracted to roughish trade (guiltily but excitedly succumbing to the crotch and smile of a hunk who cruises him in the jeans section of a department store, and having quick sex with him in the fitting rooms); and he has a socially fatal propensity to take her out on the (edges of) the Madrid gay scene, leading to a chilly encounter between her and his handsome, creative ex. Botto is unambiguously positioned as a sex object as well as a sensitive soul in this film, and the balance is tipped towards a homo- rather than a heterosexual economy of desire. Marga comments several times on how different he is to other men, and the montage keys that into his look—his soulful eyes again, smooth skin, shy smile—rather than his character. Commentary on their relationship by a caricature gay friend—an airline steward of dubious political correctness and a queeny manner—casts aspersions on Iñaki's 'conversion' and insists, in a spirit of only half-humorously misogynistic, gay homosociality, that Marga is no more than a cover ('una tapadera'), and that gayness will out. In their first bashful (and nicely comic) sex scene on the sitting-room floor Marga casts exaggerated glances of admiration down at Iñaki's erect penis and remarks on its size—a moment that might have affirmed heterosexual erotic bonding were it not for Iñaki's just lowered black leather underpants, and for the matching emphasis on penis size in the classic gay pick-up scene just mentioned (a match underscored by a scene in the same fitting rooms later where he and Marga will themselves kiss and cuddle). When at the end of the film, at a gay wedding (the conclusion of a clumsy sub-plot relating to the then current campaign for the civil recognition of same-sex couples in Spanish cities) Marga and Iñaki—who has returned from another excursion into gayness— dance together to the tune of 'Moon River' it is in one way a closure (the fulfilment of Marga's dreams, which have been calqued on *Breakfast at Tiffany's*) but in another it leaves Botto's character floating free and ambivalent. The tune and the camera-moves (in tight as the two embrace; swirling with them; swooping up) camp up the moment. Audience reactions at two mainstream screenings in the film's first week in Madrid to Botto's engagements with gayness in the film—nervous giggles at his look and clothing; intakes of breath and open laughter at the fitting-room sex scene—suggested that the transgression of Botto's usual image were being duly registered and internalized.

Of this younger (though now not the youngest) generation of male actors it is Botto who has the fullest and most varied filmography, ranging from romantic comedy in Joaquín Oristrell's *Novios* (Girlfriend and Boyfriend) (1998)—winning him a reputation as Spain's best screen kisser— through the twist on that genre in *Sobreviviré*, through well-made history and dramatic heritage movies,[11] to the psychological and physical violence of *Historias del Kronen* and *Plenilunio*, which form a chronological bridge. He has an actorly presence and is developing perhaps into a cross between Gómez and Banderas. The theatrical story at the core of *Éxtasis* (1995: discussed in Ch. 4), where Botto has a minor role as an aspiring actor, and the arch-theatrical associations of the adaptation of the classic early renaissance dramatic piece *La Celestina* (Gerardo Vera, 1995)—in which, however, Botto romps rather carelessly through the role of a Calisto with well-shampooed hair and a markedly contemporary, gruff Madrid tonality (Gómez Sierra forthcoming)—make of Botto an actors' actor, as does the substance of most interviews and reports, turning as they do to his continuing combination of stage and screen roles.[12] He has his own company, 'Nuevo Repertorio' (The New Rep), and is a frequent stage performer (recently under the direction of his mother Cristina Rota, the renowned artistic director, and founder of the

---

[11] Including, more recently, Montxo Armendáriz's *Silencio roto* (Broken Silence) (2001), on the *maquis*, the anti-Franco guerrilla, set in 1944, which I have been unable to view.

[12] For recent examples see: *Fotogramas*, 1,880 (2000): 89–95, 92–5; *Blanco y negro* (*Dominical*), 29 April 2001: 21–5; *La mirada*, 2–3 June 2001: 50–6; http://www.tentaciones.elpais.es/t/d/20010330/seccion/p01.htm (10 Feb. 2002).

Cristina Rota Actors' Studio).[13] Credited second to Javier Bardem in John Malkovich's *The Dancer Upstairs* which premièred at the Sundance Festival 2002, Botto is starting to gain not only an international profile but fame by association in what is becoming a traditional pattern of star bonding and tutelage of the contemporary Spanish industry.

[13] In, for example, a Spanish version of *Rosencrantz and Guildenstern Are Dead*, Compañía Nuevo Repertorio, Madrid, 2000 and on tour.

TABLE 7.1. *Filmography: Eduardo Noriega*

Year	Title	English title(s) (official in italics; literal in roman)	Director	Billing	Audience figures and takings	Other information
1994	*Historias del Kronen*	Stories of the Kronen	Montxo Armendáriz	Minor	771,950 / €2,344,136	
1996	*Cuestión de suerte*	A Question of Luck	Rafael Moleón	2nd	50,884 / €187,565	
1996	*Tesis*	*Snuff* / Thesis	Alejandro Amenábar	3rd	854,735 / €2,646,146	
1997	*Abre los ojos*	Open Your Eyes	Alejandro Amenábar	Top	1,793,934 / €6,441,571	
1997	*Más allá del jardín*	Beyond the Garden	Pedro Olea	Minor	312,891 / €1,068,698	
1998	*Cha cha chá*		Antonio del Real	Top	855,715 / €3,036,142	
1999	*Carretera y manta*	To the End of the Road	Alfonso Arandia	2nd	56,573 / €222,436	
1999	*El invierno de las Anjanas . . . de amor y de sueños*	The Winter We Prayed to the Angels . . . and of Love and Dreams	Pedro Telechea	Top	46,847 / €191,170	
1999	*La fuente amarilla*	The Yellow Fountain	Miguel Santesmases	Top	84,243 / €311,464	Co-pro Spain, France
1999	*Nadie conoce a nadie*	Nobody Knows Anybody	Mateo Gil	Top	1,409,621 / €5,526,483	
2000	*Plata quemada*	Burning Money / Burnt Money	Marcelo Piñeyro	Top	102,073 / €424,727	Co-pro Argentina, Spain, France
2001	*El espinazo del diablo*	The Devil's Backbone	Guillermo del Toro	Top	699,519 / €2,960,034	
2001	*Visionarios*	Visionaries	Manuel Gutiérrez Aragón	Top	56,659 / €260,547	
2001	*Guerreros*	Warriors	Daniel Calparsoro	Top	195,673 / €865,442	

Shorts

Allanamiento de morada (House Clearance) (Mateo Gil, 1998)
Cita (Date) (Luis López Varona 1996)
En casa de Diego (At Diego's Place) (Carlos Montero, 1996)
Luna (Moon) (Alejandro Amenábar, 1994)
Soñé que te mataba (I Dreamt I Was Killing You) (Mateo Gil, 1994)
Una historia más (Domenico Clolfi, 1994)

TABLE 7.2. *Filmography: Fele Martínez*

Year	Title	English title(s) (official in italics; literal in roman)	Director	Billing	Audience figures and takings	Other information
1996	*Tesis*	*Snuff* / *Thesis*	Alejandro Amenábar	Top	854,735 / €2,646,146	Goya for Best New Actor
1997	*Abre los ojos*	*Open Your Eyes*	Alejandro Amenábar	Top	1,793,934 / €6,441,571	
1997	*El tiempo de la felicidad*	The Time of Happiness	Manuel Iborra	7th	206,674 / €687,916	
1997	*Insomnio*	Insomnia	Chus Gutiérrez	6th	103,974 / €350,937	
1998	*Los amantes del círculo polar*	*Lovers of the Arctic Circle*	Julio Medem	2nd	749,277 / €2,788,826	
1999	*Lágrimas negras*	Dark Tears	Ricardo Franco	2nd	153,889 / €587,135	
1999	*¿Tú qué harías por amor?*	What Would You Do for Love?	Carlos Saura Medrano (aka Carlo Saura Jnr.)	Top	52,132 / €207,235	
1999	*El arte de morir*	The Art of Dying	Álvaro Fernández Armero	Top	820,230 / €3,240,823	Co-pro Spain, Peru
2000	*Tinta roja*	Red Ink	Francisco J. Lombardi	Top	39,758 / €181,152	
2000	*Tuno negro*	Dark Player	Pedro Luis Barbero and Vicente J. Martín Perán	Top	562,414 / €2,239,600	
2001	*Capitanes de abril* / *Capitães de Abril*	Captains of April	María de Medieros		74,077 / €318,582	Co-pro Portugal, Spain

Shorts

Pasaia (Mikel Aguirresarobe, 1996)
Amigos (Friends) (Manuel Martínez Marcos, 1998)

TABLE 7.3. *Filmography: Liberto Rabal*

Year	Title	English title(s) (official in italics; literal in roman)	Director	Billing	Audience figures and takings	Other information
1995	*Así en el Cielo como en la Tierra*	On Earth As It Is In Heaven	José Luis Cuerda	Minor	200,741 / €584,299	As the angel Raphael; with Fernando Fernán Gómez (as God the Father) and Francisco Rabal (as St Peter)
1995	*Alma gitana*	Gypsy Soul	Chus Gutiérrez	Minor	231,710 / €667,942	As a student
1996	*Pon un hombre en tu vida*	Put a Man in Your Life	Eva Lesmes	6th	121,504 / €381,035	
1996	*Más que amor, frenesí*	*Not Love, Just Frenzy*	Alfonso Albacete, Miguel Bardem, and David Menkes	8th	311,889 / €1,040,528	
1996	*Tranvía a la Malvarrosa*	*The Tram to Malvarrosa Beach*	José Luis García Sánchez	Top	186,779 / €621,446,83	
1997	*Carne trémula*	Live Flesh	Pedro Almodóvar	1st	1,433,173 / €4,990,272	
1997	*El tiempo de la felicidad*	Happy Years	Manuel Iborra	8th	206,674 / €687,916	With Fele Martínez
2000	*Todo menos la chica*	Everything Except the Girl	Jesús Delgado	2nd	3,408 / €13,702	
2000	*Tangos robados*	Stolen Tangos	Eduardo de Gregorio	1st	32,330 / €157,304	Co-pro France, Spain

Television series

A las once en casa (Home by Eleven) TVE 1998/1999

Non-Spanish language productions

Mare largo (Fernando Vicentini Orgnani, 1998)

TABLE 7.4. *Filmography: Juan Diego Botto*

Year	Title	English title(s) (official in italics; literal in roman)	Director	Billing	Audience figures and takings	Other information
1984	*Los motivos de Berta*	Berta's Reasons	José Luis Guerín	7th	4,807 / €8,467	
1986	*El río de oro*	The Golden River	Jaime Chávarri	6th	65,680 / €115,200	
1986	*Teo el pelirrojo*	Teo the Redhead	Paco Lucio	4th	58,905 / €82,149	
1989	*Si te dicen que caí*	If they Say I Fell	Vicente Aranda	10th	340,702 / €700,184	
1989	*Ovejas negras*	Black Sheep	José María Carreño	3rd	19,756 / €43,635	
1991	*Cómo ser mujer y no morir en el intento*	How to be a Woman and Not Die in the Attempt	Ana Belén	Minor	689,779 / €1,673,380	
1992	*1492: The Conquest of Paradise*		Ridley Scott	Minor	971,935 / €2,789,918	Co-pro Spain, France, UK
1994	*Historias del Kronen*	Stories of the Kronen	Montxo Armendáriz	Top	771,950 / €2,344,136	Goya for Best New Actor
1995	*La sal de la vida*	The Salt of Life	Eugenio Martín	3rd	71,994 / €188,742	
1995	*La Celestina*	Celestina	Gerardo Vera	2nd	443,979 / €1,393,595	
1996	*Más que amor, frenesí*	More Than Love, Just Frenzy	Alfonso Albacete, Miguel Bardem, and David Menkes	8th	311,889 / €1,040,528	
1997	*En brazos de la mujer madura*	In the Arms of Older Women	Manuel Lombardero	Top	92,104 / €303,333	
1997	*Martín (Hache)*	*Martín (H)*	Adolfo Aristarain	2nd	576,020 / €2,083,925	Co-pro Spain, Argentina
1999	*Sobreviviré*	I Will Survive	Alfonso Albacete and David Menkes	2nd	1,080,029 / €4,116,053	
1999	*Asfalto*	Big City Streets	Daniel Calparsoro	2nd	139,282 / €552,865	
2000	*Plenilunio*	Full Moon	Imanol Uribe	3rd	169,575 / €682,374	
2001	*Silencio roto*	*Broken Silence*	Montxo Armendáriz	2nd	426,310 / €1,829,642	

Shorts

Hace quince años (Fifteen Years Back) (José Luis Escolar, 1987)

English language productions

The Dancer Upstairs (John Malkovich, 2001)

Conclusion

Spanish readers in particular, because of the huge range of actors' names that have been given prominence in the media and in conversations in bars, coffee shops, and cinema queues over the past twenty-odd years, may think that there are some strange choices made in this book. I have not (this time around) chosen to write about any of the great actresses, even though some of them—Victoria Abril, Carmen Maura, Marisa Paredes—clearly construct as many masculinities as the best of their male counterparts; and have only been able to allude in passing to the importance of such pairings as Emma Suárez and Banderas, Botto, or Gómez (discussed by Allinson (1999: 34)). The men chosen are themselves by no means the only representatives—although I have judged them to be the most famous—of the issues and modes of expression I have been exploring. While the book has been in preparation (mainly between 1999 and 2001) Sergi López (b. 1965), for instance, has quickly become one of the most interesting actors, and one that I might have discussed, despite his late association with mainstream Castilian-language cinema; Liberto Rabal (b. 1975), on the other hand, since I embarked on the section on younger actors, has come to less than I and others imagined he might do. José Coronado (b. 1957) must surely be the epitome of the old-style leading man to a significant segment of the audience (filmgoers, television watchers, and magazine buyers now in their forties and fifties), not least for his roles opposite tragic national diva (widow of the bullfighter Paquirri) Isabel Pantoja in the musical-within-a-film *Yo soy esa* (I Am the Other Woman) (Luis Sanz, 1990), as Don Juan in the eponymous miniseries for television (1997), as the extremely expert lover in Vicente Aranda's erotic literary adaptation *La Mirada del otro / The Naked Eye* (1998), or as the young Goya in Saura's *Goya en Burdeos / Goya in Bordeaux* (1999). He is described, perhaps not without some vagueness and partiality, in the standard dictionary of Spanish stars of the 1990s (Clemente 1998) as Spain's number one leading man and as having all the physical characteristics (green eyes, brown hair, a perfect match of weight to height) to be the prototypical, ideally suited to, and much needed by, 'una cinematografía como la nuestra' (an industry like our own) (70): but because of his relatively slim filmography and lack of sustained association with major box-office hits I have excluded him.

Range, or perceived range, of roles has come into my selection criteria too: while Antonio Resines (b. 1954), Juanjo Puigcorbé (b. 1955), Fernando Guillén Cuervo (b. 1961), and Gabino Diego (b. 1966) are versatile, peaked in the post-Franco period, and rank consistently highly in popularity polls, their main association is with comedy, which merits a separate study.[1] Karra Elejalde (b. 1961) is another marginal case, an actor of some presence—with his 'tipología dura y de perfiles bien reconocibles' (tough type of look and recognizable character traits) (Borau 1998: 307)—who is relegated here because of the predominance of supporting, if very striking, roles rather than in co- and lead position. A similar case is, perhaps, that of Pepón Nieto (b. 1968) whose usual work is in comedy. Nancho Novo (b. 1959), with hindsight, I ought really to have included, not least for his connection to Julio Medem, and to popular music. He and López are among the book's more unfortunate omissions.

By way of a different kind of corrective observation I should also remind the reader that my view of these actors and my selection of films and scenes is partial in the sense of being an extrapolation of issues that I felt would open up plots and performances and help to explain the construction of this aspect of contemporary Spanish cinema around these two sets of terms of 'stars' and 'masculinities'. For theoretical purposes and for the sake of structure there has been some considerable elision here, and I have steadily set aside substantial quantities of the more standard instances of overlap between acting and acting the man. It is also worth bearing in mind, looking back over this book, that there is, in criticism of Spanish cinema in English, at least, a general tendency to look rather too hard for signs in the new stars of a 'New Spain' of leftist, liberal, or libertarian departures from the rule-bound, normalizing past (both that of the Franco era seen from the early 1980s and that of parts of the 'Socialist' era, seen from the disappointed 1990s). This arises partly out of the subversive reputations of such directors as Bigas Luna and Almodóvar, and partly out of a loose and anachronistic but still powerful association in the minds of intellectuals and graduate film audiences (within Spain, but spreading outwards) between indigenous film production and political leftism or intellectual liberalism. The legacy of the perceived 1980s supremacy of *cinematografía liberal* (liberal film-making) still holds sway (on its illusory qualities, see Hopewell 1989: 158–9). I hope that I have been able to signal from time to time that such a quest for dissidence in these stars needs a little adjustment against the reality of

---

[1] There is a proliferating archive of comment and analysis on the comedies of Alex de la Iglesia and Santiago Segura, as well as on Almodóvar (e.g. Allinson 2001: 125–38; P. Evans 1996: 10–26). A useful guide in English is Jordan and Morgan-Tamosunas (1998: 68–86); Soria (1986) offers a context; there is general coverage in Gubern *et al.* (1995: 432–5); also, more substantially, see Carty (2001).

what they enshrine and choose to represent; and I hope that the focus on the less social politics of masculinities has helped in this adjustment. Although Arias is openly committed in his public life to a number of anti-establishment and anti-authoritarian causes, many of the roles he has chosen need a lot of hard spectatorial work on them before they become anything other than smug or disturbingly authentic representations of reactionary or dysfunctional masculinity. Banderas, once the (wishfully supposed) polymorphous and delightful disrupter of sexual, narrative, and moral conventions under Almodóvar's direction did, after all, move to America and into an industry infamously jumpy on such disruptive matters (and, like Arias, but unlike the others, has practised settling down and getting married). Even Bardem is sometimes not entirely distanced even now from an old-style unreconstructed *machismo* in laddish interview and in hypermasculine performance. Sanz is so good at being the epitome, in comic roles, of failed *macho* awfulness that the paint sticks. Gómez's prominent roles either plant him in the Franco era anyway or explore—usually via the trope of police work—something that the publicity blurbs might not hesitate to label 'evil', 'inner turmoil', or 'despair': none of which are especially propitious for a socially progressive cinema. Mollà is the only one who might be susceptible of exploration as a consistently unconventional presence in and out of character (at least, that is, until his somewhat fatuous role in the colourful heritage movie and expensive pot-boiler *Volavérunt* (Bigas Luna, 1999)).

None the less, it is a curiosity of the Spanish case that at one stage or other all my main actors have engaged in roles that give a memorable counter-cultural edge to their star personae, the early Banderas the most (as rebellious youth and sexual adventurer; as icon of an age of change), Mollà next (for example as the ingenious, psychopathic, independent bomber of traditionalist Seville in *Nadie conoce a nadie*), then Arias (good at both heroic and ice-cruel criminality). Bardem and Gómez, in *Jamón, jamón* and *Tierra* respectively, have memorably imprinted onto them different sorts of telluric wildness (though some 450,000 fewer cinema viewers have seen those of *Tierra*); Sanz has occasionally gone against type to cross the line from his usual roguishness into genuine dissidence. These rebel types, raising various questions about angst in the individual and society, about escapism and displacement, about anomie (see Dyer 1998: 52–4), also respond with a noticeable frequency to issues in Spanish political and social life in ways clearly destined to elicit identifications and sympathies as well as activate critical engagement in their audiences. But above all they raise questions of sexual and representational politics. This the case in other actors born in the 1970s whose performances do not figure in this book, and who are not (yet) stars: Coque Malla as disaffected youth in *Todo es mentira* (1994);

Javier Albalá in *Chevrolet* (Javier Maqua, 1997) as the classic 'rebel male' (McCann 1991) and image of ruined youth; Gustavo Salmerón alongside Botto in *Asfalto*; Ernesto Alterio in *Los lobos de Washington*, and Alterio with Adriá Collado, as different types of rebel (Lorca and Dalí) in Saura's *Buñuel y la mesa del rey Salomón* (Buñuel and King Solomon's Table) (2001)—and so on.

As is common across much of world cinema, it is to typicality, and to representativeness (as well as sexual attractiveness and familiarity of image) that the Spanish magazines turn in their annual reviews of new, upcoming actors (Castellano and Costa 1995; Asúa 1998; Heredero 1999; Martialay, Ponga, and Ulled 2000). Dyer's arguments (1998) that the typicality of the actor, more than charisma or marketing, is most significant in making him or her a star have been usefully inflected by Spicer (1997: 144): 'Male stars represent easily recognised types of masculinity which have been socially, culturally and historically constructed, embodying important beliefs about power, authority, nationality and class [and their] combination of typicality and uniqueness encourages audience identification, admiration and desire.' As condensations of such constructions, and as 'clues to the changing construction of masculinity' of a period (144) (Spicer is concerned with the late 1940s), the actors of the Spanish 1980s and 1990s and beyond emerge from and point to specific articulations of individuals, audiences, consumers, constituencies (urban filmgoers; admirers of Banderas; enthusiasts of Spanish culture, and so on); to communities, and to elements of nationhood. But there is a concomitant thrust to the effect these men's images have. As well as reaching out into and adjusting the layered collective sense of identity by way of typification and the rehearsal of beliefs, in performance and in circulation they also (seem to) speak to and for 'me' through those operations of identification, admiration, and desire. Arias as the 1960s and 1970s folk hero El Lute; Banderas as restless youth in 1980s San Sebastian, or making good in suddenly modern Madrid; Bardem as late twentieth-century *macho* youth or 30-something A-gay man; Mollà as love- and AIDS-stricken dispossessed 1990s male or power-broking eighteenth-century Prime Minister; Sanz in wartime: these do not simply relate indexically to such types and times, and help watching individuals to gain a sense of self in history. As 'mediators between the real and the imaginary' (Hayward 1996: 344), as objects of desire that exceed their representations of type and of character, and as identificatory processes imprinted on page, screen, and affective memory, these actors not only conform and reflect Spanish masculinities, their triumphs and their crises, but have got under the skin of their characters and their audiences and are stars, bright stars, in the cultural imaginary of Spain.

References

(See Preface on the abbreviation FOA, and the Filmoteca Nacional, Madrid.)

Abelleira Briz, José Antonio (1986). 'Antonio Banderas: "Vine a Madrid con 15.000 pesetas y sin conocer a nadie"', *Ya (Vivir)*, 24 Jan.: FOA.

Academia (1996). 'Vicente Aranda: Una búsqueda permanente' [Extract of unattributed interview], 13: 47–8.

Advocate [unattributed] (1999). '*Live Flesh*' [Review], http://www.advocate.com/html/video/live_flesh.asp (25 Jan. 2001).

Aguilar, Carlos, and Jaume Genover (1996). *Las estrellas de nuestro cine: 500 biofilmografías de intérpretes españoles*. Madrid: Alianza Editorial.

Alameda, Soledad (1992). 'Antonio Banderas: capricho español', *El País (Semanal)*, 26 April: 18–31 and front page.

Albert, Antonio (1994). '*Todos los hombres sois iguales*' [Review], *Cinerama*, 24: 28.

Alcover, Norberto (1997). '*Carne Trémula*' [Review], *Reseña de literatura, arte, y espectáculos*, 288: 26.

Alfeo Álvarez, Juan Carlos (2001). 'El enigma de la culpa: la homosexualidad y el cine español, 1962–2000', *Journal of Contemporary Iberian Studies*, 13/3: 136–47.

Allen, Richard, and Murray Smith (1997). 'Introduction: Film Theory and Philosophy', in Allen and Smith (eds.), *Film Theory and Philosophy*. Oxford: Clarendon Press, 1–35.

Allinson, Mark (1997). 'Not Natural Born Killers, Not Matadors: Violence in Three Films by Young Spanish Directors', *Bulletin of Hispanic Studies* (Liverpool), 74/3: 315–30.

—— (1999). 'Pilar Miró's Last Two Films: History, Adaptation, and Genre', in Rix and Rodríguez-Saona (eds.) (1999: 33–45).

—— (2000). 'The Construction of Youth in 1980s and 1990s Spain', in Jordan and Morgan-Tamosunas (eds.), 2000: 265–73.

—— (2001). *A Spanish Labyrinth: The Films of Pedro Almodóvar*. London: I. B. Tauris.

Altares, Guillermo (2001). 'Toda historia de guerra es una historia de fantasmas' [Interview with Guillermo del Toro], *El País (El Espectador)*, 15 April: 10–11.

Álvarez, José Luis (1986). 'Antonio Banderas: "Deseo compartir mi vida con una mujer"', *La Revista del Mundo*, 22 Dec.: FOA.

Ángulo, Jesús, Carlos F. Heredero, and José Luis Rebordinos (1994). *Entre el documental y la ficción: el cine de Imanol Uribe*. San Sebastian and Vitoria: Filmoteca Vasca and Fundación Caja Vital Kutxa.

Antón, Elvira (2000). 'Gendered Images: Constructions of Masculinity and Femininity in Television Advertising', in Jordan and Morgan-Tamosunas (eds.) (2000: 205–13).

Arroyo, Carmen (1987). 'Imanol Arias: La seducción de una mirada', *Imagen Semanal*, 14 June: FOA.

Arroyo, Jose (1992). '*La ley del deseo*: A Gay Seduction', in Richard Dyer and Ginette Vincendeau (eds.), *European Popular Cinema*. London and New York: Routledge, 31–46.

—— (1996). 'The Auteur and the National Cinema', *Tesserae*, 2: 269–72.

—— (1998). '*Live Flesh / Carne trémula*' [Review], *Sight and Sound*, 8:5: 51.

Asúa, Alfonso (1998). 'Generación Y: Los cachorros del cine español'. *Cinerama*, 74: 74–9.

Aznar, Paloma (1997). 'El actor de moda y el nuevo chico Almodóvar: Liberto Rabal, otro tranvía llamado deseo', *Época* (*Sociedad*), 21 April: 86–7.

Babington, Bruce (2001). 'Introduction. British Stars and Stardom', in Babington (ed.), *British Stars and Stardom: From Alma Taylor to Sean Connery*. Manchester: Manchester University Press.

Babington, Bruce, and Peter W. Evans (1989). *Affairs to Remember: The Hollywood Comedy of the Sexes*. Manchester and New York: Manchester University Press.

Belategui [aka Belategi], Oskar (1999). 'Nadie Conoce a Nadie', *El Correo Digital*, 19 Nov.: http://www.diario-elcorreo.es/servicios/cine/evasion/eva991119a.html (7 Jan. 2000).

—— (2001). 'Javier Bardem, Actor: "Los premios sacan lo peor de uno"', *El Correo Digital*, 25 Feb.: http://www.diario-elcorreo.es/cine/datos/protagonistas/prota250201.html (3 July 2001).

Bellido, Adolfo (1999). 'Del thriller al terror (Esos chicos y esas chicas tan malos/as)', *En cadena dos* 12 (Dec.) [Dossier sobre el cine español de los 90], http://www.puntapunt.com/Club/encadenados/12_encadenados/rashomon.htm (23 Jan. 2001).

Belluscio, Marta (1996). *Seductores y amantes: historia del 'Latin Lover' y otros galanes*. Valencia: La Máscara.

Beneke, Timothy (1997). *Proving Manhood: Reflections on Men and Sexism*. Berkeley, Calif.: University of California Press.

Berger, Maurice, Brian Wallis, and Simon Watson (eds.) (1995*a*). *Constructing Masculinity*. New York and London: Routledge.

—— (1995*b*). 'Introduction', in Berger, Wallis, and Watson (eds.) (1995*a*: 1–8).

Borau, José Luis (ed.) (1998). *Diccionario del cine español*. Madrid: Alianza.

Bordwell, David (1996). 'Contemporary Film Studies and the Vicissitudes of Grand Theory', in Bordwell and Noël Carroll (eds.), *Post-Theory: Reconstructing Film Studies*. Madison, Wis.: University of Wisconsin Press, 3–36.

Boyero, Carlos (1989). 'Imanol Arias: de perfil', *Diario 16*, 13 July: FOA.

Brooksbank Jones, Anny (forthcoming). 'Sensing and Ending: Predestination in Imanol Uribe's *Días contados*', *Revista Canadiense de Estudios Hispánicos*.

Butler, Judith (1993). *Bodies That Matter: On the Discursive Limits of 'Sex'*. London and New York: Routledge.

Caparrós Lera, José María (1992). *El cine español de la democracia: de la muerte de Franco al "cambio" socialista (1975–1989)*. Barcelona: Anthropos.

Carty, Gabrielle (2001). 'Female Roles in the Comedy Films of Fernando Colomo', unpublished doctoral thesis. London: Queen Mary and Westfield College.

Casado, Nuria (2000). 'El cine español no llena', *El País Digital* (*Cultura/Foro 21*), 20 Dec.: http://www.elpais.es/ayuda/escuela/galeria/periodico20–24.pdf (18 Jan. 2002).

Casanova, María (1998). 'Jordi Mollà: "Si me dijeran que un premio sirve . . ."'. *Cinemanía*, 31: 118–20.

—— (1999). 'Liberto Rabal', *Cinemanía*, 43: 113.

Castellano, Koro, and Jordi Costa (1995). 'La nueva cosecha', *El País* (*Semanal*), 5 March: 16–20.

Castilla, Amelia (1996). 'Busca y captura de estrellas: El cine español renueva su fórmula de selección de actores', *El País*, 14 April: 32.

Castro, Antonio (1987). 'Testimonio de una época: *El Lute: Camina, o revienta*', *Dirigido*, 151: 19–24.

Cendrós, Teresa (2001). 'Javier Bardem aceptó encarnar a Reinaldo Arenas porque le dolió su vida', *El País*, 28 Feb.: http://www.elpais.es/articulo. html?anchor=elpepiesp&xref=20010228elpepiesp_1&type=Tes&date= (12 Jan. 2002).

Cinerama [unattributed] (1995). 'Javier Bardem', 40: 34.

—— (1996). 'Diccionario de actores' [Supplement in instalments].

Clemente, Beatriz (1998). *Diccionario de las estrellas cinematográficas españolas de los años noventa*. Madrid: Cacitel.

Cohan, Steven (1993). 'Prologue. Masculinity as Spectacle: Reflections on Men and Mainstream Cinema', in Cohan and Hark (eds.) (1993: 9–20).

Cohan, Steven, and Ina Rae Hark (eds.) (1993*a*). *Screening the Male: Exploring Masculinities in Hollywood Cinema*. London and New York: Routledge.

Cohan, Steven, and Ina Rae Hark (1993*b*). 'Introduction', in Cohan and Hark (eds.) (1993*a*: 1–8).

Connell, Robert W. (1995). *Masculinities*. Cambridge: Polity Press.

Conway, Madeline (2000). 'The Politics and Representation of Disability in Contemporary Spain', in Jordan and Morgan-Tamosunas (eds.) (2000: 251–9).

Cook, Pam (1980). 'Star Signs', *Screen*, 20/3–4: 80–8.

Cook, Pam (ed.) (1995). *The Cinema Book*. London: British Film Institute.

Corner, John, and Sylvia Harvey (eds.) (1991), *Enterprise and Heritage: Cross-currents of National Culture*. London and New York: Routledge.

Cortijo, Javier (1997). 'Carmelo Gómez: "Me gusta ayudar a mi padre a cultivar la tierra"', *Blanco y negro*, 13 April: 50–5.

Dawson, Graham (1994). *Soldier Heroes: British Adventure, Empire and the Imagining of Masculinity*. London and New York: Routledge.

de Laiglesia, Juan Carlos (1992). 'Javier Bardem: El actor revelación de la temporada', *Man* (Madrid), Sept.: 118–22.

Deia Igandia [unattributed] (1994). 'Jorge Sanz: La madurez cinematográfica de un eterno adolescente' (Vizcaya), 18 Sept.: 8–12.

Deleyto, Celestino (1999). 'Motherland, Space, Femininity, and Spanishness in *Jamón, jamón* (Bigas Luna, 1992)', in P. Evans (ed.) (1999*a*: 270–85).

Diario de León [unattributed] (1994). '"Me gusta soñar"', 19 Oct.: 49.

Diez Minutos [unattributed] (1987). 'Imanol Arias: "Pastora me quiere mucho y a mí me gusta sentirme querido"', 10 Feb.: 10–15.

D'Lugo, Marvin (1999). 'Re-imagining the Community: Imanol Uribe's *La muerte de Mikel* (1983) and the Cinema of Transition', in P. Evans (ed.) (1999*a*: 194–209).

de Cordova, Richard (1990). *Picture Personalities: The Emergence of the Star System in America*. Urbana, Ill. and Chicago: University of Illinois Press.

de Lauretis, Teresa (1984). *Alice Doesn't: Feminism, Semiotics, Cinema*. Bloomington, Ind.: Indiana University Press.

Diosdado, Ana (1988). 'Imanol Arias: "La gente cree que soy el protagonista de << Anillos de oro>>"', *Blanco y negro*, 6 March: 75–9.

Donald, Ralph (1992). 'Masculinity and Machismo in Hollywood's War Films', in Steve Craig (ed.), *Men, Masculinity, and the Media*. Newbury Park, Calif., London, New Delhi: Sage, 124–36.

Dyer, Richard (1986). *Heavenly Bodies: Film Stars and Society*. London and Basingstoke: Macmillan and British Film Institute.

—— (1998). *Stars*, 2nd augmented edn. London: British Film Institute.

Echevarría, Rosa María (1996). 'Carmelo Gómez: "De no haber triunfado en el cine, ahora estaría sembrando trigo"', *Blanco y negro*, 9 June: 42–5.

Ellis, John (1992). *Visible Fictions: Cinema; Television; Video*. London and New York: Routledge.

Esterberg, Kristin (1996). '"A Certain Swagger When I Walk": Performing Lesbian Identity', in Seidman (ed.) (1996: 259–79).

Estrella Digital, La [unattributed] (2000). '*Segunda piel* analiza las "formas de convivencia oxidadas" de los matrimonies falsos' [Interview with Gerardo Vera], 12 Jan.: http://www.estrelladigital.es/000112/articulos/cultura/Bardem.htm (4 Oct. 2000).

Evans, Jo (1999). 'Imanol Uribe's *La muerte de Mikel*: Policing the Gaze/Mind the Gap', in Fiddian and Michael (eds.) (1999: 101–9).

Evans, Peter William (1995*a*). *The Films of Luis Buñuel: Subjectivity and Desire*. Oxford: Clarendon Press.

—— (1995*b*). 'Back to the Future: Cinema and Democracy', in Graham and Labanyi (eds.) (1995: 326–31).

—— (1996). *Women on the Verge of a Nervous Breakdown (Mujeres al borde de un ataque de nervios)*. London: British Film Institute.

—— (ed.) (1999*a*). *Spanish Cinema: The Auteurist Tradition*. Oxford: Oxford University Press.

—— (1999*b*). '*Furtivos* (Borau, 1975): My Mother, My Lover', in P. Evans (ed.) (1999*a*: 115–27).

—— (1999*c*). 'The Dame in the Kimono: *Amantes*, Spanish Noir and the Femme Fatale', in Fiddian and Michael (eds.) (1999: 93–100).

Fergo, María Helena (1985). 'Antonio Banderas: el galán de Ana Belén', *Semana*, 20 Nov.: FOA.

Fernández-Alemany, Manuel, and Andrés Sciolla (1999). *Mariquitas y marimachos: Guía completa de la homosexualidad*. Madrid: Nuer Ediciones.

Fernández-Santos, Ángel (1997). 'Esplendor en la palabra' [Review of *El perro del hortelano*], *El País Digital (Tentaciones)*, 5 Feb.: http://www.udel.edu/leipzig/perro.htm (28 Oct. 2001).

Ferrando, Carlos (1987). 'Imanol Arias: "Mi vida privada no tiene precio"', *Interviú*, 14 April: 106–9.

—— (1994). 'Javier Bardem: "Se puede ser muy macho y muy sensible"', *Gente*, 24.: FOA.

Fiddian, Robin, and Ian Michael (eds.) (1999). *Sound on Vision: Studies in Spanish Cinema*, Special Issue of *Bulletin of Hispanic Studies* (Glasgow), 76: 1.

Finney, Angus (1996). *The State of European Cinema: A New Dose of Reality*. London: Cassell.

Fotogramas [unattributed] (1993). 'Chicos que son chicas/Chicas que son chicos', 1,783: 56.

—— (1994*a*). 'Antonio Banderas: Nuestro hombre en Hollywood', 1,807: 68–9.

—— (1994*b*). '20 nuevos rostros pidiendo paso', 1,810 [Summer Supplement]: 28–37.

—— (2000). 'El cine español va bien. Las cifras, y las opiniones de los productores' [Dossier], 1,880: 218–26.

Fouz-Hernández, Santiago (1999). 'All that Glitters is not Gold: Reading Javier Bardem's Body in Bigas Luna's *Golden Balls*', in Rix and Rodríguez-Saona (eds.) (1999: 47–62).

—— (2000). 'Generación X? Spanish Urban Youth Culture at the End of the Century in Mañas's/Armendáriz's *Historias del Kronen*', *Romance Studies*, 18/1: 83–98.

—— (2002). 'Representations of Masculinity on Contemporary Spanish and British Cinema', unpublished Ph.D. thesis. Newcastle upon Tyne: University of Newcastle.

Fouz-Hernández, Santiago, and Chris Perriam (2000). 'Beyond Almodóvar: "Homosexuality" in Spanish cinema of the 1990s', in David Alderson and Linda Anderson (eds.), *Territories of Desire in Queer Culture: Refiguring Contemporary Boundaries*. Manchester: Manchester University Press, 96–111.

Frosh, Stephen (1994). *Sexual Differences: Masculinity and Ideology*. London: Routledge.

Fuchs, Cynthia J. (1993). 'The Buddy Politic', in Cohan and Rae Hark (eds.) (1993: 194–210).

Fuente, Inmaculada de la (1984). 'Imanol Arias: Un seductor que odia ser galán'. *El País (Semanal)*, 9 Sept.: 7–10.

Fundación Octaedro (2001). 'Entrevista a Carmelo Gómez', http://www.octaedro.org.ec/carmelogomez1.htm (6 Nov. 2001).

Fuss, Diana (1991). 'Inside/Out', in Fuss (ed.), *Inside/Out. Lesbian Theories/Gay Theories*, New York: Routledge, 1–10.

Gallardo, Teresa (1996). 'Jordi Mollà: La humanidad del antihéreo', *Tendencias* (Madrid), 1 March: 35–9.

García, Cecilia (1996). 'Carmelo Gómez: La aventura de la interpretación', *Cinerama*, 48: 28–31.

García Lorca, Federico (1986). *Obras completas*. Madrid: Aguilar, ii.

Garrido, Inma (2000). 'Pasiones ocultas' [Report on *Segunda piel*], *Cinemanía*, 52: 94–5.

Gil, Carlos (1994). 'Javier Bardem: "Ser buen actor es hablar con dios"' [Report on San Sebastián Film Festival], *Ya*, 23 Sept.: 43.

Gil, Cristina (1996). 'Imanol Arias: "He tenido la suerte de pasar de ser galán a hacer de padre"', *Ya*, 9 Jan.: 51–3.

Gilmore, David (1990). *Manhood in the Making: Cultural Concepts of Masculinity*. New Haven: Yale University Press.

Gledhill, Christine (1991). *Stardom: Industry of Desire*. London and New York: Routledge.

—— (ed.) (1997). *Home Is Where the Heart Is, Studies in Melodrama and the Woman's Film*. London: British Film Institute.

Goicoechea, Maite (1987). 'Amar a un homosexual: Informe', *Dunia*, 242: 64–6.

Gómez Sierra, Esther (forthcoming). '*Celestina*: adaptación cinematográfica y cliché cultural'.

González, Marisa, and Juan Pasquín (1990). 'Imanol Arias: "Estoy deseando tener otro hijo"', *Pronto*, 20 Oct.: 91–2.

Gracia, Silvia (1992). 'Jorge Sanz: "No doy la talla para ser galán"', *Pronto*, 10 Oct.: 95.

Griffith, Richard (1970). *The Movie Stars*. Garden City, NY: Doubleday.

Guardian Unlimited (2001). 'Why am I doing this absurd job?' [interview with Javier Bardem], *Guardian Unlimited*, 21 March: http://film.guardian.co.uk/oscars2001/storynav/0,7677,461137,00.html (2 Dec. 2001).

Gubern, Román, *et al.* (1995). *Historia del cine español*. Madrid: Cátedra.

Hayward, Susan (1996). *Key Concepts in Cinema Studies*. London: Routledge.

Heredero, Carlos (1992). 'Antonio Banderas: La fuerza del deseo', *Diario 16*, 8 March: 10.

—— (1997). '*La buena Estrella*: Un sensible y emotivo retrato de desplazados', *Dirigido*, 258: 26–8.

—— (1999). 'Cine español: nueva generación', *Dirigido*, 278: 50–66.

Hernández Ruiz, Javier (1998). 'Sinfonía de esferas' [Review of *Los amantes del círculo polar*], *Dirigido*, 271: 30–1.

Holland, Jonathan (1999). '*Nadie conoce a nadie / Nobody Knows Anybody*' [Review], *Variety*, 20 Dec.: http://www.findarticles.com/m1312/6_377/58459266/p1/article.jhtml (21 Dec. 2000).

—— (2000). '*Segunda piel / Second Skin*' [Review], *Variety*, 21 Feb.: http://www.findarticles.com/cf_0/m1312/1_378/59975785/p1/article.jhtml (13 Dec. 2000).

Holmlund, Chris (1993). 'Masculinity as Multiple Masquerade: The "Mature" Stallone and the Stallone Clone', in Cohan and Hark (eds.) (1993: 213–29).

Hopewell, John (1986). *Out of the Past: Spanish Cinema after Franco*. London: British Film Institute.

—— (1989). *El cine español después de Franco, 1973–1988*. Madrid: Ediciones El Arquero.

Isasi, Teresa (1999). '*Los amantes del círculo polar*: Experiencia emocional', *Academia*, 26: 52–6.

Jacobs, Lea (1987). 'Censorship and the Fallen Woman Cycle', in Gledhill (ed.) (1987: 100–12).

Jagose, Annamarie (1996). *Queer Theory: An Introduction*. New York: New York University Press.

Jordan, Barry (1999). 'Refiguring the Past in the Post-Franco Fiction Film: Fernando Trueba's *Belle Époque*', in Fiddian and Michael (eds.) (1999: 139–56).

Jordan, Barry, and Rikki Morgan-Tamosunas (1998). *Contemporary Spanish Cinema*. Manchester and New York: Manchester University Press.

—— (eds.) (2000). *Contemporary Spanish Cultural Studies*. London: Arnold.

Kinder, Marsha (1993). *Blood Cinema: The Reconstruction of National Identity in Spain*. Berkeley, Calif.: University of California Press.

—— (1997). 'Refiguring Socialist Spain: An Introduction', in Kinder (ed.), *Refiguring Spain: Cinema, Media, Representation*. Durham, NC, and London: Duke University Press, 1–32.

Knights, Vanessa (2001). 'El bolero: expresión de la modernidad latinoamericana', *Actas del III Congreso de la Asociación Internacional para el Estudio de la Música Popular*, http://www.hist.puc.cl/historia/iaspm/pdf/Knights.pdf (14 Jan. 2002).

Krutnik, Frank (1991). *A Lonely Street: Film Noir, Genre, Masculinity*. London and New York: Routledge.

Labanyi, Jo (1997). 'Race, Gender, and Disavowal in Spanish Cinema of the Early Franco Period: The Missionary Film and the Folkloric Musical', *Screen*, 38/3: 215–31.

LaPlace, Maria (1987). 'Producing and Consuming the Woman's Film: Discursive Struggle in *Now Voyager*', in Gledhill (ed.) (1997: 138–65).

Lehman, Peter (1993). *Running Scared: Masculinity and the Representation of the Male Body*. Philadephia: Temple University Press.

Leyra, Paloma (1994). 'Carmelo Gómez: "Me gusta protestar"', *El Semanal* (Madrid), 28 Aug.: 32.

Llamas, Ricardo, and Francisco Javier Vidarte (2001). *Extravíos*. Madrid: Espasa Calpe.

López, Carlos (1992). 'Antonio Banderas: "Ser actor es una renuncia a madurar"', *La Esfera*, March: 56, 58–64.

Losilla, Carlos (1999). '*Boca a boca*: Actualidad de la comedia', *Dirigido*, 240: 8.

McCann, Graham (1991). *Rebel Males: Clift, Brando and Dean*. New Brunswick, NJ: Rutgers University Press.

McDonald, Paul (1998). 'Reconceptualising Stardom' [supplementary chapter], in Dyer (1998: 177–211).

—— (2000). *The Star System: Hollywood's Production of Popular Identities*. London: Wallflower.

Macnab, Geoffrey (2000). *Searching for Stars: Rethinking British Cinema*. London: Cassell.

Mandrell, James (1995). 'Sense and Sensibility, or Latent Heterosexuality and *Labyrinth of Passions*', in Kathleen M. Vernon and Barbara Morris (eds.), *Post-Franco, Postmodern: The Films of Pedro Almodóvar*. Westport, Conn. and London: Greenwood Press, 41–57.

Maqua, Javier (1994). 'La estrella: un discurso a pedazos', *Archivos de la filmoteca* (Valencia), Oct.: 25–33.

Martialay, Julieta (2000). 'Fele Martínez: Un chico con suerte', *Fotogramas*, 1,879: 91–7.

Martialay, Julieta, Paula Ponga, and Toni Ulled (2000). 'El relevo: 14 actores para 2001', *Fotogramas*, 1,882: 78–89.

Martín, Ángel (1993). 'Javier Bardem: "Sólo un muerto puede creer que lo sabe todo"', *El Periódico* (*La Gente*), 3 Oct.: 6–12.

Martín-Lunas, Milagros (1998). 'Arrancan los dos proyectos más esperados de cine español', *El Mundo*, 10 May: 53.

Martín-Márquez, Susan (1999). *Feminist Discourse and Spanish Cinema: Sight Unseen*. Oxford: Oxford University Press.

Martínez-Expósito, Alfredo (1995). 'La construcción del personaje en *La muerte de Mikel*: Un comentario a la teoría de mundos posibles', *Journal of Iberian & Latin American Studies*, 1/1–2: 93–8.

Mayne, Judith (1993). *Cinema and Spectatorship*. London and New York: Routledge.

Merikaetxebarria, Antón (1994). 'Javier Bardem: El cine en vena', *El Correo Español* (Vizcaya), 2 Oct.: 4.

Metz, Christian (1983). 'The Imaginary Signifier' (tr. Ben Brewster), in Metz, *Psychoanalysis and Cinema: the Imaginary Signifier*, tr. Ben Brewster, Celia Britton, Alfred Guzzetti, and Annwyl Williams. London and Basingstoke: Macmillan, 1–87.

Mir, Fernando (1988). 'Del macho al hombre: La transición a través de la publicidad', *Ajoblanco*, 12: 20–9.

Mira, Alberto (1999). *Para entendernos: Diccionario de cultura homosexual, gay y lésbica*. Barcelona: Ediciones de la Tempestad.

Modleski, Tania (1988). *The Women Who Knew Too Much: Hitchcock and Feminist Theory*. New York and London: Methuen.

Molina Foix, Vicente (1994). '*Días contados*' [Review], *Fotogramas*, 1,812: 9.

Monk, Claire (1997). 'The Heritage Film and Gendered Spectatorship', *Close Up: The Electronic Journal of British Cinema*, 1, pts. 1 and 2, http://www.shu.ac.uk/services/lc/closeup/monk.htm and . . . /monk2.htm (6 Nov. 2001).

Monterde, José Enrique (1987). 'El deseo, el sexo, y la muerte: *La ley del deseo*', *Dirigido*, 145: 10–12.

Morgan, Rikki (1995*a*). 'Pedro Almodovar's *Tie Me Up! Tie Me Down!*: The Mechanics of Masculinity', in Pat Kirkham and Janet Thumim (eds.), *Me Jane: Masculinity, Movies and Women*. London: Lawrence & Wishart, 113–27.

—— (1995*b*). 'Nostalgia and the Contemporary Spanish Musical Film', *Revista Canadiense de Estudios Hispánicos*, 20/1: 151–66.

Morgan, Rikki, and Barry Jordan (1994). '*Jamón, jamón*: A Tale of Ham and Pastiche', *Donaire*, 2: 57–64.

Morgan-Tamosunas, Rikki (forthcoming). 'Narrative, Desire, and Critical Discourse in Pedro Almodóvar's *Carne trémula*', *Journal of Iberian and Latin American Studies* (*Tesserae*).

Morin, Edgar (1960). *The Stars*, tr. Richard Howard. New York: Grove Press.

Mundo, El [unattributed] (1997). 'Almodóvar apuesta por Liberto Rabal', *El Mundo* (*Revista*), 2 March: FOA.

Narváez, Raquel (1989). 'Antonio Banderas: "No despierto el morbo"', *La Gente*, 14 May: 3–4.

Navarro, Nuria (1997). 'Jordi Mollà: "Soy propenso al surrealismo"', *El Periódico* (*Dominical*), 26 Jan.: 26–9.

Neale, Steve (1993). 'Prologue: Masculinity As Spectacle', in Cohan and Rae Hark (eds.) (1993: 9–19). (First published in *Screen*, 24 (1983): 2–16.)

Nieva de la Paz, Pilar (1997). 'Pilar Miró ante el teatro clásico' [seminar series: 'Teatro y cine: la búsqueda de nuevos lenguajes expresivos']: http://www.csic.es/prensa/teatroycine.html (28 Oct. 2001).

Oliva, Ana, and Gloria Fernández (1995). *Antonio Banderas: Tan sólo un actor*. Manresa: Grata Lectura.

Pagés, Rosa (1993). '*Belle Époque*' [Review], *Amante Cine*, 2/15: 4.

Palacios, Jesús (2000). '*Asfalto*' [Review], *Fotogramas*, 1,876: 24.

Parker, Andrew (1996). 'Sporting Masculinities: Gender Relations and the Body', in Máirtín Mac an Ghaill (ed.), *Understanding Masculinities: Social Relations and Cultural Arenas*. Buckingham and Philadelphia: Open University Press, 126–38.

Parrondo, Jorge (1994). '*Entrevista con el vampiro*' [interview with Antonio Banderas], *Imágenes de la actualidad*, 125: 98–101.

Perriam, Chris (forthcoming). 'Alejandro Amenábar's *Abre los ojos / Open Your Eyes* (1997)', in Antonio Lázaro-Reboll and Andy Willis (eds.), *Spanish Popular Cinemas*. Manchester: Manchester University Press.

Pineda Novo, Daniel (1991). *Las folklóricas y el cine*. Huelva: Festival de Cine Iberoamericano.

Ponga, Paula (1994). 'Jorge Sanz: Cine en las venas', *Fotogramas*, 1,806: 64.

—— (1997). 'Jordi Mollà: "Soy complicado"', *Fotogramas*, 1,846: 40–4.

—— (1999). 'Eduardo Noriega: el galán sensato', *Fotogramas*, 1,867: 16–22.

—— (2000). '*Segunda piel*: Radiografía de la homosexualidad oculta', *Fotogramas*, 1,875: 104–7.

—— (2001). 'Eduardo Noriega: Irrestiblemente listo', *Fotogramas*, 1,891: 94–102.

Powrie, Phil (1997). *French Cinema in the 1980s: Nostalgia and the Crisis of Masculinity*. Oxford: Clarendon Press.

Preston, Peter (2001). 'It's Love: But Don't Tell Fidel' [Review of *Before Night Falls*], *The Observer* (17 June), http://www.observer.co.uk/review/story/0,6903,507918,00.html (12 Sept. 2001.)

Pretorius, William (2000). '*Second Skin*', *News 24* (Johannesburg), 30 Sept.: http://news24.com/News24/Offbeat/Movies/0.1637.2-16-141_889070.00.html (15 July 2001).

Rebello, Stephen (1995). 'Antonio Banderas: Red-blooded Male', *Attitude*, Jan.: 20–4.

Reboiras, Ramón (1996). 'De gañán a galán'. *Cambio 16*, 1,278: 50–2.

Retamar, Ángel (2001). 'Elegidos para la gloria: Javier Bardem', *Zero*, 25: 9–12.

Reuters/Variety [staff reporters] (2001). 'Homegrown pics gain in Europe', http://dailynews.yahoo.com/h/nm/20011226/en/film-europe_1.html (7 Jan. 2002).

Reviriego, Carlos (2000). '*Segunda piel* de Gerardo Vera', *El Mundo* (*Cultural*), 9 Jan.: 56–8.

Rey, Juan (1994). *El hombre fingido: La representación de la masculinidad en el discurso publicitario*. Madrid: Fundamentos.

Rigalt, Carmen (1997). 'Javier Bardem: "En este país somos cuatro actores cono-cidos y nos lo compartimos todo: el bueno, el malo, la puta, y el gracioso"', *El Mundo (Revista)*, 17 Aug.: 16–19.

Rivera, Alfonso (1994). 'Un paso adelante: Javier Bardem', *El País (Tentaciones)*, 23 Sept.: 5–10.

Rix, Rob, and Roberto Rodríguez-Saona (1999). *Spanish Cinema Calling the Shots.* Leeds: Trinity and All Saints College.

Rodowick, David (1991). *The Difficulty of Difference: Psychoanalysis, Sexual Difference and Film Theory.* New York: Routledge.

Romney, Jonathan (2000). '*Lovers of the Arctic Circle / Los amantes del círculo polar*' [Review], *Sight and Sound*, 10/2: 48–9.

—— (2001). 'Masque of the Living Dead', in Ginette Vincendeau (ed.), *Film/ Literature/Heritage: A Sight and Sound Reader.* London: British Film Institute, 37–43.

Rubio, José Luis (1984). 'Imanol Arias: Historia de un seductor'. *Cambio 16*, 664: 76–9.

Rubio, Teresa (1985). 'Antonio Banderas: "Quiero ser el Butragueño del cine"', *El Periódico*, 22 Dec.: 50–4.

Salaman, Naomi (1994). 'Regarding Male Objects', in Naomi Salaman and Linda Williams (eds.), *What She Wants: Women Artists Look at Men.* London: Verso, 13–26.

Sanden, Robert van der (2000). 'Antonio Banderas', *Glossy* (Amsterdam/Gilze), 13: 62–3.

Santaolalla, Isabel (1999). 'Julio Medem's *Vacas* (1991): Historicizing the Forest', in Evans (ed.) (1999a: 310–24).

Sartori, Beatriz (1993). 'Imanol Arias: "He vivido una crisis muy profunda de la que he salido reforzado"', *El Mundo (Magazin)*, 4 April: 47–50.

Segovia, Alberto (1996). '*Éxtasis*' [Review], *Cinerama*, 45: 41.

Seidman, Steven (ed.) (1996). *Queer Theory/Sociology.* Cambridge, Mass.: Black-well, 1996.

Serrano, Vicente (2001). 'Eduardo Noriega: "Creo que en mi profesión soy un priv-ilegiado"', *Interfilms*, 13/151: 18–24.

Siles, Luis Eduardo (1987). 'Antonio Banderas: "Lucho por una carrera ascendente como actor"', *Garbo*, 28 Feb.: 27, 29.

Siminovich, Maya (1996). 'Imanol Arias y la fuerza de sus cuarenta', *Cosmopolitan* (Madrid), 1 Feb.: 405–8.

Smith, Paul (1995). 'Eastwood Bound', in Berger, Wallis, and Watson (eds.) (1995: 77–97).

Smith, Paul Julian (1992). *Laws of Desire: Questions of Homosexuality in Spanish Literature and Film, 1960–1990.* Oxford: Clarendon Press.

—— (2000). *Desire Unlimited: The Cinema of Pedro Almodóvar*, 2nd edn. London: Verso.

—— (2001a). 'Blood of a Poet', *Sight and Sound*, 11/6: 30–1.

—— (2001b). 'Ghost of the Civil Dead' [Review of *The Devil's Backbone*], *Sight and Sound*, 11/12: 38–9.

Solomon-Godeau, Abigail (1995). 'Male Trouble', in Berger, Wallis, and Watson (eds.) (1995: 68–76).

Soria, Florentino (1986). *La comedia en el cine español*. Madrid: Ayuntamiento de Madrid, Artes Gráficas Municipales.

Spicer, Andrew (1997). 'Male Stars, Masculinity and British Cinema', in Robert Murphy (ed.), *The British Cinema Book*. London: British Film Institute, 144–53.

Stein, Arlene, and Ken Plummer (1996). ' "I Can't Even Think Straight": "Queer" Theory and the Missing Sexual Revolution in Sociology', in Seidman (ed.) (1996: 129–44).

Stone, Rob (2002). *Spanish Cinema*. Harlow: Pearson Education.

Tasker, Yvonne (1993). 'Dumb Movies for Dumb People: Masculinity, the Body, and the Voice in Contemporary Action Cinema', in Cohan and Rae Hark (eds.) (1993: 230–44).

Tiempo [unattributed] (1988). 'Antonio Banderas: No quiere más papeles gay', 4 July: 130–1.

Todocine [unattributed] (2000a). 'Javier Bardem', http://www.todocine.com/bio/00093457.htm (18 Dec. 2000).

—— (2000b). '*El portero*' [Review], http://www.todocine.com/mov/00202763.htm (6 Nov. 2001).

Torrecillas, Mario (1994). 'Javier Bardem: "A mí nunca me han dirigido" ', *La Vanguardia (Suplemento Cultural)*, 18 Oct.: 2.

Torreiro, Mirito (2000). 'Perdedores y ganadores' [Review of *La gran vida*], *El País (El espectador)*, 15 Oct.: 3.

Torres, Maruja (1993). 'Javier Bardem: Actor. "Sólo me ofrecen papeles de chulo" ', *El País*, 18 Oct.: 26.

Turner, Graeme (1988). *Film as Social Practice*. London and New York: Routledge.

Umbral, Francisco (1985). 'Imanol Arias', *Interviú*, 26 March: 84.

Uruena, Silvia (1994). 'Antonio Banderas: "No creo que un homosexual sea muy diferente a mí" ', *El Correo Español (Sábado)*, 17 Dec.: 20.

Vanguardia, La [unattributed] (1986). 'Hotel: Antonio Banderas'. 13 April: 6–12.

Verchili, Elena (2000). 'Javier Bardem: "Jordi Mollà tiene un buen par de glúteos" ', *El Mundo (Cultura)*, 1 Jan., www.el-mundo.es/2000/01/11/cultura/11NO118.html (30 Sept. 2000).

Vidal, Jaume (2000). 'Gerardo Vera muestra en *Segunda piel* el dolor del enamoramiento', *El País*, 11 Jan.: 35.

Villalobos, Ruiz de (1993). '*Intruso*' [Review], *Imágenes de actualidad*, 119: 41.

Vincendeau, Ginette (2000). *Stars and Stardom in French Cinema*. London and New York: Continuum.

—— (ed.) (2001). 'Introduction' in Vincendeau (ed.), *Film/Literature/Heritage*. London: British Film Institute, pp. xi–xxv.

Walker, Alexander (1970). *Stardom: The Hollywood Phenomenon*. New York: Stein & Day.

Willemen, Paul (1981). 'Anthony Mann: Looking at the Male', *Framework*, 15–17: 16–20.

Williams, Linda (1983). 'When the Woman Looks', in Mary Ann Doane, Patricia Mellencamp, and Linda Williams (eds.), *Re-vision: Essays in Feminist Film Criticism*. Frederick, MD: University Publications of America, 83–99.

Wright, Patrick (1985). *On Living in an Old Country: The National Past in Contemporary Britain*. London: Verso.

Index

Bold numbers denote reference to illustrations.